W9-CCU-295

NOTRE DAME
Communication and Theatre

the third theatre

the third theatre

by
ROBERT
BRUSTEIN

ALFRED A. KNOPF

New York   1969

In memory of
my father

Preface

*Despite the polemical nature of some of the
opening articles, this book cannot lay claim to a
consistent theme. I offer it frankly as a collection
of pieces written between 1957 and 1968—
pieces that deal not only with theatre but also
with literature, culture, and the movies—
which I hope have sufficient relevance to be
worth preserving in book form. The only unity
I can find in the collection, aside from a unity
of style, proceeds from my obvious reluctance
to discuss works of art without some reflection on
the civilization that gave them birth. I am an
incorrigible about intruding cultural generalities
on artistic subjects, and I hope the reader will
forgive me for this, and for whatever other
errors, lapses, or excesses he may find in this book.*

contents

III OBSERVATIONS

Introduction:
The Third Theatre Revisited

This book takes its title from what has come to be its
most controversial essay: a salute to a new theatre that
was just beginning to evolve in opposition to the existing
theatre on Broadway and in the culture centers. At the
time I wrote this essay, in the middle sixties, the third
theatre was a fringe movement whose continued survival
was as problematical as its antiwar posture was unpopular, so it was with considerable surprise that I
watched it, soon after, begin to capture the bulwarks of
theatrical power and insinuate itself into the mainstream.
This development closely paralleled a failure of nerve
among the middle classes, as the forces of the establishment grew guilty and enfeebled before the culture of
the young, and the American avant-garde, for the first
time in its history, became the glass of fashion and the
mold of form. What was once considered special and
arcane—the exclusive concern of an alienated, argu-
mentative, intensely serious elite—was now open to easy
access through television and the popular magazines;
vogues in women's fashions followed hard upon, and
sometimes even influenced, vogues in modern painting;
underground movies became box office bonanzas, and
Andy Warhol's factory was making him a millionaire.

This narrowing of the traditional distance between
high and mass-middle culture was accompanied, in the
third theatre, by a growing callowness, sloppiness, and
arrogance which had the effect of arousing my suspicious-
ness of it. Thus, the opening sections of my book reflect

not only my efforts to document this movement but also my growing disenchantment with it. I developed much the same ambivalence toward the antiwar and Black Power movements as they changed from noble acts of nonviolent resistance by highly serious individuals to disruptive and histrionic acts by half-baked, infantile "revolutionaries." For just as the frustrations over the endless conflict in Vietnam and the unresolved dilemmas of the black people have given an extremist, vaguely totalitarian coloration to certain cadres of the left, so the success of the third theatre, which reflects these frustrations, has tended to sanctify its failings and conventionalize its virtues. What once seemed daring and original now often seems tiresome and familiar; stereotyped political assertions, encouraged by easy audience acceptance, have replaced instinctive, individualized dissent; and the complex moral and metaphysical issues of great art are being obliterated by a simple-minded nihilism that reduces everything to zero.

Does this suggest that I am ready to repudiate the assumptions of my earlier essay? Only insofar as I must repudiate all theatre movements that begin to take an ideological direction. While the new theatre as a whole has taken a wrong turn, however, there are still a number of young American playwrights with the gifts to blast this theatre out of its formulas: Jean-Claude van Itallie, Sam Shepard, Charles Dizenzo, Ronald Ribman, and Leo Rutman, to name but a few. Similarly, while I overvalued *Viet Rock* in my relief to discover a play that mentioned the Vietnam war at all, I still regard *America Hurrah, Dynamite Tonite,* and *MacBird* as works of real imagination and originality, and will continue to defend these plays against hostile critics who attack what is genuine in this movement along with what is spurious. On the other hand, it is becoming increasingly clear, now that the new theatre has begun to rigidify, that it may spell as great a danger to dramatic art as the old theatre: it already embodies similar defects. Its anti-intellectualism, its sensationalism, its sexual obsessiveness, its massacre of language, its noisy attention-getting mechanisms, its indifference to artistry, craft, and skill, its violence, and, above all, its mindless tributes to Love and Togetherness (now in the form of "group gropes" and "love zaps") are not adversary demands upon the American character but rather the very qualities that have continually degraded us, the very qualities that have kept us laggard and Philistine in the theatre throughout the past three decades.

It is ironic that these qualities, already so conspicuous in the commercial theatre, should be offered as expressions of a new sensibility—even more ironic that one should find them embedded in the work of the Living Theatre upon the return of this company after an exile of four years. Initiating a tour designed to revolutionize not only the stage but the various university and civic centers that were being visited, the Living Theatre proved, upon its very first appearance, to have changed its style in a manner very similar to the changes in the new theatre. Indeed, it soon became clear that it was the original source of many Off-Off-Broadway conventions. Having eked out a precarious existence for seventeen years as an embattled minority troupe dedicated to the great classic and contemporary European works as well as to the more experimental American plays, the Living Theatre returned with a fierce antagonism to all dramatic texts that could not somehow be translated into its special anarchistic program. The company had developed an almost symbiotic unity in its years of traveling together over the European continent; it had become a self-generating, self perpetuating organism whose existence was more important than any work it performed; and it was inflamed with a sense of mission that was less theatrical or even political than it was religious and evangelical.

These changes were reflected physically as well. Julian Beck's features now contained an ascetic calm usually associated with Hindu gurus and Confucian monks, while his wife, Judith Malina, had taken on the look of an unprotected street urchin, her eyes sometimes ablaze with fervency, sometimes limpid with compassion for all martyrs, not excluding herself. The Becks—as well as the entire company—had developed an extraordinary physical integrity that was at once the most immediate, and the most long-lasting impression, one had of them. Dressed like gypsies, hippies, and nomads in clothing from every quarter of the earth, the men sometimes indistinguishable from the women, and even the children beaded, bangled, and long-haired, they moved with a beauty that testified to an inward grace, as well as to months of arduous training on breathing and the body.

Unfortunately, the Living Theatre had little of substance to contribute beyond its physical athleticism and its exotic style of life. Although two of the four works presented on this tour (*The Mysteries* and *Frankenstein*) showed original techniques, none added up to a viable artistic experience or fulfilled its initial promise, largely because a gifted playwright was lacking to shape it. It was disconcerting to discover that the Becks no longer seemed very interested in coherent theatrical productions. What obsessed them now was their missionary program; they were more eager to convert their audiences, through whatever means, to their special brand of revolutionary politics. In production after production, the company demonstrated its remarkable capacity to manipulate minds. Playing upon a general sense of emptiness in a world without absolutes, where even individual salvation seems far too complicated and difficult, the Living Theatre proselytized among the young in the manner of hip evangelists, encouraging each spectator to make his decision for love, freedom, and anarchy. And the most depressing thing of all was how easily university students, and even some faculty members, responded to the baldest of slogans and the most simplistic interpretations of reality.

After *The Mysteries*, a series of process exercises which for me was the most interesting and least pretentious of its offerings, the Living Theatre proceeded to demonstrate in *Antigone* (a version of the story which reduced it down to the most melodramatic confrontation between political evil and oppressed good), in *Frankenstein* (a camp horror tale with Radio City Music Hall prestidigitation techniques about how civilization turns man into a monster), and particularly in the audience-participation epic, *Paradise Now,* that it had virtually abandoned all desire to create artistic imitations. It was now clear that the Becks' previous efforts to examine the boundaries separating art from life (in such pre-exile productions as *The Connection* and *Tonight We Improvise*) had been expanded into a full-scale assault upon any separation whatsoever between the spectator and the stage. Audiences were invited over the footlights to join some performers while other performers wandered through the house; actors whined plaintively about their inability to travel without a passport, live without money, smoke marijuana, or take their clothes off, after which they stripped to loincloths and bikinis; students peeled down, upon this encouragement, to jockey shorts; mass love-zaps and petting parties were organized on stage among couples of various sexes and sexual dispositions; and after the endless, loveless, sexless groping was finally over, everyone was exhorted to leave the theatre and convert the police to anarchism, to storm the jails and free the prisoners, to stop the war and ban the bomb, to take over the streets in the name of the people—and, then, to disperse quietly lest any of this end (as it did one night in New Haven) with somebody in jail for disturbing the peace.

Needless to say, unfulfillable demands of this kind

were extremely irresponsible, given the impressionable nature of young audiences; they were also extremely meretricious, since the Living Theatre invariably took refuge in its theatrical function whenever things threatened to get out of hand. For all its emphasis on reality, the company never quite managed to escape out of performance; for all its emphasis on spontaneity and accident, it still followed a semi-fixed pattern which ended similarly every evening. To extend a theatrical action into the audience is not to annihilate the performance, it is to annihilate the audience—everyone becomes a performer, the seats become part of the stage. This paradox was not lost on Jean Genet, whose play *The Balcony* was based on his understanding that since revolution is dedicated to the destruction of artifice, its greatest enemy is playacting. But it was a paradox from which the Living Theatre was never able to escape. And when the Becks appeared recently on the Merv Griffin Show, outlining their political theories between a series of nightclub acts, they only dramatized further their imprisonment in show biz—in Genet's image, they were still in the brothel.

What was finally most disturbing about the Living Theatre was the content of the ideology it was marketing under the name of anarchism. In spite of all the invitations to participate in free theatre, it was constraint and control that remained most conspicuous: no spectator was ever allowed to violate the pattern of manipulated consent. At Yale, we saw a female student launch into a passionate denunciation of the Living Theatre, only to be hustled offstage by a group of performers who embraced her into silence—unbuttoning her blouse, feeling her legs, and shutting her mouth with kisses. Another student, beginning an impersonation of Ed Sullivan while navigating around the interlocked bodies on the stage, was prevented from introducing a note of satire into the evening by an actor who drowned him out with an imitation of the Kennedy assassination. The company, particularly vulnerable to ridicule because of its total lack of humor, allowed no alien laughter ever to penetrate its relentless solemnity, self-righteousness, and self-importance. Love and brotherhood were continually on the lips of the actors, but no actors in my experience have bristled with so much aggression or more successfully galvanized the aggression of the spectator. As for love and brotherhood, all one saw was herd-love and brotherhood among the anonymous. It was, finally, not a vision of human freedom that one took away from *Paradise Now* but rather vague, disturbing memories of the youth rallies in Hitler's Nuremberg. The return of the Living Theatre described a full circle insofar as the company had now taken on the very authoritarian qualities it had once denounced, the very repressiveness that had driven it from the country four years before.

The unprecedented success of the Living Theatre with the radical young—and with those who follow the radical young—has, however, of momentous significance because it indicated precisely what these audiences were now demanding of the stage. For these impatient generations, with their inability to sustain frustration for a moment, it was the opportunity for participation that proved most attractive. The passive role of spectator had become insufficient. Now theatrical production had to satisfy the thirst for an elusive "relevance" and convince its audiences that they were helping to enact an episode in history. The Living Theatre promised the theatricalization of campus revolts, confrontations, and occupations—the theatricalization of those numerous quasi-revolutionary gestures by which students are persuading themselves today that they are having a significant impact on their times. That these gestures are aimed not against the Pentagon or the napalm-producing factories, but rather against the university itself (for all its faults, still one of the last outposts of civilization and humaneness) only indicates that the desire for effectiveness *somewhere* far transcends the desire for effective change.* But it also indicates that with the day of the protest upon us, the conditions necessary for the creation of great art may very well be over, at least for a time. As one gifted acting student told me, upon withdrawing from Yale: "I don't give a shit about art. I want to create events."

For myself, I regard this development with mingled feelings, mostly sad ones. This extraordinary generation, upon whom so much praise and attention have been lavished, cannot help inspiring feelings of respect—but my respect is becoming mixed with great apprehension. At once so vital and idealistic, and so childish, irrational, and overindulged, the radical young are questioning the very roots of our civilization, but what they would sub- stitute, apart from continuous improvisation and an ethics of experience, is far from known. The silent and conservative students of the fifties are no more, thank heavens; they have gone off to join the system and con- solidate its errors. But some of the more demonic students of the sixties may very well, in their impatience for change, destroy what is valuable in our culture along with what is despicable—destroying even the valuable things their contemporaries have helped to create. While the theatre, along with popular music, has benefited enor- mously from an infusion of young energy that has trans- formed our way of seeing and hearing, the more radical theatre is less an advance than a throwback. With this theatre, we have returned to the thirties, watching the same abuse of truths that do not serve political ends, the same contempt for writers who do not try to change their times, the same monolithic modes of thought, the same

---

* This is not to say that some of the more extreme revolutionists are not preparing, at least in their fantasies, for assaults on the Pentagon. My sixteen-year-old stepson met a girl the other day who was practicing jiu-jitsu in preparation for encounters with the U.S. Army. "Can you throw a tank?" he asked.

assaults on any expression that is not a form of consent. The theatre of commitment, which had just begun to shake itself free from dependence on narrow ideology, is again becoming a theatre of naked slogans and raw emotionalism, and death knells are once more being heard for the works of Western civilization.

These works will, hopefully, survive—they are certainly among the few things worth preserving. But they will survive only through renewed efforts at conservation, and this means renewed efforts of intelligence and will. The threatening apocalypse is something for which many of us must share the blame: by radically questioning the prevailing humanism, we helped to start violent engines in motion which may end by pushing everything we value over the precipice. Secure in our powerlessness, and secure that thought would never lead to action, we let our minds play upon questionable alternatives, never suspecting that those alternatives might soon be upon us, more swiftly and irrevocably than we dreamt. These were errors of judgment—but there were those who made less forgivable errors of power. Seeking a Mosaic role, they led these hungry generations to a violent view from Pisgah that could have no creative issue. Guilt-ridden, indecisive, flaccid, hating authority and enamored of influence, they surrendered principles they had once affirmed, accepting again what was so hateful in the past. In a time when intelligence is needed more than ever before, they encouraged a form of intellectual decomposition, becoming fellow travelers of a movement they could never hope to join, which would, in time, proceed to swallow them up.

We honor the young because without them, there is no future. But there will surely be no future either unless the more extreme of our young can cease from annihilating the past. With our civilization tottering, the temptation is strong to release one's hold on reality and credit the most fantastic flights of absurdity simply because they signify change. But the more radical inventions of a new generation are nothing if they proceed from the same violent and mindless sources that originally brought our civilization to this terrifying juncture. We fail the future when we surrender what we know and value for the sake of fashion and influence, and we fail the theatre when we countenance the rejection of language, form, and accomplishment in favor of an easy, instant culture. The third theatre I describe in the opening pages of this book contains, in Synge's words, "reality and joy"—which is to say, it synthesizes the principles of work and of pleasure, discipline and imagination, form and process, reflection and improvisation, age and youth. It is a theatre that spans the generations—a theatre, in other words, that has yet to appear in this country of divided spirits.

I

polemics

The Third Theatre

More than half a century ago, the Irish dramatist John Millington Synge had occasion to lament the separation between sense and sensuality in the contemporary theatre: "On the stage one must have reality and one must have joy; and that is why the intellectual modern drama has failed, and people have grown sick of the false joy of the musical comedy, that has been given them in place of the rich joy found only in what is superb and wild in reality." Synge was a trifle premature in judging the fatigue of audiences with these two forms of theatre—the intellectual modern drama still manages to retain some vitality, and the musical stage continues to attract hordes of spectators—but he was certainly accurate in perceiving that "reality" and "joy" tend to be separate theatrical pursuits. Until very recently, in fact, most Americans treated theatre as an escape, shunning reality and seeking out the "false joy" of musicals and light comedies, but even now, when the intellectual modern drama is more tolerated and esteemed in this country, it fails to achieve the proper synthesis and condemns its adherents to strict puritan rigors. The superficiality of Broadway show business will not concern us here—it is the inevitable consequence of an enterprise based purely on profit—but the whey-faced solemnity of our serious theatre is a problem that needs some airing. Why are our more ambitious dramatic efforts often so stiff and pious? Why is it so difficult for patrons of the serious theatre to enjoy themselves at a play?

The "rich joy" of which Synge spoke, of course, has always been a quality of the greatest forms of theatre. "Hamlet and Lear are gay," observed Yeats in a poem, "gaiety transfiguring all that dread," and anyone who has

ever had a genuine tragic experience at a play knows
that it involves a good deal of ecstasy. But it is not gaiety
that infuses such works as *Tiny Alice* and *After the
Fall,* it is the heavy breathing of Meaning and Significance, while joyous is the last word one would use to
describe the mood at Lincoln Center. I am not now
discussing the merits of such plays and companies,
though I am obviously not enthusiastic about them. I
am speaking rather of the atmosphere they generate. It is
difficult to imagine anyone visiting such events with any
pleasurable anticipation; and, indeed, they create a kind
of bored dutifulness in the spectator that has hitherto
been inspired only by a church service or a commence-
ment address. There is a paradox involved here which
can be attributed to the lag between supply and demand.
For just as an interest in the beautification of America has
developed only after much of the nation has become a
sewer, so an interest in dramatic art has been generated
at a time when none is being produced. We are, as a result, giving unprecedented support to a theatre void of
any excitement or vitality, which males will attend in the
way husbands have traditionally visited Wagnerian opera,
as drowsy sacrifices to the insatiable female thirst for
cultural improvement.

Now this is far from the situation in Europe. In
England, where theatregoing is an intimate part of daily
life and not a status anxiety or a cultural compulsion,
the theatre represents a major source of artistic pleasure.
And it is to the subsidized repertory theatres—not to the
West End showshops—that spectators flock for enjoyment. To witness Paul Scofield with the Royal Shakespeare Company investigating the impotency of old age
in *King Lear* or *The Government Inspector;* to see
Albert Finney, at the National Theatre of Britain, alternating between a brutal valet in *Miss Julie,* a homosexual designer in *Black Comedy,* and a peanut-vendor

Duke in *Much Ado About Nothing;* to watch Robert Stephens, also at the National, deepening his art with each successive role; to follow the development of the Royal Shakespeare Company *Marat/Sade* from an experimental acting exercise to a triumphant full-dress production; to observe the English Stage Company at the Royal Court continually endangering its existence to test the limits of the Lord Chamberlain's power over stage censorship; even to see a relatively inferior company at the Mermaid Theatre staging a sanguinary reenactment of the Passion in the *Wakefield Cycle Plays*— these are the events that tell us what Synge meant by "rich joy." For those who still prefer the "false joy" of the musical stage, there is always *Hello Dolly* and *Funny Girl* and a few English musicals, but it is at the Old Vic and Aldwych theatres that tickets are most in demand and the real fun is to be had.

Something of the same light spirit can be found in the theatres across the Channel, and particularly among the more gifted playwrights of France and Germany. There is, I suppose, no more uncompromising a dramatist than Bertolt Brecht, whose artistic seriousness has made him a major particle in our own cultural explosion, not to mention a seminal figure in contemporary world theatre. But one would never gather from the ponderous, reverential way that Brecht is usually staged in this country that he is a master of comic wit who uses vaudeville turns, clown shows, and circus numbers as structural elements of his art, or that he very frequently populates his plays with lusty rogues and mischievous scoundrels. Eugène Ionesco, often described as a pivot of the theatre of the absurd, is essentially a *farceur* whose absurdities stem from Molière and the Marx Brothers. Samuel Beckett writes of human futility using the devices of the music hall and characters based on the silent-movie *personae* of Chaplin and Keaton. And when Peter Weiss or Jean Genet or Frederic Duerrenmatt wish to make moral or political statements, they do so with supreme theatricality and a large degree of impishness.

By contrast, the more ambitious American drama is almost invariably solemn and grave, as if our authors feared to be caught in a moment of carelessness or relaxation. Eugene O'Neill—the source of so much that is worthwhile in our theatre—is also partly responsible for this: it was only toward the end of his career that he learned how to separate seriousness from portentousness. That there was a more buoyant side to O'Neill's nature can be inferred from his later plays—particularly from *Ah Wilderness!* and *A Touch of the Poet*—but as long as he thought himself a candidate for the chair of Aeschylus, he always felt compelled to present an extremely doleful countenance to his auditors. In this regard, Arthur Miller looks like O'Neill's true heir, since he too tends to confuse earnestness with humorlessness. Miller writes about "reality" without having the slightest notion of what is "superb and wild in reality," and while his plays usually aspire toward tragedy, they lack all tragic gaiety. One could multiply examples, from Anderson's *Winterset* to MacLeish's *J.B.*, of plays by playwrights who pursued the tragic muse with leaden running shoes before tripping clumsily over their laces.

Our new enthusiasm for repertory theatre has also been a spur to false seriousness, not to mention false joy. There are a few companies studded around the country that have managed to provide enjoyment without compromising their aims; but the repertory notion, for the most part, has functioned as a springboard either to excessive lightness or excessive heaviness. The APA (Association of Producing Artists) strikes me as a group that has been most successful when most lightweight, reviving old melodramas like *The Tavern* or vintage Broadway comedies like *You Can't Take It with You*, while the Blau-Irving troupe—though casual and relaxed in

San Francisco—became glum and sodden at Lincoln Center. Papp's Shakespeare company, whatever its failures with individual productions, has always miraculously preserved a sense of youth and vitality, but the "festival" atmosphere surrounding the American Shakespeare Company at Stratford has turned the area into a picnic ground.

Is there something in the American character that pushes our culture toward extremes? Certainly, we are much too anxious about our artists, too ready to crown them with unearned laurels, too eager to invest them with an Olympian role, while our lighter talents are continually being encouraged to churn up commodity froth. In either case, we are notoriously unwilling to accept our theatre artists as they are, to let them perform their most natural roles.

I don't mean to question the motives of playwrights or performers in seeking to enlarge their possibilities or explore new areas; I am merely trying to demonstrate that traditional splits in theatrical culture are not easily healed. The difficulties at Lincoln Center since its inception demonstrate this even more powerfully, Kazan's failure indicating that a lifelong dedication to the commercial theatre is not sufficient basis for an important dramatic art, and the failure of Blau and Irving suggesting that even the most lofty intentions are not enough without theatrical expertise and creative relaxation. Lincoln Center has proved a battleground between the two warring factions of the American theatre; it cannot succeed without some synthesis of "reality" and "joy"; and yet an official culture emporium is just about the last place where such syntheses occur.

Fortunately, America has a third theatre, supported primarily by the young, which combines the youthful properties of intensity, exuberance, and engagement. It is a theatre that came to life during the Off Broadway movement of the fifties, reached its culmination in the work of the Living Theatre, faltered for a moment after the trial and exile of Judith Malina and Julian Beck, gathered a little momentum with the experimental cabaret offerings of the Off Off Broadway playwrights of the sixties, and has now reached full velocity in reaction to the intolerable Vietnam war. The third theatre is gradually becoming a rallying point for all those frustrated by the moral cant of government leaders and the artistic cant of cultural leaders, for its drama, though born out of a sense of ineffectualness, seeks relief from political impotence in untrammeled free expression. Its outspokenness, in fact, is its most significant identifying characteristic—artistic license becomes an alternative to commercial acceptance. Where a previous generation had to be satisfied with intermittent sniping at political abuses in such disguised allegories as *The Crucible*, the new generation has its targets located precisely and scorched with mockery. Despite the political nature of its subject matter, however, the third theatre is generally created by those who feel disaffiliated from political structures— radical in tone but not ideology, anarchical in posture but not program, equally impatient with the liberal and conservative establishments.

Characteristic of the third theatre are three recent works: *Viet Rock*, a blistering assault on the Vietnam conflict; *Dynamite Tonite*, a lighthearted satire, in opera form, on the Cold War; and *MacBird*, a remorseless parody of *Macbeth* along American political lines. *Viet Rock* is a play with songs by Megan Terry which was worked up out of improvisations by the Open Theatre, itself an offshoot of the Living Theatre, using some of the experimental techniques of the Becks as points of departure. The action, developed through disjointed episodes, cabaret numbers, and actors' "transformations," follows the careers of seven American soldiers from birth to death, wandering from induction centers to training camps to senatorial investigating rooms and finally to the battlefield itself, where the soldiers are introduced to enemy propaganda, Saigon whores, and Vietcong guerrillas. Satirical of both sides of the conflict, *Viet Rock* antagonizes the absurdity and obscenity of war itself, not to mention the pious platitudes of those who foment it.

Dynamite Tonite, by Arnold Weinstein and William Bolcom, is an "actors' opera" which proceeds by means of a childlike naïve verse, using such unfashionable rhythms as the tango, the waltz, the soft-shoe, and the gigue, all with an undercurrent of atonality. Musically, it is an accomplishment which makes the typical commercial musical look old-fashioned and conventionalized, while dramatically, it combines an amiable jocularity with real depth of feeling. The scene is a bunker during an imaginary war—a war very much like that between Freedonia and Sylvania in the Marx Brothers movie *Duck Soup*—but one that nevertheless has disastrous consequences. Despite its wacky scenic devices and its surrealist development, *Dynamite Tonite* is a poignant examination of how belligerent nations resolve their quarrels with human lives.

Certainly, the most explosive play thus far turned up by the third theatre is Barbara Garson's *MacBird*. This work immediately establishes its young author as an extraordinarily gifted parodist, for in converting *Macbeth* to her own uses she demonstrates an unusual ear for Shakespearian verse and an impressive ability to adapt the rhythms and accents of a past age to modern idioms. But Mrs. Garson's purpose is hardly aesthetic: *MacBird* is a savagely angry work, venting the author's fury, in the most abandoned possible manner, at the past six years of American politics. Imagine a *Macbeth* in which Lyndon Johnson plays the title role, John Kennedy is Duncan, and Bobby Kennedy is Macduff, while characters such as the Egg of Head (Adlai Stevenson) enjoy Hamlet-like soliloquies about whether to leave the new

administration or work for change from within. The
seditious implications of *MacBird* are clear and apparent
—it is a work in which all political leaders are seen as
calculating, power hungry, and bloody, and nobody comes
off well. But although the play is bound to start a storm
of protest (not all of it unjustified), it will very probably
go down as one of the brutally provocative works in the
American theatre. As such, it is altogether typical of the
third theatre—that underground expression now being
developed in the cabarets, workshops, and studios—
where all assumptions are questioned, all shibboleths rejected, all dogma destroyed. A theatre, in short, where
reality and joy are once more being combined and drama
is once again becoming superb, gay, and wild.

1966

Does America Want a Theatre?

Does America want a theatre? The question is becoming
urgent, even fateful, since a country without a theatre
is a country without a soul. Is theatre to be a casualty
of a brutalized society, where Americans enact violent
dramas daily at home and abroad, and where everything
but reality is forced to be soothing? Or can it again become a creative, meaningful force in our lives, providing
us with the symbolic acts of a communal existence? If
it is true that we are now on the verge of redefining
ourselves as a nation, will the theatre have a share in

this process? Or will it continue to serve our need for escape from the more painful imperatives of the time?

The evidence suggests answers which are, at the same time, heartening and discouraging. In a country founded by Puritans hostile to the idea of theatre as expressly counter to the laws of God—where stage activity has therefore been pretty much confined to one cosmopolitan urban center—there have recently been stirrings of interest in the drama all over the land, with the result that new theatre buildings and resident companies have been created, and financial support has been forthcoming from private foundations, the government, and local municipalities.

But just as we have begun congratulating ourselves on a new cultural maturity, we discover that many of these companies are in serious trouble. The Actors Workshop in San Francisco has closed and the Living Theatre is in semi-permanent European exile; the Lincoln Center Repertory Theatre is undergoing its third reorganization in almost as many years; the Pittsburgh Playhouse has announced what is coming to be an almost annual change in its artistic directorship; the Theatre of Living Arts in Philadelphia has fired its enterprising artistic director and lost most of its actors; the Front Street Theatre in Memphis and the Long Wharf in New Haven have been saved from extinction only by last-minute activity on the part of supporters; William Ball's American Conservatory Theatre, designed to shuttle between two cities, has lost its Chicago base and is uncertain of its home in San Francisco; the new Mark Taper theatre in Los Angeles is already experiencing censorship harassment from its board; and even the relatively sturdy Guthrie Theatre in Minneapolis is suffering from steadily declining patronage. In each city, the alternatives of the resident company seem to be the same: either adapt to the entertainment needs of the local spectators or look for another home.

This option has become the basis of a debate now being conducted among people concerned for the theatre's future in this country, and the opposing viewpoints show a deep split between those who represent the interests of the audience and those intent on guaranteeing the freedom of the theatre artist. Representatives of the first position argue something like this: Audiences have many moods and are therefore capable of enjoying both serious art and light entertainment. Theatres have been failing because they neglected to satisfy the audience's need for relaxation, and offered only Brecht, Beckett, and weird versions of the classics. "One must avoid the directorial mentality," as one critic puts it, "that insists upon imposing the penitential hair shirt as a permanent garb." Artistic directors should balance whatever is new, difficult, or classical in the schedule with works that have already proven themselves with their audiences, on the assumption that spectators will more readily accept the "disillusionment" of *Endgame* when it is tempered with the lightheartedness of *Charley's Aunt*.

The argument is attractive for its moderateness and practicality (it is, after all, based on an inexorable box-office logic), and also for its democratic faith in the good sense and catholic taste of theatre audiences. It would be nice to share this faith, but I am afraid I cannot take such a sanguine view of the average American theatre-goer. Ideally, this spectator *should* be open to a variety of theatrical experiences, both abrasive and palliative, and, hopefully, he *will* be if his habits ever change. But the available evidence makes such a prospect unlikely at the present time. Certainly, on Broadway, where audiences are at least more accustomed to theatre than in Pittsburgh or Houston, the variety being offered at the moment consists of ten musicals, six light comedies, and one serious play from England. Nor is this a particularly unusual season: I can think of only one play of consequence, either contemporary or classical, that Americans have produced on Broadway in the last ten years to any popular acclaim.

In England, where serious theatregoing is a habit nurtured over many years, nobody would dream of suggesting that the Royal Shakespeare Company balance *The Homecoming* with *The Barretts of Wimpole Street* or alternate *Marat/Sade* with *Sailor Beware* in order to satisfy a spectator's desire for entertainment. There the assumption is that a good play is entertaining by its very nature, and that spectators with lighter tastes have every opportunity—as they do here—to satisfy their palates in the commercial theatre. No, I am afraid the balanced-schedule argument is one advanced by critics who never liked *Endgame* in the first place, speaking on behalf of audiences that have persistently rejected anything but the most innocuous plays. This is not to say that resident theatres should avoid *Charley's Aunt*—I myself share the general affection for vintage farces and melodramas, and believe they can be accommodated in the schedule of any serious company (a brilliant production of *Room Service*, in fact, was in Andre Gregory's schedule the year he was fired in Philadelphia). It is the principle I object to. For the principle of arguing from the audience's point of view prepares the way for any meretricious piece of goods on the pretext that more ambitious ventures will naturally follow. I seem to remember television producers, years ago, claiming heatedly that quiz shows and situation comedies would make it possible for quality plays to appear regularly on the networks. We are still waiting. The brute fact is that the bad invariably drives out the good.

Proof that this may be happening already in the resident theatre movement has recently come in the announcement by one of the most adventurous companies in the country that its next season will consist of *Our Town, The Crucible, Arsenic and Old Lace, U.S.A., Two for the Seesaw,* and *Dear Liar*—a season indistinguishable, in short, from that of any summer stock company. Of course, the company is in financial trouble; of course, such a program will help it to survive; of course, some of these plays are solid works of theatre. But none of them brings us beyond the status quo, and to maintain the status quo, in a time of crisis, is to edge the American theatre a little further toward extinction.

Let us argue for a moment from the artist's point of view, admittedly a very impractical coign of vantage. From this point of view, it is an aesthetic sin to follow public taste; it is a duty and an obligation to lead it. Without a large amount of development and exploration, art remains in a permanent state of stagnation; without men like Joyce, Eliot, Stravinsky, and Picasso, the arts they revolutionized would probably never have moved out of the Victorian age. Similarly, it has been a handful of hair-shirted fanatics in the theatre—Antoine, Stanislavsky, Ibsen, Brecht, George Devine, the Becks, Grotowski—who have made it a place worth arguing about at all, and their advances were hardly achieved by currying popular favor. Audiences proved grateful—*afterward*. Lest this sound undemocratic, elitish, or intellectually snobbish, we should remind ourselves that creative work is not subject to democratic laws; it is a lonely and isolated activity that gains adherents slowly, and collects a plurality only years after it has accomplished its purpose. (Even political democracy was originally conceived not as an instrument of a lazy-minded majority, but rather of an informed and intelligent electorate.)

Are American theatre companies entitled to claim the prerogatives of artists—ignoring and even defying the taste of the public? They have certainly been making such claims, with varying degrees of justification. It can hardly be said that the resident theatre movement has achieved any whopping breakthroughs in the past few years, but—along with the Off Off Broadway movement—it seems to be producing the only native theatre that arouses any hope for the future. Much of this work is self-indulgent, much deliberately provocative, much poorly performed; but some of it is genuinely vital and original, and there is something exhilarating in its courage to strike out along new paths, regardless of community reactions. The experimentation of André Gregory when he was in Philadelphia; the directorial intensity of William Ball in his work with the ACT; Paul Sills' work with game theatre in Chicago; the development of the Open Theatre under the leadership of Joseph Chaikin; the interesting first season of Gordon Davidson's theatre in Los Angeles; the schedule of avant-garde plays planned by Joseph Papp in his new winter headquarters on New York's Lafayette Street—these are the activities that keep one's interest alive in a form that just a short while ago was in danger of drying up.

It would be folly to believe, however, that there is yet a very large audience for this kind of work, though it may sometimes attract considerable attention. Theatre-going is not yet an activity to which Americans take naturally, unless on a quest for after-dinner amusement or cultural status, and the new theatre is often a source of bafflement and annoyance. It is for this reason that artistic directors find themselves engaged in such a bitter conflict with their boards, as subscriptions dwindle and deficits mount. Nor has outside financing from philanthropic agencies been a very dependable source of support. The government-sponsored National Council of the Arts, though it made a laudable grant to Joseph Papp for his winter season, prefers to keep aloof from anything controversial, while the private foundations, though occasionally imaginative and adventurous, lean toward projects that have already found favor with audiences. By far the greatest beneficiary of grants this year—with $900,000 from Ford, $200,000 from the government, and over $170,000 from a variety of other foundations—

is the APA, a company that has been struggling for nine
years and that now produces a standard repertory on
Broadway.

The outlook is not happy, the probability being that
many of these companies will collapse. Others will survive by reverting to community theatre status, offering
a combination of Broadway plays from the Samuel French
catalogue and genteel productions of the classics, with
an occasional unconventional work thrown in to keep
the company from falling into despair. There are, however, some alternatives to the present system—one that
I personally favor is an alliance between the resident
theatre movement and the great universities. This does
not solve the money problem—private universities are in
almost as much financial trouble these days as resident
theatres—but it could provide a solid base of operations
and a relative freedom from the pressure to produce
immediate results or to meet the entertainment demands
of a community. Under the umbrella of the university,
men in science and the humanities have traditionally
conducted research, with the time to pursue their work
and the facilities to pursue it efficiently. Why should this
not be possible in the theatre as well? The condition of
our stage is such, in my opinion, that nothing short of
radical transformation will save it. It has lost its greatest
power as an art form—the power to alter destinies, to
affect men in a direct and meaningful way. Experimental
research, therefore, has become as essential to its development as to the development of chemistry, biology,
or medicine. Under an enlightened university administration, a theatre might be able not only to help preserve
the past, but to make some experimental probes into the
future as well.

The university also offers the advantage of a literate
audience on the premises—but this advantage is more
potential than actual. For although it is true that the
academic community is relatively familiar with the great

works of the stage, and many faculty members and their wives have a passionate interest in the theatre, it is not necessarily true that the university world is any more open to new experiences than any other social unit. As trustees of the past, some professors tend to be conservative in their notions of art, and particularly suspicious of the modern, so that classics are regarded with awe and reverence, and any departure from orthodox procedures becomes a source of disquiet. Yet, if dramatic art is not being continually refreshed, and if new links are not being continually forged between the past and the present, then the theatre will stiffen into a museum. As one correspondent recently warned me, "Beware of the ivy. It has the power to crumble stone."

Still, there is a vast, and as yet untapped, reservoir of spectators in the student body of a university. At present, students are abdicating their place in the theatre to the middle-aged, and going to the movies instead. Hopefully, they will soon discover the more direct and electrifying satisfactions of the stage. For the stage is just beginning to reflect the concerns and obsessions of certain pockets of the younger generation: their outrage over Vietnam; their boredom and indifference to the Cold War; their sense of disenfranchisement and urge to freedom; their discontent with a social inheritance of inequality, race hatred, and violence; their passion for electronic music; their interest in the conventions of pop films; even their less attractive predilections for psychedelic experience, being cool, copping out, and making war between the generations. I am not one who believes in idealizing youth, but there is no question that, for the first time in many years, large numbers of the young are developing a real moral beauty—particularly in the sacrifices they are making to protest the current war. And I am certain that it is from among the young that theatres must draw their audiences if they are to survive.

The audiences do not yet exist, the serious theatre

movement in this country is stalled, the future promises only small and scattered achievements. To the question Does America want a theatre, then, we must answer: No, not yet. But a few Americans do, passionately; others may begin to want one soon; and in the promise of this new awakening, the hope of the theatre lies.

1967

No More Masterpieces

Perhaps one of the most controversial statements of the revolutionary French theatre theoretician Antonin Artaud was his call for "no more masterpieces." For, taken literally, this position implies a complete break with all classical Western literature. It was Artaud's conviction that traditional theatre had reached a dead end, that the works of Molière and Racine had become less a living heritage than a source of rot and deterioration, and that the theatre would never be reborn in modern form until it had burrowed its way back past the written works of civilization to primitive, even preliterary roots. Like all polemicists, Artaud was overstating his case. Actually, it was not the great French classical writers who disturbed him so much as the stodgy staging of their plays by such companies as the Comédie Française. And it was out of his desire to recapture some of the great ages of the theatre—including the French Neoclassic age of Molière and Racine—that he was compelled to make such a blanket repudiation of all beloved masterworks.

Artaud had become convinced that the greatest enemy of vital theatre was the contemporary middle-class notion of "art." In Artaud's mind, art was an excrescence, a limb of man rather than his vital center—it was something cut off from the inmost heart of the people. For the mildewed concept of *art*, Artaud wished to substitute his dynamic notion of *culture*, a word he used in a very special sense. Art was the expression of one man, culture the expression of all; art divided mankind, culture united it. For Artaud, culture was closely related to primitive religion, and would ideally take the form of ritual, ceremony, and sacrificial rites. Connecting with the entire populace and not just the well-fed bourgeoisie, culture was to produce a theatre that would shock and dismay, exteriorizing the dream life through theatrical images dredged from the deepest roots of man's psychic experience.

One does not have to accept Artaud whole, or join him in rejecting the whole corpus of Western dramatic literature, in order to understand his hostility to masterpieces. As a metaphor rather than a literal fact, Artaud's position makes a lot of sense, for it enjoins us to make the maximum demands on the theatrical event, to ask that everything performed on the stage—including classical plays—have the power and immediacy of living experiences, catching the audience up in an emotion of multitude. His is a cry against the institutionalization of dramatic art, against the piety reflected in the very word "masterpiece." Artaud's battle cry, in short, asks us to free the energies of the great classical plays, asks us to liberate these works from libraries and museums, asks us to explore the hidden links that exist between every successful work of art and the deep sensual life of every spectator.

The questions raised by Artaud are of particular moment to us now that we are caught in a period of theatrical unrest, for until we can answer those questions properly we will never properly formulate an American theatre. If theatre, which so recently seemed close to extinction in this country, is now shaking itself into wakefulness like a long-sleeping animal, what form will this new awakening take for the production of the classics? If radical departures are now taking place in playwriting, acting, and staging, how will these affect the presentation of works from another time and country? Certainly, this seems like the proper time to be raising these questions. The decline of the commercial system has resulted, at least temporarily, in a certain tolerance for experimentation; numerous arts councils are agonizing over the meaning of culture and the nation's responsibility to support it; and, although theatre boards and paying audiences are still demanding the more conventional forms of entertainment, artistic directors in various resident theatres around the country are searching for a new sense of theatrical identity. We are now in a crisis which will inevitably lead to change, and Artaud's questions must be raised again if we are ever to advance past the safe, the tired, and the predictable in the programing of plays. What is the proper relationship between the past and the present? Is history something to be memorialized or must it be renewed with each succeeding generation? How do we build a bridge to the past without turning into prisoners of culture centers and slaves to masterpieces?

The answers I am going to suggest may at first seem unacceptable, since the literate community is traditionally opposed to any tampering with the past. But I do not see any way out of our present dilemma unless we are willing to approach classical works with complete freedom, even if this means adapting them into a modern idiom. I should add, by way of a preparatory footnote, that I advance this notion tentatively, and with a little astonishment at myself, since I have often been critical of the extensive liberties directors have taken with classical plays. As a teacher of dramatic literature, I have always felt that a classical play was relevant to the present by virtue of its concern with universal values and timeless traits of character, and as a critic of production, I have frequently cried out against the mutilation of the classics, either through updating, bowdlerizing, or adapting them to the musical stage. I still have strong objections to certain of these approaches. But I have also had to concede lately that excessive familiarity with one's favorite plays, either in the study or in the theatre, can have the result of neutralizing their power. Certain works that used to have a lot of meaning for me—say, *Lysistrata* or *Romeo and Juliet*—have by now lost a good deal of their charm. After seeing a dull but respectable enough production of *Measure for Measure,* performed by the Bristol Old Vic, I became curiously reluctant to read that play as well. And I am even growing gradually estranged from *Hamlet,* a work I thought would never lose its magnetism. To put it bluntly, I have sometimes found myself—during an evening at the theatre—half inclined to shout, "No more Shakespeare!"; and this about an author of the greatest depth and brillance, whom I have loved since childhood. I think we must conclude that the Shakespeherian Rag, as T. S. Eliot called it, is a rhythm that begins to surfeit like any rhythm played too often, and that the famous parody of the history plays performed by the Beyond the Fringe company is a form of protest that becomes more meaningful with each successive conventional production of Shakespeare's plays.

Actually, we have reached the end of a cycle in the staging of the classics, and if we don't attempt some renewal in our thinking about these works, we run the risk of becoming as paralyzed in the theatre as captive husbands now are at Wagnerian opera. Ideally, such renewal should take place every ten or twenty years, and indeed *has* been taking place throughout history; in fact, it is only in recent times that literature has assumed the inviolability of scripture—perhaps because it has begun to take the place of scripture. But even scripture, in previous times, was susceptible of interpretation and adaptation. Just as the gospels of Matthew, Mark, Luke, and John were adapted by medieval guilds in the Passion plays, so the Homeric myths—which constituted scripture for the Greeks—have been in a constant state of development and change. The Electra story, for example, was dramatized by Aeschylus, then by Sophocles, and then by Euripides, each treatment a brand-new departure which reflected each writer's own religious, social, and psychological obsessions. Roman drama is little more than a free revision of Greek comedies and tragedies, particularly those of Menander and Euripides, performed in Greek dress but clearly Latin in tone and temperament. Racine adapted Euripides and Seneca to his own purposes, while Molière Frenchified Terence and Plautus. In seventeenth- and eighteenth-century France, England, and Italy, almost every writer with literary pretensions revised or adapted the Greco-Roman drama; in the nineteenth century, the Germans joined the parade; and in our own day, the tradition of myth drama—which is to say, the updating of classical plays by contemporary hands—reached its peak.

Nobody, for example, dares to produce Greek originals more radically than Cocteau, Anouilh, Giraudoux, T. S. Eliot, and Eugene O'Neill dared to rewrite them. To turn Oedipus into a willful neurotic with a mother fixation, as Cocteau did in *La Machine Infernale*, or to make Agamemnon into a returning Civil War officer, as O'Neill did in *Mourning Becomes Electra*, or to bring the Alcestis story into the modern drawing room with Herakles transformed into a spiritual advisor and psychological counselor, as Eliot did in *The Cocktail Party*, is to wreak havoc on the original intentions of the original authors of these plays. But despite the fact that the adaptation mania possessed the world of literature, art, music, and drama for the first half of our century, no professor of classics has ever been anywhere nearly as outraged by the reworking of Aeschylus as professors of literature, including myself, have been by the reworking of Shakespeare.

It could, of course, be argued that the Greeks themselves set a precedent for the elastic interpretation of their plots, and that, anyway, there is a world of difference between the plots of Shakespeare and the myths of the Greeks. But it could also be argued that Shakespeare himself borrowed his plots, and that the great stories of the Western tradition—the stories of Lear, Macbeth, Candide, and the Underground Man—are *our* myths, as deeply imbedded in our racial unconscious as the myths of Oedipus, Orestes, and Antigone were in the minds of Athenians.

As a matter of fact, it is only recently that Shakespeare has become a sacred, inviolable text. In the Restoration period—the first age in which the Elizabethans were revived on anything approaching a significant scale—plays by Shakespeare and his contemporaries were treated with about as much respect as the first story idea for a Hollywood movie. John Dryden, whose admiration for Shakespeare was second to none, had no compunction at all about translating his great predecessor's works into an idiom more acceptable to his formal and decorous age. He made a hash of *Troilus and Cressida;* he totally revised *The Tempest,* with the aid of William Davenant; and he rewrote *Antony and Cleopatra* so as to make it no longer a sprawling colossal epic but rather a well-organized and unglamorous moral lesson, during which Antony's wife, accompanied by her children, arrives on stage to plead tearfully for the preservation of her marriage. Nor was Dryden unique in this; with the exception of *Hamlet* and *Macbeth,* which remained more or less untouched, every play of Shakespeare's suffered a sea change in this period. As Verdi was later to do with *Othello, Henry IV,* and *Macbeth,* Purcell adapted *The*

Tempest and *A Midsummer Night's Dream* into operas. Colley Cibber revised *Richard III,* adding new characters and a famous line still mistakenly attributed to Shakespeare ("Off with his head! So much for Buckingham!"). And in a later version by Nahum Tate, which held the stage for a century and a half, *King Lear* was given a happy ending which found Lear conquering the forces of Goneril and Regan, Cordelia marrying Edgar, and everyone but the villains living happily ever after.

A similar fate overtook Shakespeare for the next hundred years and yet he managed to survive; in fact, it was not until the romantic period, when the word masterpiece was invented, and a large middle-class public began seeking cultural improvement through books, plays, newspapers, and magazines, that Shakespeare became an object of jealous devotion. It was at this time—during the late eighteenth and nineteenth centuries—that Shakespeare developed into "the immortal Bard," and thus sanctified, was approached in the most conventionalized manner. The famous roles became material for the declamatory acting of actor-managers; scenery became ponderous and extravagant and atmospheric; costumes were made of velvet and brocades, flowing headpieces, and beautifully carved daggers and swords. It was the beginning of the "historical" Shakespeare, in which audiences were somehow persuaded they were seeing an authentic re-enactment of the play in its own period, even though Shakespeare's plays had originally been performed on a bare stage with a minimum of props, and with costumes that continually violated historicity (Shakespeare's original Cleopatra, for example, was known to have worn a hoop skirt).

This movement found its apotheosis in twentieth-century England in the institutionalized Shakespeare of the Old Vic Company and the Stratford Memorial Theatre. Both these institutions produced genuine achievements, particularly the Old Vic during the Olivier years in the late forties and early fifties when Ralph Richardson, Peggy Ashcroft, Joyce Redman, and Harry Andrews were members of the company, and the great productions of *Oedipus Rex, Henry IV,* and *Uncle Vanya* were being organized under the direction of Michel St. Denis and Glen Byam Shaw. But like the Comédie Française, which was also regenerated from time to time, these companies were more often dedicated to perpetuating the past than illuminating it, and, as a result, ended up looking more like museums than living organisms. The Stratford Memorial Theatre, until its recent transformation by Peter Hall (who took the word "Memorial" out of the title and the atmosphere, renamed the group the Royal Shakespeare Company, leased a London theatre, and introduced new plays into the repertory), was invariably overrun by tourists and schoolchildren who had already paid their fealty to the homes of Ann Hathaway and Mary Arden, and to Shakespeare's grave. As for the Old Vic, this company, once it had been abandoned by Olivier and his boisterous companions, degenerated into a collection of effeminate leading men and genteel leading ladies who offered a Shakespeare calculated to rouse no one from somnolence, and who were ultimately absorbed into the quasi-official National Theatre without the slightest protest from anyone.

The academic approach to the classics suggested by the productions of these two companies was more than a period or a costume problem: it was essentially a problem of attack. In the simplest terms, it amounted to a failure to probe and explore the classics in new and daring ways. This is not to say that institutional Shakespeare was impervious to novelty. Quite the contrary, it was at Stratford, and particularly at the Old Vic, that a practice known as "jollying Shakespeare up"—a particularly noxious form of streamlining—first took hold. The "jollying" techniques were especially adored by directors who were doing a Shakespeare play perhaps for the fourth time in as many years, and who therefore undertook to amuse themselves during a rather arduous chore not by trying to penetrate the play more deeply, but rather by changing its physical environment—not by determining a true modern equivalent for the action, but rather by redesigning its costumes, props, and settings. Tyrone Guthrie—responsible for many genuinely exciting productions of Shakespeare—was also largely responsible for the "jollying" approach, which has always seemed to me one of the emptiest and least concentrated ways to produce a classic.

It was, nevertheless, an approach that soon became immensely popular with many of the classical repertory companies in England and America—not only at the Old Vic and Stratford, but at the Bristol Old Vic, the Minneapolis Theatre, the Phoenix Theatre in New York—in fact, everywhere that Mr. Guthrie visited. "Jollying up" reached epidemic proportions with the American Shakespeare Festival at Stratford, Connecticut, where the plays were almost invariably set during some time and in some geographical location totally foreign both to the spirit and the letter of the text: *Measure for Measure* in nineteenth-century Vienna, *Twelfth Night* in Brighton during the Napoleonic Wars, *Much Ado About Nothing* in Spanish Texas around the time of the Alamo. I myself had no purist objections to updating Shakespeare; rather I objected to updating Shakespeare for no discernible reason other than the desire for novelty. And when these techniques occasionally worked for comic or thematic emphasis—as did Franco Zefferelli's treatment of *Much Ado About Nothing* at the National Theatre, in which the characters became nineteenth-century Italian noblemen, peanut vendors, and *carabinieri*, or Guthrie's own production of *Troilus and Cressida*, which analogized the corruption of the Trojans through images from turn-of-the-century Europe—then I felt that this was justification enough. But it was rare indeed when the "jollying" approach illuminated the plot, theme, or characters in the slightest way.

While this was going on in the Anglo-Saxon world, another approach to the classics was being explored elsewhere, particularly by Bertolt Brecht and the Berliner Ensemble, which demonstrated that there is an alternative both to academic conventionality and to irresponsible "jollying up." For what Brecht proved through his own example was the possibility of refreshing the past by fortifying it with a new vision, the possibility of rejuvenating a classical idea by discovering for it a strong modern equivalent. Like T. S. Eliot, Brecht was a writer who used literary fragments to shore against his ruins: his own work is virtually a pastiche of plundered literature. Brecht, in fact, worked very much the way Shakespeare did, striving not so much for originality of plot as for originality of conception, and just as, say, *Hamlet* is a reworking of an earlier play, probably by Kyd, so *The Threepenny Opera* is a modern version of Gay's *Beggar's Opera, Edward II* is a new look at Marlowe's play, *Trumpet and Drums* is a modern adaptation of Farquhar's *Recruiting Officer,* and *The Caucasian Chalk Circle* is an elaboration of the old Chinese play *The Circle of Chalk.* Looting his way through the past, Brecht emerges as one of the great buccaneers of literature, for as he remarked when accused of plagiarizing a contemporary's work without acknowledgment: "In literature as in life, I do not recognize the concept of private property."

Given Brecht's manner of working, it was inevitable that he should turn his attention to Shakespeare himself, just as it was inevitable that the style of the Berliner Ensemble should be based on a distillation of epic Shakespearian production. In the *Little Organum for the Theatre,* Brecht speaks of the need of the theatre "to speak up decisively for the interests of its time," and goes on to give a reading of *Hamlet* in which the chief character's internal struggles take second place to the external struggle taking place between Fortinbras and the Polish forces, advising that cuts and interpolations be made to justify this reading. In his adaption of *Coriolanus*—uncompleted at his death but, finished by another hand, now one of the chief glories of the Berliner Ensemble—Brecht shifts the emphasis of the play from considerations of human fallibility to considerations of economic problems caused by a rise in the price of corn, all played out against a background of battle in which Marcius and Aufidius stalk each other like two Kabuki warriors. As a Marxist, Brecht's motive for adapting Shakespeare was primarily political—he wanted food and money to replace love and power as the prime dramatic concerns; and because of his ideology, he was anxious to bring Shakespeare's feudal sense of economics and primitive nationalism into some sort of conformity with the latest "scientific" findings on these subjects. Nevertheless, despite his narrow ideological views, Brecht brought fresh eyes to the staging of Shapespeare's plays, and gave artistic authority to a whole new method of producing the classics.

This authority was soon transferred to England, after a visit of the Berliner Ensemble in the fifties, and is now finding full expression in the work being done by the Royal Shakespeare Company. Under the direction of Peter Hall,* and in association with such brilliant directors as Peter Brook, Clifford Williams, Trevor Nunn, and John Barton, this group has been creating a quiet revolution in the production of Shakespeare—a revolution which makes the more glamorous productions of the National Theatre look a little staid and old-fashioned. Like the Berliner Ensemble, the Royal Shakespeare Company is not a company of stars but rather of directors and actors producing out of workshop conditions; projects

* Peter Hall has since resigned from the directorship of the Royal Shakespeare Company, and given over the reins to Trevor Nunn.

are initiated less in order to provide roles for lead actors than to establish the identity of the company as a whole. Settings are spare and abstract, using metal, wire, and aluminum; costumes are constructed out of burlap and leather; the acting is terse, ironic, cold, and contemporary; the style of the new plays (like *The Homecoming*) is almost indistinguishable from the style of the old (like Marlowe's *Edward II*).

And indeed the style of the new determines the style of the old. In Royal Shakespeare productions, Shakespeare and his contemporaries are seen through the eyes of Beckett, Pinter, Genet, Brecht, and their contemporaries. Peter Brook's celebrated production of *King Lear*, for example, was such a modernized treatment of Shakespeare based on a serious new reading of the play. Brook, deeply influenced by Jan Kott's unconventional interpretations in *Shakespeare Our Contemporary*, offered *King Lear* in a barren primitive landscape where no birds sang—visually realized by a single geometric sheet of corroded metal suspended near stretched canvas. All action was excised from the play and all empathy forbidden; compassionate speeches, including Edmund's repentance, were simply cut. The battle scenes became offstage cries, and the storm was realized by means of three shaking pieces of metal. Time stood still, activity became meaningless, life inchoate, and the most significant sounds to be heard were the soughing and wheezing of an arthritic old man. It was *King Lear* as if written by Samuel Beckett—a Lear of stasis, ordeals, frustration—in which the repeated negatives of the play (no, never, nothing) became the token syllables of life upon a lonely, abandoned planet.

In America, we are just beginning to probe the possibilities of the modernized classic, though, to be fair, the Living Theatre was experimenting with new classical styles long before the English. Most of these experiments were dismal failures (I am still trying to forget a pro-

duction of Sophocles' *Women of Trachis,* translated by
Ezra Pound into twenty-three-skidoo colloquialisms,
which sent me running from the theatre), but when the
principle was transferred to the production of a modern
classic like Pirandello's *Tonight We Improvise,* it worked
very well indeed (Pirandello's play was reset in New
York, and Doctor Hinkfuss, the Reinhardtian director,
became Julian Beck, a precious avant-garde aesthete).
Similarly, the recent production of *MacBird* could be
considered a radical reworking of Shakespeare, which
uses *Macbeth* for its remorseless political purposes as
freely as Brecht's *Arturo Ui* uses *Richard III.*

To speak from closer experience, a recent production
of *Volpone* at Yale, directed by Clifford Williams of the
Royal Shakespeare Company, made an interesting
(though incomplete) effort to find analogies for Jonson's play in the modern experience. Taking note of
Jonson's emphasis on distortions and transformations of
nature, Williams set the play in a fantasy Venice out
of the imagination of Fellini and Antonioni—a Venice
of aristocratic vice and corrupt daydreams. In this version, Volpone's dwarf, eunuch, and hermaphrodite became a monstrous pipe-smoking hunchback in a skirt,
an outrageously campy queer, and a short-cropped lesbian
in a leather suit who sang tuneless rock-and-roll; Mosca
became a cunning Machiavellian pimp, obsessed with a
loathed body and its excretions; Volpone turned into a
vulgar middle-class charlatan with a bit of the pitchman
in him; and the whole parade of suitors, judges, notaries,
lawyers, and whores found their equivalents among the
denizens of *la dolce vita.* Thus, Volpone's famous apos-
trophe to Celia before the attempted rape ("Come my
Celia, let us prove") was sung and danced to the tune
of *bossa nova,* and Volpone came before the judges, im-
potent, in a hospital gown, being pumped with plasma,
and drawn in a wheelchair by a male nurse.

In the Yale production of Aeschylus' *Prometheus*

Bound, as adapted by Robert Lowell, the director, Jonathan Miller, chose to dispense entirely with the Greek setting, including the white-robed Greek chorus and the conventional notions of the gods who hover over the action. "I want to escape from that deadening limbo of metaphysics," he told an interviewer. "It has less and less resonance for us, those huge, vague, sort of nimbic figures, it's all rather sweet in an unsettling way. I want to go all the way along with Cal's [Lowell's] conception. Not any of this Caucasus, rocks, and crags, and all that operatic nonsense. We thought it would be far more exciting if we could set it in some institution that represents tyranny."

The setting he chose was a vague seventeenth-century background—probably Spain during the Inquisition. Michael Annals' design for the play was of an awesome hugeness, starkly geometric, with niches and platforms of tortured, aging brick ascending upward and downward to what looked like infinity. "It's supposed to suggest a structure far larger than you can see," Miller said, "sort of a brick kiln, a Pharos or huge lighthouse on the Mediterranean going up thousands of feet and going down thousands of feet into the sea; no specific time, but some sort of decaying seventeenth-century culture that has gone bad. The characters are prisoners, they put on the play in this eternal imprisonment as entertainment."

The notion as stated is reminiscent of *Marat/Sade,* where prisoners or inmates also enact a play; in performance, it proved to be much more vague, blurry, and imprecise. What Miller had in mind was the memory theory of Frances Yates,* which assumes that each culture remembers the past by imagining a theatre and associating parts of speech with parts of the theatre. Using the seventeenth century as a kind of "booster message center," men could thereby argue their way back to antiquity.

* Cf. her *The Art of Memory* (Chicago: University of Chicago Press; 1966).

The *Prometheus* production cautiously avoided bringing any recognizable gods on the stage—Ocean became a tired, self-serving, and wheedling old man, Hermes like an S.S. trooper out of an old anti-Nazi movie, Hephaestus a crippled Negro who buzzed and hummed while he worked putting wedges into Prometheus' side—but the Greek gods were nevertheless continually present as cracked statuary in niches well above the heads of the actors.

Miller was anxious to let the action resonate in the minds of the auditors without allowing them to decide on any single interpretation. A lot of good rehearsal ideas, in fact, were thrown out because they were too precisely analogical. Originally, for example, Miller wanted to open the play with Prometheus adjusting a gag in his mouth, being tortured by Hephaestus to muffled screams, and then removing the gag as though nothing had happened. The torture itself was to be effectuated not through any physical contact but through analogy: Hephaestus broke some twigs at the feet of Prometheus as a metaphor for breaking his limbs and beat a leather pallet to signify the painful driving in of a wedge. But the device for Miller was too distinctly Oriental, and it was therefore discarded, rather to my own regret, with the torture scene finally being performed in relative darkness.

Other devices remained intact. In Lowell's text, the daughters of Ocean were changed to three Seabirds— Miller further enlarged their roles by turning them into recording angels who inscribe Prometheus' utterings and prompt the other actors, as well as fulfill their own function as questioners and observers. Io—raped by Zeus and pursued by flies—became the victim, in Miller's hands, of a kind of celestial malaria, in a frequent state of heat and delirium. And Prometheus himself was turned less into a demigod, raging against his fate, than a bitter, self-hating but brilliantly intellectual young man, biting out his words in scorn, reluctant even to give the gods the benefit of his indignation. The result of this was a thoroughly modernized version of the ancient play, with contemporary resonances in the echoes thrown out toward all forms of tyranny (including certain aspects of L.B.J.'s America), but a version which still maintained a certain historical distance.

The dangers of this line of attack are obvious: everything depends upon the tact, taste, and talent of the director. If new values are not unearthed by a new approach, then the whole effort is worthless; and if these new values are merely eccentric or irresponsible, then it is careerism rather than art that has been served. Then again, romantic and light comedies do not lend themselves handily to such treatment, and neither do plays with very particularized environments. I do not look forward with any anticipation to the all-male production of *As You Like It* being produced at the National Theatre this season, and I do not look backward with any affection at the APA's translation of Chekhov's *Seagull* into Noel Coward's England.

But when something in the play itself stimulates the director to pursue a radical new line of inquiry, then even the most radical transformations can be justified. I think we might be more tolerant of these modernized interpretations if we stopped regarding each new production as definitive. Changing Shakespeare is not the same thing as painting a mustache on the Mona Lisa, for if an artwork has been desecrated by such behavior, a dramatic work still continues to exist purely, as a text. If we regard each new production of a classical play less as a total re-creation of that work than as a directorial essay upon it, then I think we will begin to regard mutilated masterpieces with more permissiveness and relaxation. Peter Brook's production of *King Lear* is no more final than Jan Kott's chapter on the play: it is merely one more perspective on a profoundly complicated tragedy, a perspective that will undoubtedly inspire other productions in reply. And it is this continuing dialogue that keeps masterpieces alive on the stage, just as the dialogue among such Shakespearian critics as Coleridge, Bradley, T. S. Eliot, and F. R. Leavis has helped to keep the plays alive on the page.

What "no more masterpieces" means for us, then, is no more piety, no more reverence, no more sanctimoniousness in the theatre. It means the freedom to approach the most sacred text as if it had just been written. It means trying to re-create not so much the original environment of a work as the original excitement with which spectators attended it, and that means establishing a link less with the spectator's educated life—the passages he memorized in school and college—than with his psychic life—the passages burned into his soul by the acid of experience. "No more masterpieces" means treating the theatre as informally as a circus tent, a music hall, a prize ring—a place in which the spectator participates rather than worships, and offers the stage something more than the condescension of applause. "No more masterpieces" means not a disrespect for the past, but rather an effort to rediscover some of its vitality. For masterpieces are the sedatives of a time half dead at the top, and only when they cease to lull us will our time begin to come alive.

1967

Politics and the New Theatre

The past four or five years have witnessed the break-down of existing forms of theatrical production and the emergence of new theatre expressions, originating in coffeehouses, cabarets, lofts, warehouses, and garages. The radical development of what has been called the New Theatre coincides with unrest in our political life and our large centers of learning, and may, indeed, be motivated by similar dissatisfactions. There has, unquestionably, been a serious failure in American institutions, a failure dramatized by the Vietnam war and the Negro riots, and by the unwillingness of the present administration to deal meaningfully with these events, either to end the war or to redress the grievances of black people. An increasing polarization is resulting between the voter and the politician, between the student and the university bureaucracy, and between the intelligent spectator and the commercial stage—all testifying to a loss of faith in a mass society based on money and dedicated to spreading American power throughout the world.

Under these circumstances, the need for some overhaul of existing institutions is undeniable. But will—and, indeed, should—the attempt to restructure the theatre take the same form as the attempt to restructure society? I ask this question because I detect a correspondence between the New Theatre and the New Politics: the Off Off Broadway movement, even at its most Bohemian, seems to be developing an ideological understructure that is helping to determine a number of its conventions. The question is also pertinent because some of these

New Theatre conventions are about to enter the mainstream: the commercial success of *Hair* will surely be followed by a rash of similiar entries on Broadway in the near future. Partly because the old commercial forms have calcified, partly because the "cultural explosion" has fizzled, a vacuum has been created that the New Theatre seems destined to fill. While Neil Simon comedies and David Merrick musicals will continue to hold the Broadway stage in future years, an enclave of the commercial theatre has been captured by a movement radically opposed to the facile myths of conventional New York entertainment.

It remains to be seen whether this movement will help to transform the commercial theatre or will eventually be absorbed by it. To judge from the past, both alternatives are probable. In the twenties, the little theatre movement sent its playwrights and directors to Broadway to gain in wealth and acclaim what they lost in freedom and daring (O'Neill alone managed to preserve some of the integrity of his original vision). In the thirties, the Group Theatre developed those playwriting and directing talents (Odets, Kazan, Clurman) that were eventually to dominate the commercial stage in the forties and fifties. And in the fifties, the Actors Studio grew from a training ground for a new realistic acting technique into a filling station for Broadway, Hollywood, and television vehicles. In each case, a group of innovators brought new life to an enfeebled institution which then proceeded to rise, like a juggernaut, and crush them into marketable commodities.

What of the New Theatre? Certainly it is too early to prophesy its future. At the moment, it displays great strengths and great weaknesses, and, given my worrisome temperament, it is naturally the weaknesses that trouble me most. Among its strengths are the large number of interesting writers it has produced. Although none can yet be called a major talent, the very accumulation of names is impressive: Sam Shepard, John Guare, Rosalyn Drexler, Rochelle Owens, Jean-Claude van Itallie, Charles Dizenzo, Sally Ordway, Maria Irene Fornes, Megan Terry, Lanford Wilson, Paul Foster—the list is too large to complete. All share a passion for experimentation, all are original, all possess an individualized vision, and few would have had quite the same freedom to develop had they not found a home at the Open Theatre, Cafe La Mama, Theatre Genesis, Judson Church, or any of the other numerous theatre hostels studded about the city.

Then, the New Theatre, at its best, is capable of some exciting production techniques. Since Off Off Broadway actors are essentially amateurs without much training in their craft, they do not have the opportunities of more professional actors—and lacking professional opportunities, they lack professional opportunism as well. This gives them the luxury of remaining together as a group, and a theatrical presentation that results from a collaboration between a writer and a permanent troupe, in which directors and actors contribute to the evolution of a work, is bound to prove a more organic experience than one coming from a prepared script and a pickup cast. The Open Theatre production of *America Hurrah* was effective precisely because it emerged out of a workshop in which the author participated along with the performers, thus evolving a precision of attack and an ensemble unity that would otherwise have been impossible.

It is here, however, in the precarious balance between the contribution of the playwright and the contribution of the producing unit that danger lies. And what worries me about some of the more recent manifestations of the New Theatre is that this balance has been upset, with the creative partner (the writer) being eclipsed by the interpretive partners (the director and the actors). This is particularly evident, I think, in the work of Tom

O'Horgan, who is rapidly becoming the most influential exponent of the New Theatre and its most celebrated figure. As a director, Mr. O'Horgan has managed to assimilate a great number of avant-garde influences—including Grotowski, Peter Brook, Oriental theatre, Brecht, and Artaud—but he has adopted these less for interpretive purposes than for the sake of formulating his own mannerist style. Thus, his various productions have served to reflect his own obsessions and techniques rather than to communicate a particular writer's vision, with the result that they have seemed to me virtually indistinguishable. Whether he is disintegrating the story line of *Hair* and reducing that work to a series of musical-choreographic set pieces, or dissolving Paul Foster's *Tom Paine* into his own theatricalist stew, or drowning the language of Rochelle Owens' *Futz* with a thunder of film effects, transformations, raga music, and Balinese dances, Mr. O'Horgan manages to use the same sensationalist effects: nude tableaux, human pyramids, Yoga exercises, and the more androgynous forms of sexual exhibitionism. There is unquestionable expertise in the way this director creates his effects, but they seem to me without lasting impact or any ostensible purpose other than to put on the tourists out front.

The Performing Group's production of *Dionysus in 69* has similar limitations, although here the actors rather than the director have captured the stage from the writer. This very loose adaptation of *The Bacchae* uses less than one-third of Euripides' text, and fills the rest of its three-hour length with improvised interpolations concerning the players' opinions on politics, sex, their own neuroses, and their director, Richard Schechner (I once argued for a more elastic approach to the classics in order to make these works more than pious rituals and cultural yawns—my own articles have a way of returning to haunt me). I would like to be able to report that the Performing Group has discovered some relevant modern metaphor for *The Bacchae,* but its only function is as a springboard for calisthenics, puberty rites, group therapy, and a prolonged orgy with Pentheus as the passive victim of male and female seducers (even this is irrelevant to Euripides, since the Bacchantes were not orgiasts so much as violent women possessed by dreams and drunkenness). The orgy, by the way, is really a petting party in which the spectator is invited to join. As the author fades from the scene, the audience becomes more and more visible. Just as the actors try to engage us in a bull session on current events in *Tom Paine,* so they are crawling all over our laps in *Dionysus in 69,* in a specially constructed environment meant to break down the traditional barriers between the spectator and the stage.

Kenneth Tynan has reported on a similar phenomenon in the London theatre while reviewing a production of Arrabal's *The Labyrinth:* "After student revolt, this is actor revolt. The text, chosen perhaps for its feebleness, becomes a pretext for guerilla warfare, in which the audience is surrounded, infiltrated, and dive-bombed by the players. Their class enemy . . . is the author. 'To the tumbril with the wordsmiths!' is the evening's implicit message. . . . And the director, instead of supporting the king, joins forces with the mob. The result is civil war: non-verbal theatre shouting down verbal theatre, and achieving a state of deafening deadlock."

Mr. Tynan's French revolutionary imagery is very appropriate because the New Theatre style is intimately linked to revolutionary politics. What we are witnessing is the effort of the avant-garde to translate "participatory democracy" into artistic terms, demanding a new egalitarianism that gives equal rank to everyone except the author. Just as the SDS is reluctant to accept leaders or formulate programs for fear of subordinating itself to another form of authority, so the New Theatre, in its more extreme form, rejects the supreme role of the playwright as authoritarian and tyrannical. In much the same way, the performers can defend their lack of training: any discipline or craft can be considered a restriction on the uninhibited histrionic imagination. And because physical motion is spontaneous while language is reflective, the New Theatre is becoming a theatre of gesture, repudiating words as restraints on the freedom of the theatrical occasion.

All this is undoubtedly deliciously liberating for those who participate; for those who watch, it augurs a new barbarianism. While it is extremely unfashionable to say so these days, the creation of theatre art is not a democratic process: it is the work of an inspired individual functioning in close collaboration with disciplined craftsmen. Unless those involved are more talented and experienced than those who observe, then the theatre can have meaning only as a self-indulgence; unless a supreme creative intelligence is guiding the work, then it will serve only the actor's vanity or the director's style. If spontaneity is valued for its own sake, then it soon descends into crude infantilism; if the process of work rather than the results of this process are exposed to the public, then the only ones enjoying themselves will be on the stage. The youth movement in America, which produced the New Theatre, has made real creative advances, especially in popular music, and it has given us all a greater belief in the possibility that our political system can be improved. But there is an anarchic side to this movement which can make a hash of culture if it starts to run wild. To preserve the integrity of culture is still one of the prime goals of democracy, participatory or not, because without a true culture, our lives will be narrow, brutish, and flat.

1968

II

opinions

Journey and Arrival of a Playwright

THE JOURNEY OF THE FIFTH HORSE

by Ronald Ribman

The Journey of the Fifth Horse is quite a fascinating journey indeed, and it brings close to destination a very promising talent in a theatre marked by few interesting arrivals. Sometimes tedious, sometimes clumsy, sometimes distracted, the play has nevertheless been written by a man with substantial literary gifts and a fine instinct for the stage, and I'm astonished that this has not been more noted and acclaimed. Ronald Ribman, the author, is actually something of an original among our dramatists —one who seems to work neither out of his own personal life nor out of the American experience. *Harry, Noon and Night*—Ribman's first dramatic effort, produced some years ago at the American Place Theatre—is set in modern Berlin and might have been written by a decadent German dramatist of the Weimar period, while *The Journey of the Fifth Horse* is a convincing re-creation of late nineteenth-century Petersburg. Both plays are highly idiosyncratic. And though his first play—a confused concoction about an American expatriate being tracked down by his brother, and an hysterical humpbacked German queer plagued by faulty plumbing in a squalid Berlin flat—was far from satisfying, it showed

the same unusual handling of scene and the same refreshing freedom from platitude.

The Journey of the Fifth Horse combines this originality with firmer control and a better sense of purpose.
Ostensibly an adaptation of Turgenyev's short story *The
Diary of a Superfluous Man,* the play is an unmistakably
new work which nevertheless preserves the core of the
story intact. What results is something both modern and
traditional, both grotesque and lyrical, a combination the
author achieves through a highly ingenious structure.
For Ribman has absorbed the Turgenyev plot into a plot
of his own contrivance so that Chulkaturin, Turgenyev's
superfluous man, is contrasted with Zoditch, an invented
character, and Chulkaturin's story becomes a play-within-
a-play subject to Zoditch's mordant commentary.

The Journey of the Fifth Horse opens in a publishing
house where Zoditch works as first reader. Two former
servants of an aristocrat recently dead of tuberculosis
are trying to peddle his private diary to the firm, and
Zoditch—a smug, narrow Philistine with the soul of a
civil servant—is ordered to read it. As Zoditch angrily
turns the pages in his room, meanwhile indulging himself
in mean fantasies of sex and power, Chulkaturin's story
comes alive to the accompaniment of Zoditch's contemptuous snorts and barks. It is soon quite clear that no two
men could be more unalike. Chulkaturin is noble, sensitive, shy, melancholy, full of self-doubt; Zoditch is crass,
petty, envious, shallow, full of self-praise. Chulkaturin is
awkward with women, generous with friends; Zoditch is
confident with women, ruthless with friends. Chulkaturin
feels as unnecessary as a fifth horse "fastened uselessly
to the coach of life"; Zoditch has no doubts at all about
the importance of his own existence.

Yet, despite the contrasts in their station, temperament,
and quality—despite their differing approaches to life
and love—Chulkaturin and Zoditch are shown to be
brothers, as Ribman weaves the two patterns into one

human fabric. People from Zoditch's life—his employer's daughter, his rival in the firm, his handsome fellow employee—become characters in Chulkaturin's story—a young girl from the gentry, the friend of her family, the glittering cavalry officer who impregnates her. And when Chulkaturin loses the girl he loves to the family friend (played by the same actor who steals away the daughter of Zoditch's employer) and Zoditch fails in his efforts to make a wealthy match with his landlady, both men are left loveless and forlorn. The stories merge—Chulkaturin beckons to Zoditch while Zoditch screams impotently back ("Liar! I am loved. *That* is the ending")—and the play concludes, as it began, with some words about a monkey beckoning to a passing man from its cage.

Ribman has created the meanness and the poignance with something approaching dramatic poetry, and his dialogue is full of lyric grace and bitter gall. There are, besides, moments in this play which could not have been written by any other American dramatist—a character struggling with a suit that hates him because he stole it from his master, two men engaging in a tug of war over a tea tray, a peasant freezing to death on the stairs and being attacked by his landlady's dogs, a country squire desperately trying to determine the sex of his daughter's bullfinch by blowing up its tail feathers—these proceed from an imagination that is fertile and alive. Zoditch's fantasies, furthermore, have an eerie nightmare quality that is often chilling, and the alternation of reality and dream is very deftly handled.

As for the production, Larry Arrick has conceived it intelligently, with the aid of an extremely flexible setting by Kert Lundell, but while Arrick is obviously a good actor's coach, he has not coaxed consistent performances from his cast. Some of the Russian scenes have a slightly Yiddish flavor, others are colloquially American, and the mixture of styles is occasionally disconcerting. Although many of the actors are weak, Michael Tolan deserves commendation as Chulkaturin, for he seems to have largely freed himself from a habitual dependence on a resonant voice to tap considerable reserves of power. Bearded, tormented, tentative, and awkward, he sometimes reminds one of Scofield in his emotional attack, and he effectively captures the despondent nobility of the role.

But the performance of the evening is given by Dustin Hoffman as Zoditch. Having seen Hoffman now in both of Ribman's plays (he played the homosexual in *Harry, Noon and Night*, scampering around the stage in a wrapper like a neurotic roadrunner), I can testify to his powers of transformation and invention; he fits Ribman's eccentric vision as closely as Brando did Williams' in *Streetcar Named Desire*. Rigid, close-cropped, twitchy, wearing a brush mustache and rimless glasses, he catches the very essence of Zoditch's miserable self-importance, and he has found sounds and gestures—perpetually washing his hands in a basin, cackling and hopping like Hitler after the fall of Paris, viciously snapping the four locks on his room door, pushing his contempt for Chulkaturin through his nasal passages—that are perfectly adapted to the part. Hoffman presently has crude edges, but I wouldn't be surprised if he soon develops into an actor of the first rank, and even now his understanding of the relationship between character and makeup, gesture, and silhouette is hardly matched in our theatre.

So we have an actor and we have a playwright, both on the verge of something important. *The Journey of the Fifth Horse* stops a little short of complete gratification because the author has not perfectly satisfied the expectations aroused by his ambitious form. But the promise is there, and I have more confidence than I've felt in years that this promise is finally going to be fulfilled.

1966

Notes from the Underground

GORILLA QUEEN

by Ronald Tavel

Attending a performance of *Gorilla Queen* is like being present at a particularly rambunctious drag ball—the evening is as fruity as a nutcake. Emboldened by the popular success of camp, pop, and the underground film, the homosexual Mafia has now decided to advance the sexual revolution another step by exposing its privates in that most public of places, the theatre: the move is both audacious and carefully prepared. The author of *Gorilla Queen*—a former scriptwriter for Andy Warhol named Ronald Tavel (he calls himself "the Lamar Trotti of Underground Films")—has even issued a programatic document called "The Theatre of the Ridiculous" in which he defines the terms of the movement, locating its influences (Art Nouveau, Jack Smith's *Flaming Creatures,* the movies of Maria Montez, and psychedelic art), explaining its name ("We have passed beyond the absurd; our position is absolutely preposterous"), and analyzing its "pasty" and "moldy" derivations in the nether regions of rough trade. Although Tavel's language is the inflated prose of the autodidact ("so far as I could sensate"; "For me it is a claimant of joy in the witness of human freedoms") and his spelling and sentence structure are incredibly slipshod, he is protected against conventional criticism by the subliterate form in which he works: as a character in *Gorilla Queen* remarks, "Hastiness in creation is at the core of camp." Besides this, like most pop artists, he has tapped a virtually bottomless well of material, and he brings to his plays an irritating but quite genuine wit.

The audience at *Gorilla Queen* is composed mostly of Madison Avenue queers on a slumming tour; their laughter is nervous and uneasy. Homosexual theatre in America has hitherto been rather subterranean, and so the openness of this work comes as a bit of a shock to those accustomed to the codes and disguises employed on Broadway. Still, for all the refreshing novelty of *Gorilla Queen*, its honesty is not a sufficient antidote to its singlemindedly sexual emphasis, and I came away from the play feeling as if I had been pounded into the ground by a particularly merciless jackhammer. Tavel's method is based exclusively on faggot parodies of Grade B jungle flicks from the thirties and forties, using men in most (not all) of the female roles. A character named Karma Miranda does suggestive South American dances, wearing a basket on her head into which she deposits bananas; a lesbian named Paulet Coldbare is threatened with jungle sacrifice until it is discovered that burning her will raise the "smut pollution count"; a prissy Clifton Webb-type nun called Sister Carries, dressed in a grass skirt and a vinyl bib, leads a chorus of obscene gibbons called Glitz Ionas (bad Yiddish pun intended) who sit around scratching their crotches and singing off-color songs.

The action moves along propelled by a series of outrageous double entendres and word quibbles, and revolves around a gigantic male gorilla named Queen Kong, who first appears in a hair suit and black basketball sneakers, with sequins on his nipples and a diamond tiara on his head, swinging on a rope and flicking a limp paw at the audience. Some of this is amusing enough (the idea of a queer King Kong is inspired), but the puns soon get extremely fatiguing, probably because they are so relentlessly anal in origin. (*She:* "I abide in a small grass-ass shack." *He:* "I'd like to enlarge your place.") It's as if a baggy-pants burlesque routine had been inverted for homosexuals and then extended two or three hours past its normal length.

Inversion, in fact, is not only the method but the entire subject of this playful author: Tavel uses the theatre exclusively for the purposes of advertising queerdom. Homosexual exhibitionism is given full rein, and the theatrical masquerade is self-consciously reduced to a single transvestite function ("How do you feel about theatre now?" asks one character, to which another answers, "It's a drag"). Similarly, all heterosexual activity is either aborted or mocked. An animal trainer named Clyde Batty, one of the few straights in the pageant, fondles the breasts of a native woman named Taharah-nugi White Woman—but the breasts are false and the woman is a man. Karma Miranda is nuzzled by a queer chimney sweep, who is later caught up in the oral embraces of a female Venus Fly Trap. And Clyde himself is pursued by Sister Carries and the Glitz Ionas ("We'll homogenize this hetero yet"), finally being raped by Queen Kong and giving birth to another gorilla.

Since the performance is as abandoned as the writing, and quite as amateur, it is impossible to evaluate it: once again, the planned awfulness of camp makes criticism seem irrelevant. The more apocalyptic among us will probably view *Gorilla Queen* as one more crack in the disintegration of Western civilization, and they are probably right: in Tavel, one can certainly see the rough beast beginning his slouch (it is ironic that the overture to the play is Schiller's humanistic *Ode to Joy* in the setting of Beethoven's Ninth). But the humanism being murdered in *Gorilla Queen* was already dying in the forms from which camp draws its inspiration—bad movies, television, and the comic strips—and the paradox of the evening is how frequently the parody begins to approach the reality. In production numbers like "Doing the Cockamanie" and "Doing the Frigedelic," for example,

Tavel's burlesque becomes virtually indistinguishable from Broadway musicals, thus demonstrating once again how close our Bohemia is to our Suburbia. *Gorilla Queen* shows us the American Caliban looking into a mirror, enraged at what he sees there, but still unable to recognize his own features.

1967

Three Views of America

AMERICA HURRAH
by Jean-Claude van Itallie

Just a few days ago, a director friend was trying to convince me that America stood on the brink of a theatrical renaissance that would produce at least ten dramatists of the first rank in the next few years. At the time I found this notion fairly preposterous but I am much more willing to entertain it now, having just returned from Jean-Claude van Itallie's three-play sequence *America Hurrah*. I think I would respond to Mr. van Itallie's work under any circumstances—he speaks, if these plays are typical of him, more directly to my own particular obsessions than any other contemporary American playwright—but the important thing to note is that he does not function in isolation. The workshop and cabaret groups with which he has been associated have been collaborating with a surprising number of promising ex-

perimental dramatists, and one of these groups—the
Open Theatre—has partly determined the development
of his style.

The Open Theatre production of *America Hurrah*, in
fact, is inseparable from the plays themselves, and the
difficulty of the reviewer is in finding ways to praise the
playwright without helping to deliver him over to the cultural cannibals. For if Mr. van Itallie provides the mind,
spirit, and creative impulse of the evening, the Open
Theatre actors provide the technique and invention,
formed over three years of experimental work in histrionic
transformation, and it would be criminal if the playwright's success led to any dissolution of this collaboration. (That a similar collaboration produced less fruitful
results with the Open Theatre production of *Viet Rock*
can be explained by the fact that its interesting author
has there functioned as her own director, and thus
sacrificed the shaping effect of an objective hand, not
to mention the toughening effect of an unsentimental
mind.) With *America Hurrah*, the concept of theatrical
unity finally becomes meaningful in this country, and the
American theatre takes three giant steps toward maturity.

The triumph of this occasion is to have found provocative theatrical images for the national malaise we have
been suffering in Johnsonland these last three years:
the infection of violence, calamity, indifference, gratuitous murder, and (probably the cause of all these)
brutalizing war. In his first and most abstract short play,
Interview, Mr. van Itallie examines, through a form of
verbal and physical choreography, the mechanization of
life in modern urban America. The setting is chalk white,
broken by aluminum lines; four nervous job applicants
from various classes of life are questioned by four bland
interviewers in smiling shiny masks. The interview begins
to reduce the applicants to a gaping, blinking chorus,
and when they retreat into the air, the street completes
the process. A young girl trying to find her way to 14th

Street runs a gauntlet of spastics, creeps, drunks, bizarre couples; a telephone operator is given cancer surgery with the actors transforming themselves into a failing respiratory machine; one unhappy man is given the usual ritual advice by his analyst ("Blah, blah, blah, blah—*hostile!* Blah, blah, blah, blah—*penis!* Blah, blah, blah, blah—*mother!* Blah, blah, blah, blah—*money!*") while another is given customary silence by his priest; a candidate for governor dispenses hollow rhetoric on the subject of rats, red tape, foul air, and Vietnam; and the play ends with the entire cast marching in place, their mouths opening and closing in a dehumanized language ("My fault" "Excuse me" "Can you help me?" "Next") from which all emotion has been evacuated. Joseph Chaikin, who founded the Open Theatre, has directed with keen imagination, finding the exact mechanical equivalents for the automatic movement of the play.

TV and *Motel,* both directed by the gifted Jacques Levy, are more particularized works, and both make their points through the interesting device of juxtaposition. *TV,* for example, which takes place in a television rating room, juxtaposes the eventless activities of three tired employees of the company with melodramatic scenes from familiar television programs (performed behind them by actors whose faces have been made up with video lines). The effect of this is to make a commonplace office reality act as a simple counterpoint to the grotesqueries taking place on the screen, thus obviating any need for satiric exaggeration (which mars most satire on the medium). While the office workers quarrel, joke, hold a birthday party, choke on chicken bones, etc., the television people enact the fantasies, crimes, and aberrations of contemporary America. Wonderboy, aided by his Wondervision, saves a housewife threatened by her monster husband; a news program tells of the accidental killing of sixty peasants in a friendly Vietnamese village, followed by a commercial for cigarettes; the Lily Heaven show brings us a loudmouthed pop singer with a Pepsodent smile, singing an endless finale to endless applause; a Billion Dollar Movie about World War II ends with the reconciliation of two stiff lovers ("I've learned a lot . . . Maybe that's what wars are for"); Billy Graham addresses a crusade in Houston ("If you could see through the roof of this air-conditioned aerodrome, you'd see the stars"), trying to reconcile great wealth with evangelical Christianity; a situation comedy, continually interrupted by canned laughter, revolves around the momentous question of why daughter isn't going to the prom. By the conclusion of the play, the three employees have become completely assimilated into the video action, though they haven't even been watching it, thus demonstrating, I assume, how mass culture has the power to break down our reality, whether we allow it to or not.

Mr. van Itallie's final short play is the most exciting of the evening, for it is based on a metaphor so powerful that it may well become the objective correlative of the Johnson age. Entitled *Motel*, it too is based on juxtapositions—of civilization and savagery, harmony and disorder, the nostalgic past and the terrifying present. Verbally, *Motel* is a monologue spoken by a female motel keeper—the homey voice belongs to Ruth White, but the body is that of an enormous aproned doll with a huge carnival mask atop it, complete with hair rollers and glasses. The speech drones on about rooms ("rooms of marble and rooms of cork, all letting forth an avalanche"), rooms throughout history, and particularly this motel room with its antimacassars, hooked rugs, plastic flowers from Japan, television set, toilet that flushes automatically. As the motel keeper proudly catalogues the room's possessions, the door opens with a blinding flash of headlights and a young couple enters—two more Artaudian mannikins on raised shoes, their huge heads bobbing, their bodies moving with the jerky menace of animated monsters. Gradually, they undress for the night, coming together for a grotesque papier-mâché embrace, rubbing their cardboard bodies; then turn on the TV and, to the accompaniment of wild rock-and-roll, go about the cheerful destruction of the room: ripping off the toilet seat, breaking the bedsprings, pulling down doors and windows, scrawling obscenities and pornographic scrib- blings with lipstick on the walls, and finally tearing the motel keeper apart, head and all. Vladimir Nabokov ef- fectively used motel culture, in *Lolita*, as an image of the sordidness and tastelessness in the depths of our land; Mr. van Itallie uses it as an image of our violence, our insanity, our need to defile.

He has, in short, discovered the truest poetic function of the theatre, which is not, like Edward Albee or Ten- nessee Williams, to absorb the audience into the author's own personal problems, and not, like Arthur Miller, to pose old-fashioned social issues in rational, discursive form, but rather to invent metaphors which can poi- gnantly suggest a nation's nightmares and afflictions. These metaphors solve nothing, change nothing, trans- form nothing, but they do manage to relax frustration and assuage loneliness by showing that it is still possible for men to share a common humanity—even if this only means sharing a common revulsion against what is mean and detestable. It is for this reason that I am exhilarated by these plays and by what they augur for the future of the American theatre.

1966

All Hail, MacBird

MACBIRD

by Barbara Garson

The opening night of *MacBird* was for me an exhilarating experience, and in more ways than one. There was, first of all, the work itself, full of irrepressible impudence and anarchic zest—it has been beautifully produced and immediately calms one's fears that it might not act as well as it reads. But the *event* of the opening was equally impressive—a genuine happening in which an underground author confronted the overworld, exposing dangerous private fantasies to public eyes and ears. That *MacBird* has thus far remained free from political harassment suggests either that we are living in extraordinarily free times or that the present administration has learned how to ignore its critics entirely—both propositions, I think, are true, and more closely related than would first appear. But aside from the political freedom it implies, the production of the play implies a new theatrical freedom (perhaps also a new theatrical irresponsibility, but this is a price of freedom) that will doubtless make it infinitely more exciting to occupy a theatre seat from now on. Barbara Garson's burlesque of *Macbeth*, with its satiric parallels between Shakespeare's Scotland and Johnson's America, was clearly designed to be read only at protest rallies and antiwar meetings. Yet, here was a production being performed in full panoply at a swinging Greenwich Village coffeehouse before an audience composed not only of well-wishers but of Broadway celebrities, gossip columnists, theatre journalists, and political commentators—possibly the most divided audience I have ever joined. Two opposing

Americas were rubbing sleeves (I was myself, through the good offices of the Great Usher in the Sky, seated at a table with Walter Kerr), and one momentarily awaited elbow friction that might ignite the whole room.

Nothing happened, but the tension was real, and here lies one of the most signal qualities of *MacBird:* its power to provoke, energize, and upset its audiences. Mr. Kerr has attacked the play for precisely this quality ("So long as a man is breathing he can be hit where it hurts. But it is something else again to be hit where *we* hurt"), as if it were the theatre's function to cushion spectators from pain. Despite his negative opinion, however, Mr. Kerr at least seems to have divined Mrs. Garson's primary moral and aesthetic purpose in the play, which is not to convince anyone that Johnson murdered Kennedy—only the literal minded will deduce that (do they also believe she thinks Johnson arranged for the death of Stevenson and the plane crash of Teddy Kennedy?)—but rather to name the unnameable and speak the unspeakable. If we are living in a world of anguish, frustration, and senseless violence—a world which only the mad continue to find sane and reasonable—then *MacBird* helps destroy anxieties merely by making our nightmares tangible and manifest.

In short, Barbara Garson is—whether she knows it or not—a true child of Lenny Bruce, who, in turn, is proving to be the posthumous father of the new American drama. For just as Bruce threatened to explode the heavens by suggesting, say, that Eleanor Roosevelt had a venereal disease which she communicated to Chiang Kai-shek (hence his leggings), so Mrs. Garson dares to madden every reasonable, patriotic, right-thinking American by bringing the Kennedy assassination on stage as an object for satire, and making his successor the architect of the event. The degree of truth in both statements is about equal, which is to say virtually nonexistent (though, to be sure, one proposition is purely fantastical and the other has at least been suspected). What is liberating for the spectator in these statements, however, is their audacity: in each case, the author turns himself into a potential scapegoat for the tribe, evacuating poisons from the body politic, even at the cost of drinking the cup himself. In former days, this was the function of the tragic hero, and the effect on the spectator was what Aristotle called catharsis.

I doubt if Mrs. Garson would claim this function for herself—her conscious purpose is purely political. She wishes to expose the corrosive lust for power that lies behind the orderly façade of government. For this reason, as some have divined, the real object of her satire is less President Johnson than the whole Kennedy dynasty, and the play is already proving more disconcerting to Kennedy liberals than to Johnson conservatives. The emphasis is even more clear in the playing than in the reading because—in the inspired performance of Stacy Keach—the character of MacBird acquires a dimension that the character of Robert Ken O'Dunc (Bobby Kennedy) never reaches. Keach knows what Laurence Olivier knows about the playing of villains—that the actor must love the character he is portraying, no matter how black or evil—and his MacBird, as a result, transcends vulgarity, sentimentality, cornpone folksiness, and brutality to become a figure of some power and substance (actually, he turns into Macbeth, a character I should like to see this actor play some day).

But Robert Ken O'Dunc remains the sterile, mechanical conspirator—cunning, oily, sinister, and duplicitous—and explains why at the end in the accents of Macduff:

> *To free his sons from paralyzing scruples*
> *And temper us for roles of world authority*
> *Our pulpy human hearts were cut away.*
> *And in their place, precision apparatus*
> *Of steel and plastic tubing was inserted.*

The sticky, humid blood was drained and then
A tepid antiseptic brine injected.

John Ken O'Dunc, played in a stiff and lofty imperial style, is equally antiseptic, though Teddy, who "suffered complications," is merely an idiot ("Bobby, look. There's moo-moos on the lawn"). The most respected figures of both administrations are, similarly, seen with a cold eye, as if they had all sold their birthrights for a mess of political pottage. The Egg of Head (Stevenson) has a soliloquy, based on Hamlet's "To be or not to be," in which he decides to join forces with evil in the delusion that he can work from within for change, while the Earl of Warren is seen betraying the needs of his conscience in order to "bury doubt" about the real assassins. In such a world, all those in government, no matter how personally decent they may be, take corruption from the general fault, and the only honorable alternatives are withdrawal from political life or radical transformation of the existing structure. Thus, Mrs. Garson reserves her satiric spleen not so much for certain personalities in American political life as for a system of government within which it has become impossible to act with honor.

The production is excellent in all respects. Roy Levine, who invented the directorial concept, and Gerald Freedman, who completed it when he took over the show three weeks prior to the opening, have both approached *MacBird* as if it were a play by Brecht. Those who have seen the Berliner Ensemble version of *The Resistible Rise of Arturo Ui*—another work which uses Shakespeare (*Richard III*) in order to make a political comment (on Hitler's rise to power)—will notice certain similarities between the two productions in the use of makeup, props, and costumes. The actors wear pancake masks; the three witches have become a beatnik, a Black Muslim, and an old-style revolutionary who sing, dance, and perform minstrel shows; and the acting is a lovely amalgam of Shakespearian ham and contemporary reference. So are the costumes, which capture the flavor both of Shakespeare history plays and of American political conventions, sports, and movies. The Wayne of Morse, in a Ben Turpin mustache, flies on stage in red underwear, wearing a helmet and brandishing an enormous lance; John Ken O'Dunc is given an orb and scepter during his coronation which are made of gilded baseballs; Lady MacBird comes on for her sleepwalking scene with cold cream smeared on her face, wearing hair rollers and a celebrity hat; and MacBird dresses for battle by donning spiked football shoulder pads, a catcher's mask, chest protector and shin guards, and hockey gloves.

As for the performances, all are good, some are very good, the lead is superb. William Devane as Bobby bears a strong resemblance to his prototype, and adds a singular quality of smiling villainy; Jennifer Darling, as the beatnik witch, has a fine energetic bounce; and Stacy Keach brings to MacBird a pelvic strut, a rolling tongue, and a powerfully brutal presence which makes his fall harrowing as well as hilarious. The settings are imaginative, the music illustrative, and the coffeehouse comfortable (except for its impossible sight lines)—in short, *MacBird* is now bubbling up from underground in an extremely artful environment. Firmly established as a scandalous success, it is finding its way into the souls, if not the hearts, of our countrymen, and nothing can prevent it now from doing its purgative work.

1967

From Hair to Hamlet

HAIR

Book and Lyrics
by Gerome Ragni and James Rado;
Music by Galt MacDermott

Joseph Papp has planted a new theatre in New York, and the first fruit of his careful husbandry is "an American tribal love-rock musical" called *Hair*. Mr. Papp's creation of a winter headquarters and his desire to produce new plays are logical next steps for a man whose theatrical career has been dedicated to underlining the importance of process and permanency. Indeed, as he himself recognizes, these steps are essential to his continuing exploration of the Shakespearian canon. "To keep Shakespeare contemporary," he remarks in a program note entitled *From Hair to Hamlet*, "we must be a modern theatre engaged in producing plays dramatizing the potent forces of our time . . ."

It has been frequently said that the history of the theatre is the history of Shakespeare production, and what we should infer from this observation is that Shakespeare has always been vitally affected by the forms, techniques, and ideas of later dramatists. The Shakespeare of the Restoration was a writer very much under the influence of Dryden; the Shakespeare of the nineteenth century was a figure created by English, French, and German Romantics; and the Shakespeare of our own time is frequently a creature of Brecht, Beckett, and Artaud. In the same way that the Royal Shakespeare Company is continually trying to revitalize its classical productions by doing new plays, so Mr. Papp's Public Theatre is attempting to develop new writers in order

that Shakespeare's plays will not stiffen into "masterpieces," lacking contemporary purpose or meaning.

Understanding also how essential environment can be
to the creation of a theatrical community, Mr. Papp has
acquired the old Astor Place Library and completely
altered its interior for the production of plays. With two
theatres still under construction, activities this year will
be confined to the Florence Sutro Anspacher Theatre, a
stage (more accurately, a floor) handsomely designed by
Giorgio Cavaglieri and Ming Cho Lee, which has the
audience looking down on it from three sides. For *Hair*,
Mr. Lee has built a scaffolding to house the rock band,
whose five members—rather like the orchestra in the
Berliner Ensemble production of *Dreigroschenoper*—remain in full view of the audience at all times. Projected
from this scaffolding are various examples of modern
poster art, including psychedelic designs, and huge blowup photographs of Twiggy, Lyndon, and other such
makers of our fashions and nightmares.

I am sorry to say that what is currently happening on
the stage is of considerably less moment than the environment itself, but it is one of the great advantages of
permanent groups that the whole is always more important than its component parts. The concept of a hippie
musical with an electronic score is potentially very exciting, and I am convinced that the sound of rock—a
sound that has developed real drive, sophistication, and
vitality—is destined to become of tremendous importance
to our stage. But despite its effective moments, *Hair* is
still too closely linked to the meretricious conventions of
American musicals to realize this potential, and there is
something intrinsically one-dimensional in the hippie
movement which prevents the material from ever developing a texture of any thickness.

Since the hippies have recently become the victims of
a vast publicity network, there is also something intrinsically voguish about their scene, and this gives one

the recurrent feeling that *Hair* is going out of fashion even as it is being performed. Like *Viet Rock*—to which it owes its inspiration and even a few of its episodes— *Hair* is pieced together out of newspapers and magazine sections, being a series of topical allusions to contemporary politics and culture, designed less to convey information than to play imaginatively upon what is already known. Thus, the book of the musical follows the careers of two close hippie friends—one a lower-class dropout named Berger, the other a middle-class boy named Claude—as they wander, in a kind of psychedelic picaresque, through the patterned experiences of the turned-on generation: putting down their square parents, who, in turn, belittle their bizarre appearance ("And take off my beads, this is not a reservation"), trying to keep out of the army ("I want to be over here doing the things they're defending"), engaging in freewheeling erotic activity which discriminates neither between race, sex, nor partner ("If you do it with Claude tonight, I'll do it with you tomorrow"), organizing protest marches in the park ("A huge suck-in for peace . . . Bring your blankets with something to suck"), wearing crazy uniforms, necklaces, and tons of hair, and, above all, seeking escape from a hated reality in the "total self-awareness" induced by drugs. At the end, nothing can prevent Claude from service in Vietnam and certain death, and as a last sacrificial gesture, he hands Berger his shorn locks before he boards the train.

Some of this is entertaining, but in none of it do we sense that the authors have thought about or felt their material very deeply, and they are too mindless in their acceptance of the teenage version of reality. The non-hippie world is facilely identified as a society of puritan moms and dads who love war and hate love; the hippies are full of self-pity, self-congratulation, and self-satisfaction; and the book and lyrics are continually threatening to fall into sentimentality ("Follow the children, follow their smiles"). Then, for all its concern with sensation, self-awareness, new levels of feeling, *Hair* never manages to communicate the nature of the experience the characters so frequently exalt. And finally, *Hair* conspicuously fails to record the growing conviction among hippies that the movement is over—a victim of a grosser and more brutal world than flower power can redeem.

As for the production, it has its strengths, notably in Galt MacDermott's score, which, if not authentic rock-and-roll, nevertheless achieves a fine dynamic bounce. And some production numbers, particularly a pot phantasmagoria which essentializes American history from Lincoln's emancipation of the slaves to the Vietnam war, and which climaxes in the ritualized slaughter, under strobe lights, of Buddhists by nuns, then of nuns by Indians, then of Indians by soldiers, is emotionally charged and exciting. But Gerald Freedman's direction is designed more for the old musicals than the new; it reflects the razz-a-matazz of Jerome Robbins rather than the intensity of the Open Theatre; and it, therefore, establishes its links more with *West Side Story* and *Gypsy* than with *Viet Rock* and *America Hurrah* (many, of course, will be grateful for this). The singing is strong and energetic, but the acting lacks color and variety, while the presence of the belted song, the brassy production number, and the choreographed action is essentially antithetical to an authentic hippie atmosphere, which should be cool and lobbed-out rather than bouncing with chorus-boy energy.

If *Hair* does not represent a revolution in musicals, however, it does point the way toward such a revolution: it will be very hard, in the future, to compose a Richard Rodgers-type work with quite the same confidence and equanimity as before. In this sense, then, *Hair* succeeds not so much for what it accomplishes as for what it sets out to do. For a permanent theatre, a good search can sometimes be as rewarding as a good discovery, and if

Hair has any influence on the future work of the Public Theatre—*Hamlet* is Mr. Papp's next production—then it will have justified itself within a system dedicated to organic growth.

1967

The Anti-Hamlet
of Joseph Papp

HAMLET
by William Shakespeare

Joseph Papp is currently launching an anarchic assault on one of Shakespeare's best-loved plays, which, if ultimately disappointing as an event, nonetheless has sufficient originality as an experiment to compel attention. I found the whole undertaking to be pretty courageous, and while it has drawn a predictable response from those who prefer their Kulchur prepackaged, standardized, and wholly digestible like a TV dinner, I think it is bound to have an effect on the theatrical consciousness for some time to come. I should add that the evening is something of an ordeal—after its initial promise, this *Hamlet* gets rather boring—but one's quarrel is less with the intention of the enterprise than with its execution, less with the direction of the road than with the rocky nature of the terrain.

What Mr. Papp has done, quite simply, is to annihilate the play as we have come to know it, substituting a corrupt hour-and-a-half cutting that arbitrarily transposes the order of the scenes, reassigns speeches from one character to another, reduces the *dramatis personae* drastically, and explodes the familiar pattern of action. His motive is clear: it is to rescue the play from the seminar room, to withdraw it from history, to obliterate the memory of all those beautifully spoken, handsomely costumed productions that now stand like a wall between us and an immediate experience of the action. "*Hamlet* is like a sponge," Jan Kott has written. "Unless it is produced in a stylized and antiquarian fashion, it immediately absorbs all the problems of our time." Mr. Papp apparently believes that it is not simply stylization or antiquarianism that has imprisoned the energies of this play. After all, we have already had our modern Hamlets, our Hamlets in rehearsal clothes, our Teddy-boy Hamlets, our angry-young-man Hamlets—and in spite of everything, the great soliloquies still come wafting over the footlights for the audience to hum and mouth as they do arias in a Verdi opera.

It is for this reason, I suspect, that Mr. Papp has refused to invest the play with any contemporary political or philosophical meaning, or to wring it dry of what Mr. Kott calls "the problems of our time." What he has done instead is to superimpose the modern experience forcibly on top of the play. The costuming tells us where we are (the guards wear GI uniforms, Claudius the beard, cigar, and dress of a South American dictator, Gertrude appears in negligees and Ophelia in miniskirts); the props are recognizably modern; and the incidental music ranges from torch songs to rhythm-and-blues (Ophelia sings her rock dirges into a mike, dressed like a go-go girl in a straw hat and tights). But despite an effective evocation of the brutal, menacing quality of the American military presence, Papp's *Hamlet* remains conscientiously against interpretation. It emerges as an anti-*Hamlet*, antithetical to the very notion of a literary masterpiece;

a Happening, where everything is designed for environmental effect rather than for meaning; a Dadaist nightmare, where language becomes an agency not of communication but rather of ironic contradiction and comic
confusion, and where the spectator becomes one of the
most important characters in the play.

The technique of this production is to force gratuitous
vaudeville routines and bizarre bits of business into an
uneasy contrapuntal relationship with the spoken word.
Sometimes the stage business functions to literalize a
metaphor—Hamlet's contention that "Denmark's a prison" is illustrated by the manacles he wears throughout
the opening scenes. More often, the visual effects are a
distraction, designed to divert attention from the words—
it is Horatio, not Hamlet, for example, who wears the
striped garb of a convict. Hamlet is first seen emerging
from a coffin which sits at the foot of the bed of Claudius
and Gertrude, reading his "Oh, that this too too sullied
flesh" speech at breakneck speed, with no inflection whatever. The black rubber fingers of a candy-store monster
creep from beneath the bedclothes; they belong to the
Ghost, who appears here and throughout dressed in long
droopy underwear (Hamlet wears boxer shorts). Hamlet
plays his nunnery scene with Ophelia after having made
love to her (Claudius also gets his whacks at her inside
the coffin), speaking the lines while standing in the
audience and throwing peanuts at the stage. The play-
within-the-play is a production number, sung and danced
around a New Year's party table, complete with favors,
paper hats, confetti, and balloons, all photographed by
Horatio with an 8mm. movie camera.

Hamlet and the Ghost collaborate in two hilarious
music-hall routines: the first when Hamlet sits in his
father's lap like a ventriloquist's dummy and shares with
him the lines of "How all occasions do inform against
me"; the second, during the Gravedigger's scene, where
Hamlet plays a Puerto Rican janitor and the Ghost ("How

came he *loco*, paisano?") plays Hamlet. As for the duel scene, this becomes a game of Russian roulette played by the entire cast—including the audience, since Hamlet, alone among the piled bodies, must bring a spectator on stage to shoot him. "The rest is silence," he says, as an ear-crushing roar breaks over the loudspeakers and confetti falls from the ceiling.

The problem with all this is its ultimate lack of coherence. The actors have been responsible for too much, the director for too little, with the result that the evening seems splintered into interesting but uncoordinated fragments. Mere irreverence is not enough to sustain a play even a third the length of Shakespeare's text, and even absurdity must be organized toward some definable point. Part of the trouble lies with the cast, which is not really capable of sustaining and executing the horseplay. Martin Sheen, playing a Hamlet high on Methadrine—hopped up, always on the move, continually laughing—effectively captures the manic, frenetic side of Shakespeare's hero, but for all his charm and energy, he is simply underequipped technically for a role of this length and complexity. Fred Warriner as a vaudeville Ghost and Ralph Waite as a Castro-like Claudius are very amusing, but too many of the others look puzzled and embarrassed at what they are required to do. What this production needs is a cast trained in comic improvisations—like the Open Theatre, the Second City, or the Beyond the Fringe troupes. Lacking this, it could have used a little more time for its current members to develop the necessary techniques. I did admire David Mitchell's penitentiary setting, however, with its ominous grillwork and circular metal stairway, and the music of Galt MacDermott (who also wrote the score for *Hair*) proves the beneficial effect that one production can have on another in a permanent company's development.

By conventional standards, then, this *Hamlet* is a failure, but in failing it manages to be ten times more interesting than the slick, machine-honed successes of the other New York repertory companies. Mr. Papp's group remains, to my mind, the most audacious permanent organization in town, and the only one dedicated not simply to remounting familiar masterpieces but to trying to discover what theatre can mean to America in the sixties.

1968

A Theatre Slouches To Be Born

FUTZ

by Rochelle Owens;
featuring the La Mama troupe

The most significant theatre event of the past year was not a production but a reproduction—the transfer of *Hair,* newly restaged by La Mama's own Tom O'Horgan, to a Broadway house. I am not one to believe in omens and auguries but I do know when a vacuum is being filled. Next season, the commercial theatre may confidently expect a siege of hippie-rock musicals and avant-garde theatricals, complete with pansexual love-ins, nude tableaux, mixed media, Oriental dances, Yoga exercises, raga music, cunnilingus and fellatio—in brief, the whole mixed bag of the Off Off Broadway movement.

At this very moment, in fact, Broadway producers are probably combing the lofts, warehouses, and coffeehouses in search of a new sensation for the coming season: like every theatre movement of the past fifty years, Off Off Broadway has now become marketable. The man most responsible for the formularization of the movement is Mr. O'Horgan himself, whose stamp is so singularly consistent that all of this productions are virtually indistinguishable. Mr. O'Horgan's highly inventive but essentially mannerist attack sets the pattern for all OOB conventions. Plot, language, and character recede as the playwright becomes a minor collaborator in a fundamentally visual enterprise; style replaces theme as the primary motivation of the drama; political and social commentary, psychology, morality are absorbed into the central issue of erotic exhibitionism. Each production attempts to nudge further back the collapsing boundaries of what is allowable on the stage; each play is the occasion for a narcissistic contract between the director and his actors. Theatrical effects are substituted for dramatic line; gesture swamps words; the stage is a frenzy of chaotic excitation.

One wit has called O'Horgan the Busby Berkeley of Off Off Broadway, and there is some justice in the epithet: he is basically a choreographer of novel, picturesque gyrations. One sees a confluence of styles in his technique—Artaud, Grotowski, Noh, and particularly the Peter Brook of *Marat/Sade*—but O'Horgan borrows only the sensational aspects of these influences, ignoring the purpose for which they were designed. Brook, for example, invents in order to underline the text, O'Horgan to under*mine* it. If other OOB directors, like Jacques Levy and Lawrence Kornfeld, for all their flamboyance, are still subordinating themselves to the playwright, O'Horgan is clearly out to do his own thing and is therefore always intruding his personality into the work at hand. As a result, La Mama has changed, under his influence, from a writer's to a director's theatre.

What has remained constant is the awfulness of the acting. Performers seem to be accepted into the troupe less for the presence of talent than for the absence of inhibitions. Formal craft elements like voice, grace, intelligence, and interpretive ability are of less moment than dynamic elements like a capacity for self-exposure. Still, O'Horgan manages to invest the acting with a spontaneity and confidence which make the unself-conscious display of pubic hairs seem more relevant to his purposes than a brilliantly spoken speech or a finely conceived character. In O'Horgan's theatre, performance simply doesn't matter any more: each actor is part of a machine for creating gesture, doubling roles without attempting any distinction between them, and achieving individuality only when he pulls out of character (as he frequently does) to address the audience in his own voice. All of this has a certain ephemeral charm, but it is essentially mindless and meaningless. What has traditionally provided form and intelligence in the theatre—namely, the script—has become largely a springboard scenario for an entirely new work by O'Horgan, a work which loses its impact the moment you leave your seat.

Under these circumstances, a playwright should reflect carefully before placing himself into Mr. O'Horgan's overly capable hands. I don't think too much was lost in O'Horgan's production of Paul Foster's *Tom Paine,* since the work is pretty undernourished to begin with (Foster's innovation was to create an historical character about whom he knew less than many members of the audience). But Rochelle Owens' *Futz* does possess a fumbling, twisted, barrel-mouthed poetry that is virtually annihilated in the current production. What Miss Owens has written is a pornographic version of *Under Milk Wood,* complete with an omniscient narrator, an episodic structure, and a radio-style loquacity, about a rural Christian community sick with repressed sexual longings. These ungratified desires compel certain members of the community to destroy its one innocent—Cyrus Futz—who has conceived a passion for his sow, a passion verified for Futz in pagan and biblical mythology. The argument of the play ("It's pure sickness, but in its pureness it's a truth") is closer to pure nonsense; the author apparently adheres to the bizarre notion that Futz's sexuality is more primal, therefore more natural and generous, than that of the murder-minded generations who prefer human love objects; and, as a result, one character even strangles a girl in envious rage when he hears Futz and his porky concubine disporting themselves in the barn. But Miss Owens has an intense imagination, and her language combines imaginary dialect with feverish, surrealist imagery in a manner that marks her as a dramatic poet of genuine, if circumscribed, power.

Little of these virtues come through in the La Mama production, since the first thing to go is the dialogue. What with all the frenetic gesticulation, background music, dance, and filmwork that Mr. O'Horgan has introduced, I don't think I heard ten consecutive words during the entire evening. Actors read speeches standing on their heads; they clamber onto the backs of their partners, who face each other on all fours; they hum and buzz and drone, or do Balinese dances during the narrator's speeches; they pair off into heterosexual and homosexual groups, miming mouth-genital play. The calisthenics Mr. O'Horgan has devised for his actors, combined with their own exaggerated rural characterizations, turns Miss Owens' fantasy countryside into a camp version of Dogpatch, where every line is a cue for some new erotic display.

I suppose one could find some value in the openness of this experiment were it not so essentially superfluous, irrelevant, and attention demanding. If the text makes reference to cheeks, O'Horgan translates this visually into buttocks. If the text suggests incestuous feelings between a mother and her son, O'Horgan has the boy kissing his mother passionately, sucking her breast, and shoving his head up between her legs. Before this kind of busywork, the play begins to disintegrate as a dramatic occasion, and becomes instead an occasion for the exhibitionism of actors, with the audience cast as Peeping Toms.

Two years ago, I spoke, in an article, of a third theatre which would combine (the words are Synge's) reality and joy: let me say at once that this sort of thing is not what I meant at all. Mr. O'Horgan's theatre strikes me as singularly joyless and mechanical—a theatre which gives us eroticism without passion, frenzy without energy, egoism without identity, technique without craft, expertise without content, spectacle without beauty, gesture without intelligence. At this demoralizing moment in our history, it may be exactly the theatre we deserve.

1968

The Democratization
of Art

DIONYSUS IN 69

*The Performing Group at
The Performing Garage*

The title of *Dionysus in 69* is a good clue to its purpose:
the pounding of a Greek myth into the erotic mortar of
the Off Off Broadway movement. This loose adaptation
of *The Bacchae* sends up Euripides in much the same
way that Joseph Papp's *Hamlet* sent up Shakespeare, but
its sexual obsessiveness brings it closer to O'Horgan's
brand of theatre, where the pelvis becomes the actor's
primary organ of expression. Where The Performing
Group differs a little from the La Mama troupe is in the
emphasis it gives to audience participation. Richard
Schechner's notion of "environment" theatre, partly derived from Grotowski, partly from the Living Theatre,
is meant to invite the spectator into the action so as to
end his isolation from the stage. And so, after having
been admitted into the Wooster Street garage as though
into an Eleusinian mystery, you find yourself sharing a
perch with several actors atop one of various wooden
structures, or (if you are less lucky) squatting below on
a dirty rug while trying—without inhaling odors from
the assorted feet, buttocks, armpits, and mammaries that
are being exposed near your nostrils—to draw a cool
breath from the steaming atmosphere.

The steam is contributed by the New York summer, but
it is perfectly appropriate to what follows: a string of
sexual exercises in which the more intrepid are invited

to join (one or two do occasionally, very passively and very self-consciously). None of this gets past the petting stage, but it is clearly meant to suggest an orgy whose justification is to be found in the myth: Schechner sees the Dionysian impulse primarily as a libidinal affair. This interpretation would undoubtedly have surprised the Greeks, who looked upon Aphrodite, not Dionysus, as the embodiment of the erotic instinct—Dionysus was considered the source of drunken frenzy, hallucination, and irrationality, with sex as a possible result but hardly a motivating drive. For this reason, a more accurate modern parallel to Bacchic dissociation would have been the drug experience, since it is hallucinogenics rather than fraternity-house sex play that induces the kind of transcendent religious possession sugggested by Euripides. In any event, the effect of all these perambulations is not to involve the spectator but rather to isolate him further as a voyeur in a stag show, watching Pentheus become the victim of some overheated Bacchantes who make passes at his genitals and of Dionysus, who tries to bugger him.

At the same time that the actors are flexing their sexual muscles, they are also doing physical preparations: much of this long uninterrupted evening is taken up with isometrics, Yoga, calisthenics, and posturepedic exercises. Here The Performing Group has the opportunity to demonstrate the process by which it evolved the show, but it is curious to note once again how small a part words play in this process. *Dionysus in 69* uses only about a third of Euripides' play in the Arrowsmith translation, supplementing this with sections from *Hippolytus* and *Antigone*, and with a considerable number of ad libs from the actors; yet, language is always being buried under gesture. The more interesting images—Pentheus being dragged through the greased legs of four or five women in a rite of birth or puberty, or running frantically around the environment trying to stifle the whispers and hisses of the Chorus—have virtually nothing to do with any coherent dramatic purpose that I could divine.

Obviously, these performers are not interested in interpreting a play—however audaciously—so much as in expressing themselves: we are exposed to quite a bit of group therapy as the actors withdraw from their roles and begin to discuss their personal hang-ups. As in the O'Horgan production of *Tom Paine*, where the action is broken off for a bull session with the audience on current events, this discussion remains at the intellectual level of the actors—which is not very high. Hippie colloquialisms alternate with the psychiatric jargon of Dr. Rose Franzblau. One actor tells another, "You've got a thousand and one insecurities," others discuss their "frustrations" and their need to "verbalize." I hope these analyses prove therapeutic for the actors; I can testify that they do nothing for the observer, except to convince him that it's more fun to be on stage than in the audience. Naturally, I recognize the need for spontaneity in the theatre, but if process is to take the place of results, and an audience is present, then this process had better be interesting. Most of the time, however, The Performing Group is merely indulging private moments, revealing lives of considerably less significance than one has a right to demand in the theatre.

Still, by relative standards, there is a looseness about this company that makes me prefer it to the more mechanical La Mama troupe, along with flashes of wit that occasionally illuminate. No member of the group is a finished actor—or even a started one, for that matter— but all the performers are relaxed and athletic, and one is even personable. William Finley, who plays Dionysus, has an owlish hipster charm with his steel-rimmed glasses and long hair, and he has the capacity to improvise cogently ("I am running for President, that's right, who else have you got?"). Haranguing the other actors with a bullhorn, Finley manages swift subtle shifts between his role and his own personality that provide the evening with its only focus. His final peroration, however: "There is an urge in America—to have freedom—not bullshit freedom but real freedom. . . . This might mean burning down a slum and listening to the screams. . . . Freedom from responsibility—get guns" is a violation of the Artaud-ian principles on which this project is presumably built, since it incites to violence instead of evacuating violence in the theatre through significant myths. But then, the American avant-garde seems more and more to be reflecting the convulsive nature of the country, on the right and the left, as it leaves the world of art and tries to become contiguous with life.

Alas, I must still try to measure theatre by the standards of art, and by these standards it is presenting a sorry spectacle. The Off Off Broadway movement, which began so promisingly with *America Hurrah*, *MacBird*, and the experimental probes of the Open Theatre, is now cultivating its worst faults, developing an anarchic Philistinism which virtually throws the writer out of the theatre. The playwright John Osborne, commenting on a similar development in the English theatre, calls this "democracy gone mad. It ignores the premise of art, which is that somebody can do something better than you. The assumption of all those happenings is that everybody can do it as well as everybody else. Some clod flashing lights on a wall is doing something as significant as putting pen to paper." The democratization of art (and sex is popular with the avant-garde because it is the great equalizer) is the inevitable consequence of a culture where everybody is encouraged to do his own thing, and excellence gives way before permissiveness. But while all this self-expression is undoubtedly exhilarating to those who practice it, it could spell the end of history, literature, and tradition while banishing craft and inspiration from the arts. For the arts, including the theatre, are the culmination not of self-indulgence and accident but of discipline and imagination. What may be coming now is a theatre of liberated, arrogant amateurs—a theatre where there will be no more spectators, only performers, each tied up in his own tight bag.

1968

BROADWAY

Albee's
Allegory of Innocence

MALCOLM
by Edward Albee;
adapted from the novel by James Purdy

By closing *Malcolm* five days after it opened, Edward
Albee has cleverly disarmed criticism: nobody wants to
be caught flogging a corpse. There has been general agreement over the dreadfulness of the play; even the author
seems half inclined to forget that it was ever written; and
Malcolm is now destined for that oblivion reserved for so
many miscarriages of the postwar American dramatic
imagination. Albee's rather good-natured detachment
from the fate of his play is a more appealing posture
than his defensive acerbity over the reception of *Tiny
Alice,* but I do not think his responsibility for the work
can be so lightly evaded. Since Albee is now a "leading
American dramatist" (a description that seems lately to
have rather lost its distinction), his failures must be
scrutinized as well as his successes, especially when these
proceed from the same sort of assumptions and suggest
a similar thematic purpose.

Albee has adapted *Malcolm* from James Purdy's novel,
a book which, after seeing the play, I found myself unable to open (Albee's declared intention was to attract
readers to Purdy's writings, but he seems to have had
precisely the opposite effect). In the playwright's hands,
at any rate, the story takes the form of a *Bildungsroman*
about a fifteen-year-old Innocent who has lost his father,

and is now sitting on a golden bench, staring into space and wondering how to find him. There he is accosted by a mysterious astrologer-magician named Cox—a figure inexplicably made up to look like Uncle Sam—who sends Malcolm on a Quest for Experience ("You must begin your education—education for life, dear boy"). Malcolm's education consists in meeting various people who try to "sell," "use," or "corrupt" him (Albee's imagery remains exclusively sexual throughout), largely because he is still unblemished and undefiled. These include an ancient in a Confederate uniform who has married a whore with orange hair—these two argue interminably over whether the old fellow is 97 or 192; a wealthy society lady named Mme. Girard who has a philandering husband and four young lovers—she finds Malcolm to be "the one decent thing in this entire world" and so inevitably tries to seduce him; a Bohemian lady who paints Malcolm's portrait ("It has a certain *him* about it, don't you think?"); her husband, an ex-con who fondles Malcolm's golden hair while protesting that he is not a queer; and finally a nymphomaniac nightclub singer named Melba who warbles hot songs ("I wanna do it, baby, do it to you") and who "does it" to Malcolm so often that she kills him. Malcolm is prepared for this unusual martyrdom by one of Melba's ex-husbands who takes him to a cathouse; and thus anointed, Malcolm is plied with aphrodisiacs and delivered over to the inexhaustible Melba ("We do a lot of being married, don't we?" queries Malcolm wanly from the bedclothes), finally expiring of acute alcoholism and sexual hyperaesthesia, the latter defined by Albee as a "violent protracted excess of sexual intercourse." At the curtain, Malcolm is being mourned by Mme. Girard ("What have we not lost?"), thus demonstrating that in Albee's world a character may begin by seeking Dad, but always ends by finding Mom.

The work, in short, is one of those squashy allegories of lost innocence first introduced into the theatre by

Tennessee Williams, and thereafter perpetuated on the American stage by Arthur Laurents (*A Clearing in the Woods*), Arthur Kopit (*Oh Dad* and *Sing to Me Through Open Windows*), and Albee himself (*The American Dream*). Although the idea of innocence corrupted is strong in Milton and Henry James, the execution of it in American plays owes more to the Brothers Grimm, for such works are often full of clowns, astrologers, and fairy godmothers, and they are always aching with sentimental nostalgia over childhood or some such Edenic period before the onset of sinful puberty. The theme is meant to be of universal application, but what makes it so difficult to credit these allegories is the absolute passiveness of their central figures and the masked, guarded nature of their real themes: an Everyman of this type is brought not to the brink of the grave but rather to the edge of some unnamed sexual aberration. *Malcolm* is even more vague about its true purpose than previous examples of the genre, partly because it is written in those portentous, meaningless epigrams that authors use when they have nothing to say ("Between simile and metaphor lies all the sadness of the world," notes one character, thus confounding those who might think sadness lies between triphthongs and hieroglyphs), but mostly because it is Albee's most deeply homosexual work. As Albee gets closer and closer to his true subjects—the malevolence of women, the psychological impact of Mom, the evolution of the invert—he tends to get more abstract and incoherent until he is finally reduced, as here, to a nervous plucking at broken strings.

Alan Schneider's production matches the play in one sense: it is a disaster. The direction alternates between the tasteless (Mme. Girard's four lovers kiss her breasts) and the clichéd (Melba's ex-husband is dressed in tight jeans, boots, and studded jacket, and menaces like Brando in *The Wild One*); the setting—a geometric series of moving Japanese panels and treadmills—has no illustrative relation to the play; the costumes are both excessively gaudy and curiously inconsistent (some are Victorian, some modern); even the makeup lacks care (the old Confederate is played by a young actor with obviously powdered hair). As for the actors, they represent the most disappointing aspect of the evening, since the majority are usually excellent performers playing well below their usual level of competence (Jennifer West's raucous, vulgar Melba rises somewhat above hers), and the central role is impersonated by a young man who communicates innocence primarily through a wide-eyed stare and a piping voice which rises on final syllables. Innocence, however, is a concept that has eluded the author too; let us fervently hope that he is now experienced enough never to essay it again.

1966

Albee
Decorates an Old House

A DELICATE BALANCE
by Edward Albee

Edward Albee's recent work poses a number of problems
for the reviewer, one of them being that it is virtually impossible to discuss it without falling into repetition. Looking over the anthology of pieces I have written about his
annual procession of plays, I discover that I am continually returning to two related points: that his plays
have no internal validity and that they are all heavily
dependent upon the style of other dramatists. At the risk
of boring the reader, I am forced to repeat these judgments about *A Delicate Balance*. The fourth in a series of
disappointments that Albee has been turning out since
Who's Afraid of Virginia Woolf?, this work, like its predecessors, suffers from a borrowed style and a hollow
center. It also suggests that Albee's talent for reproduction
has begun to fail him until by now the labels on his
lendings are all but exposed to public view. Reviewers
have already noted the stamp of T. S. Eliot on *A Delicate
Balance* (a nametag that was somewhat more subtly im-
printed on *Tiny Alice* as well), and it is quite true that
Albee, like Eliot before him, is now trying to invest the
conventional drawing-room comedy with metaphysical
significance. But where Eliot was usually impelled by a
religious vision, Albee seems to be stimulated by mere
artifice, and the result is emptiness, emptiness, emptiness.

    A Delicate Balance is, to my mind, a very bad play—
not as bad as *Malcolm*, which had a certain special awfulness all its own, but boring and trivial nevertheless. It is

also the most remote of Albee's plays—so far removed from human experience, in fact, that one wonders if Albee is not letting his servants do his living for him. Although the action is supposed to take place in suburban America—in the living room and conservatory of an upper middle-class family—the environment is more that of the English landed gentry as represented on the West End before the Osborne revolution. Leatherbound books sit on library shelves, elbowing copies of *Horizon;* brandy and anisette and martinis are constantly being decanted between, over, and under bits of dialogue; the help problem becomes an object of concern, as well as problems of friendship, marriage, sex, and the proper attitude to take toward pets; and characters discuss their relationships in a lapidary style as far from modern speech as the whistles of a dolphin.

The failure of the language, actually, is the most surprising failure of the play, especially since Albee's control of idiom has usually been his most confident feature. Here, on the other hand, banal analogies are forced to pass for wisdom: "Friendship is something like a marriage, is it not, Tobias, for better or for worse?" The plot is signaled with all the subtlety of a railroad brakeman rerouting a train: "Julia is coming home. She is leaving Douglas, which is no surprise to me." A relaxed idiom is continually sacrificed to clumsy grammatical accuracy: "You are a guest," observes one character, to which the other replies, "As you." If colloquialisms are spoken, they are invariably accompanied by self-conscious apologies: One character drinks "like the famous fish," while another observes, "You're copping out, as they say." Empty chatter is passed off as profound observation with the aid of irrelevant portentous subordinate clauses: "Time happens, I suppose, to people. Everything becomes too late finally." And the play ends with one of those vibrato rising-sun lines familiar from at least a dozen such evenings: "Come now, we can begin the day."

It is clear that Albee has never heard such people talk, he has only read plays about them, and he has not retained enough from his reading to give his characters life. More surprisingly, he has not even borrowed creatively from his own work, for although a number of Albee's usual strategies are present in *A Delicate Balance,* they do not function with much cogency. One character, for example, tells of his difficulties with a cat that no longer loved him—a tale that recalls a similar tale about a dog in *The Zoo Story*—but here the narrative is no more than a sentimental recollection. Similarly, a dead child figures in this work, as in so many Albee plays, but it has no organic relevance to the action and seems introduced only to reveal the sexual hang-ups of the protagonist and to fill up time.

Too much of the play, in fact, seems purely decorative: there simply isn't enough material here to make up a full evening. *A Delicate Balance* concerns a family of four—a passive husband, an imperious wife, an alcoholic sister-in-law, and a much divorced daughter—whose problems are exacerbated when they are visited by some married friends. This couple has just experienced a nameless terror in their home, and when they move in on the family for comfort and security, a delicate balance is upset, all the characters learning that terror is infectious, like the plague. This plot has a nice touch of mystery about it, but its main consequence is to move various sexually estranged couples into each other's rooms after various impassioned dialogues. What finally puzzles the will is how very little Albee now thinks can make up a play: a few confessions, a few revelations, a little spookiness, and an emotional third-act speech.

Alan Schneider's production is stiff and pedestrian. One senses discomfort in the staging as well as in the performances: these are not roles that actors fill with pleasure. Rosemary Murphy has some vigor as the alcoholic sister-in-law, coming on like one of those sardonic (male) drunks that used to appear in the plays of Philip Barry, but like the other performers, she has a difficult time recovering the portentous rhythms of the play when she stumbles over a line. Hume Cronyn, usually one of our most dependable actors, is dry and uninteresting as the father; Jessica Tandy is delicate but high-pitched as the mother; and Marian Seldes as the daughter is vocally and physically angular. The director occasionally tries for an effect, as when he arranges four ladies with their coffee cups in the attitude of an Eliot chorus, but most of the time we are spared such tableaux and the stage is left as empty as the play. It is an emptiness that no amount of activity can fill. *A Delicate Balance* is an old house which an interior decorator has tried to furnish with reproductions and pieces bought at auction. But the house has never been lived in and the wind murmurs drily through its corridors.

1966

Albee
at the Crossroads

EVERYTHING IN THE GARDEN
by Edward Albee

When the actors and the director were first announced
for *Everything in the Garden,* I couldn't believe my ears:
Was Edward Albee concocting a formula Broadway hit?
Barbara Bel Geddes and Barry Nelson—previously co-
starred, to quote from the program notes, "in two of the
modern theatre's most popular, long-running comedies:
The Moon Is Blue and *Mary, Mary*"—were to be "reunited"
in a play by the author of *The Zoo Story* and *Who's Afraid
of Virginia Woolf?* And Peter Glenville, who frequently
wears the colors of David Merrick, had interrupted Alan
Schneider's long, unbroken collaboration with Albee to
spread his directorial gloss over *Everything in the Garden*
as he had previously over *Tchin Tchin, Becket,* and
Take Me Along. These were suspicious enough signs.
What made it even more possible that Albee was preparing to join the company of Jean Kerr and F. Hugh Herbert
was the bizarre development of his recent career which
found him first rewriting a Merrick musical called *Break-
fast at Tiffany's,* and then grinding out cocktail party
chit-chat, in *A Delicate Balance,* with brandy being decanted over supernatural conversations in a *House and
Garden* setting.

It was soon to become apparent that, in Albee's mind
at least, all this was a planned strategy. "Let them think
they're seeing *Mary, Mary,*" he was reported to have told
his cast during the first reading of the play. And, indeed,
that is precisely what we do think during Albee's opening

scenes. The curtain rises on another of William Ritman's Westchester settings; Nelson and Bel Geddes, cast again as a cheerful suburban couple, start wisecracking about money, sex, and gardening tools; and the audience, obviously relieved that it is being given one more inconsequential post-prandial entertainment, begins to respond with those flatulent barks that pass for laughter in our theatre. As the play proceeds, there are signs that Albee intends to jolt such expectations, but the audience keeps sniffing out the jokes, and when they don't come, slips into indifference. Melodrama follows comedy, looking false and misapplied. What was apparently intended as an indictment becomes just another pastime, and an increasingly unrewarding one. Albee has succeeded too well in his subterfuge; the audience has taken the play away from him. It fails on the only level it can be adequately recognized—as a bright Broadway hit.

Actually, *Everything in the Garden* is an American adaptation of a London play by Giles Cooper which, if no great shakes itself, at least has a certain power without Albee's commercial frosting. A straightforward attack on the values and prejudices of the mindless, country-club classes of England, the Cooper play concerns a middle-aged man and his wife, living above their means in a neighborhood where wealth dictates status. In order to increase their capacity for conspicuous consumption, the wife, Jenny, advertises for a job; a brothel madam answers, anxious to add Jenny to her stable. Attracted by the possibility of some extra cash, Jenny soon begins turning tricks. When the source of the bounty can no longer be hidden, her husband—after some initial indignation— accepts the situation with equanimity. What is more, he soon learns, during a party, that all of his neighbors derive their wealth from the same polluted wifely sources. When a bachelor friend makes the same discovery, the friend is killed and buried in the garden. Thus, the Cooper play is a variation on the theme of the skeleton in the cup-

board with Shaw-Ibsen overtones added—an examination
of the murder and greed that lie in the hearts of respectable pillars of society.

What Albee adds to this structure is a frothy atmosphere, an American idiom and environment (the Cooper
play was based on an actual story about some Long
Island matrons), and a great deal of ham-handed pounding of messages. Where Cooper makes his points *sotto
voce*, Albee yodels them in that tone of strident moral
purity he usually employs when discussing his attitude
toward South African apartheid and Pulitzer Prizes.
"You're all killers and whores," shouts Albee's heroine,
after having noticed that her husband works for a firm
that produces "germ gas" and that their publishing friends
advertise bad books. (This, I guess, is what is known as
"universalizing" a theme; like all the ideas in the play,
it remains completely unexamined.) Also underlined is
the liberalism of the couple's young son, who disapproves
of anti-Semitism and racism (a courageous line to take
with the Broadway audience). And padded, if not added,
is the character of Jack, the victim of the play, who is
permitted direct address to the audience about his wealth,
his passion for "Polish vod," and his bequest of "three and
a half mil" to the couple that helps to kill him. Albee's
play ends on a note of uplift: Jenny and her husband
discover they still love each other, Jack tells us they will
get their money in seven years "if they're tough enough."

Albee's version of *Everything in the Garden*, in short, is
without interest, and I'm not concealing very well my
reluctance to write about it. What continues to remain
somewhat interesting, because unresolved, is the author's
ambiguous relationship to his audience. As I have had
occasion to remark somewhat too often, Albee's identity
as a dramatist is highly uncertain. Lacking his own vision,
he turns to adaptation; lacking his own voice, he borrows
the voice of others. What has remained constant through
his every change of style—through the progression of his

influences from Genet to Strindberg to Pirandello to Williams to Ionesco to Eliot—is his peculiar love-hatred for those who attend his plays. Albee's desire to undermine the audience and be applauded for it is now leading him into the most extraordinary stratagems and subterfuges, just as his desire to be simultaneously successful and significant has managed by now to freeze his artistic imagination. He has two choices, I think, if he is ever to create interesting work again: either to resolve this conflict, or to write about it. But both alternatives oblige him to become a great deal less masked, a great deal more daring, a great deal more open than he now chooses to be.

1967

Love and Hate
on Broadway

LUV
by Murray Schisgal

POOR BITOS
by Jean Anouilh

The comedy that everybody loves is an agreeable trifle
which, in palmier days, might have constituted a brief
blackout sketch at the Palace between the vaudeville acts.
How it has managed to achieve its present eminence as
a celebrated American success is a question we might
take a moment to ponder. Several years ago, Murray
Schisgal demonstrated with two short plays—*The Typists*
and *The Tiger*—that he had certain modest gifts, among
them a talent for creating comic situations and offbeat
characters. This was enough to put him two steps ahead
of our usual money dramatists, who generally paralyze
one with their triteness and ineptitude. But since Schisgal
was also able to adapt the formal techniques of the
French avant-garde to a homogenized view of life, he was
immediately drafted into Walter Kerr's ideological war
against the advanced theatre—America's answer to European despair. All of Mr. Schigal's qualities, including his
blandness, are confirmed in *Luv*. The work has been
padded to twice its natural length (Schisgal is obviously
more comfortable with the one-act play), but it has an
attractive simplicity, and it is being enhanced by an
exceedingly engaging production.

I can foresee Mr. Schisgal writing a hundred such plays
in the future, each of them a gold mine. With a little

luck, and equally able support, he could become the Henri
Bernstein of our stage. But I can also foresee the swift
termination of his appeal if he begins to believe what
Mr. Kerr and other reviewers are now telling him—
namely, that he has profound things to say about marriage, romantic ideals, suicide, divorce, bohemianism, and
so forth. Actually, the Broadway success of *Luv* can be
attributed to the fact that it doesn't say a thing about
anything. While Schisgal's material is potentially satiric,
he renders everything down into a soothing demulcent,
so that the Broadway audience can have the tribute of
the avant-garde without its tribulations. Even further
removed from reality than the opiates of James M. Barrie,
Luv has value primarily as "pure" comedy—that is, as
a neutral canvas upon which a gifted director, Mike
Nichols, and a brilliant comedian, Alan Arkin, can splash
wild colors. For Nichols and Arkin are the real creative
minds behind *Luv*—if you doubt this, watch how quickly
the play fades when such routine actors as Eli Wallach
and Anne Jackson are alone on stage. Nichols and Arkin
have wisely turned away from the theatre of the absurd,
which inspired the playwright, and exploited that American comic tradition which inspired *them*: burlesque,
vaudeville, Chaplin, the Marx Brothers, and their own
previous associations with Nichols and May and the
Second City. What these two men cannot give the work—
for all their inventiveness and versatility—is an intelligent spine. But then if the work contained any intelligence, it would not be the comedy everybody loves.

   Poor Bitos is about a man whom everybody hates, and
the play has been rather universally disliked as well. It
deserves a better response, but I find it hard to work up
too much sympathy over its indifferent reception. Like
Duerrenmatt's *The Physicists*, Anouilh's *Poor Bitos* represents the failure of intrinsically fascinating dramatic
material because of the author's inability to realize his

theme in significant action, or think it through to a firm conclusion. Duerrenmatt's play concerned the moral obligation of physicists to abstain from thinking. This is a refreshing and convincing idea, but it got lost in Duerrenmatt's heavy-handed style, his indecision over whether to write a farce or a melodrama, and his witless madhouse digressions. Anouilh's concern is the French Revolution—a brilliant subject which has not been adequately explored on the stage since Buechner's *Danton's Death* in 1835—but he has not sufficiently fused his historical motifs with a parallel plot taking place in modern times. Part of Anouilh's difficulty is formal—his organization is sloppy and diffuse—but part can be traced to his undernourished historical imagination, last displayed in *Becket*. Anouilh has a tendency to see history as a series of personal relationships, with national policies being decided largely by disappointments in friendship or love.

Poor Bitos is structured along the lines of a play-within-a-play, a technique Anouilh is using now with increasing regularity, though never as well as Pirandello, from whom he first borrowed it. When the action begins, a group of upper-class financiers and playboys, bewigged like the leaders of the Revolutionary Tribunal, are awaiting the entrance of an insufferable chap named Bitos. They have arranged this "wig party" especially to humiliate him and, through him, the character of Robespierre, whom he is impersonating and with whom he is closely identified, being a humorless public prosecutor, resentful of frivolity and ruthless in the performance of his duty. As the play proceeds, each character is absorbed by his role, and the conflict between Bitos and his tormentors is enlarged into a struggle between a decadent aristocracy, for whom style is the only morality, and a utilitarian bureaucracy, fanatically devoted to an ideal. When Bitos is frightened into a faint by a man impersonating Robespierre's murderer, Anouilh provides a flashback sequence, examining Robespierre's actual career and death; and when Bitos recovers, in the final act, he swears vengeance even on the woman who tried to help him.

Unfortunately, this structure is repetitious and confused, and never permits either the historical or the modern action to gain sufficient momentum. Nor does it permit any unifying insight into the relationship between past and present, other than the rather banal conclusion that two men of similar temperament can arise at two different points in time. Though it promises a political conflict between right and left, furthermore, the play reduces everything to questions of personality, while Robespierre's character, as Anouilh sees it, is neither very complicated nor even very accurate, since the historical Robespierre, for all his bloodthirstiness, once resigned a post as criminal judge to avoid pronouncing a death sentence, and, for all his Puritanism, was once considered something of a dandy. Finally, *Poor Bitos* misses a magnificent opportunity for metaphysical speculation. Like *The Physicists* again, which also deals with men playing historical roles, *Poor Bitos* has been deeply influenced by Pirandello's *Henry IV;* but neither play delves into those deeper questions of human identity raised in Pirandello. Trying to enlarge his powers—the powers of one who is essentially a Boulevard entertainer—Anouilh seems to have extended them beyond the point where they still are manageable.

Shirley Butler's imported production is competent, but rather shabby-genteel, dull, and elocutionary. The American actors impersonate the English, the English impersonate the voice of the BBC, and Charles D. Gray impersonates Jack Hawkins. Only Donald Pleasence, as Bitos, looking like a little white rodent in his powdered wig, seems to have found his own style, a kind of nasal nattering always on the verge of a whine. Though Pleasence runs the risk of monotonousness, he has a lot of suppressed power and malevolence. And he is not afraid to be unpleasant, which, in a theatre dedicated to loving love, is itself something of a distinction.

1965

A Missed Masterpiece

THE DEVILS

by John Whiting; based upon
The Devils of Loudun by Aldous Huxley

The Devils has obviously been fashioned by a writer of subtle sensibility and superior intelligence: its characterization is interesting, its scope large, its prose full of disconsolate music, and its subject—the possession by devils of the nuns of Loudun and the subsequent execution for diabolism of Father Grandier—is one of great promise for the stage. Compared with *The Crucible*, which treats of similar subject matter, John Whiting's drama is a penetrating study of the roots of seventeenth-century religious fanaticism, for Whiting has more understanding of human motive than Miller, more intellect, more poetry, more humor, more imagination. Still, *The Crucible* is the better play. Whiting fails a large ambition—the writing of tragedy—while Miller accomplishes a smaller one— the writing of melodrama; and though Miller's material may be less profound than Whiting's, it is handled with greater authority. *The Devils* sprawls and crashes about the stage without a firm controlling hand to rein it in; the individual scenes have coherence but the whole does not; and as themes fly forth like sparks off an anvil, one ultimately feels assaulted by a profusion of rich ideas.

It is Whiting's intention to bring an entire French village onto the stage, and for this purpose he designs a series of swift episodes during which the principal and secondary characters move center for arias, duets, trios, and choruses. The bustling effect is reminiscent of the opening scenes of Rostand's *Cyrano* as, indeed, Whiting's staccato rhetoric seems to be influenced by Brian Hooker's translation of that play. But an epic style requires a strong central character to bring everything into focus, and Father Grandier is simply too passive a victim to fit the bill. In himself, Whiting's Grandier is interesting enough —an intellectual priest with a vigorous sexual appetite who tries to design his own extinction as a way of making amends to God; but these qualities have little influence on his fate, which is more the result of a fortuitous combination of circumstances: political revenge, clerical hostility, middle-class envy, and the unfounded accusations of a hysterical humpbacked nun who has never met him. Grandier is continually undergoing spiritual crises and continually making finalistic discoveries about himself, but his metaphysical agony and existential *Angst* have very little to do with those forces that are bulldozing him from the earth.

The intellectual structure of the play, in short, seems largely irrelevant to its emotional structure—and not only irrelevant but anachronistic. Just as it is rather disconcerting, in *The Crucible,* to find Miller's Puritan hero regarding witchcraft with all the skepticism of a nineteenth-century positivist, so it is disorienting to find Whiting's Catholic characters assuming an absurd universe, holding sophisticated rationalistic views about God, and offering Freudian explanations of various religious phenomena, as if the French of this time were already familiar with G. Rattray Taylor's chapters on diabolism in *Sex in History.* One character speaks of "father figures," another diagnoses a false pregnancy, and a number of others interpret the diabolical possession of the nuns as an obvious combination of repressed sexuality, histrionics, and opportunism. This is too easy, especially for an already enlightened audience; the play could use a little more mystery and a lot less causality; and it wouldn't have hurt if the author had tried to project himself historically into the mind of another time. What finally emerges is not so much an evocation of a past event as an essay on that event, filtered through the modern self-consciousness, and the action never breaks free from the author's grip to assume an ambiguous life of its own.

As for Michael Cacoyannis' production, it fails to endow the drama with the necessary focus and inevitability. The vignettes flow into one another smoothly enough and the torture of Grandier is harrowing, but the possession scenes—where Cacoyannis has his pretty *Sound of Music* nuns gaping, twitching, and snarling, bunching their habits around their crotches and showing their legs —approach the level of unintentional farce, and the evening has too many feverish climaxes. Then, while the acting is occasionally powerful in supporting roles (Shepperd Strudwick's furious, rasping Bishop; John Colicos' crisp cool Machiavellian villain), the leads are curiously flat. Anne Bancroft brings to the role of Sister Jeanne broad Bronx inflections, spasmodic gestures, and a variety of vocal hysterics which alternate among barks, coughs, and asthmatic heaves—a good tasteful director could have improved this performance considerably. As for Jason Robards, as Father Grandier, he achieves a certain mutilated grandeur at the end of the play when, his hair and beard completely shaven, his legs crushed and bleeding, he is led off to the stake; but Robards' sad boozy delivery, in which every syllable is a disconnected spondee and every speech a wry recollection, tends to get very monotonous. All in all, a pretty windy evening which tantalizes you with its unfulfilled potential.

1965

A Question of Identity

SLAPSTICK TRAGEDY
by Tennessee Williams

WHERE'S DADDY
by William Inge

THE LION IN WINTER
by James Goldman

Of the three new American works under review this week, two are quite feverish with self-consciousness; but then, so is most American drama of recent vintage. After a while, one must stop seeking causes in individual playwrights and look for some common seat of infection. This might very well be located in the amorphous Broadway audience, which has changed its character radically over the past fifteen years. To playwrights of previous generations, the customer was always a known quantity, but few dramatists today have any clear idea about who this middle-aged behemoth is or how to feed it, and this uncertainty issues in a loss of confidence, an erosion of identity, an exaggeration of manner. Uneasy toward their auditors, ambivalent toward their characters, secretive toward their themes, these writers continue to show confusion over whether to be insiders or outsiders, mirrors or models. And failing to identify themselves properly, they fail to show us who we are—fail, that is, to fulfill a major office of the dramatic artist.

Tennessee Williams, who comes from an earlier generation, is still making some effort to characterize himself and his audience, but the conclusions are remembered rather than discovered. In *The Mutilated*, the first short play in the twin bill called *Slapstick Tragedy*, he suggests that all human beings are deformed in some manner or other: this is an old pale story with him, and he fails to rub any fresh color into its cheeks. The two central characters—a breezy, loquacious hooker and a sensitive, damaged spinster with only one breast—are extremely familiar from Williams' previous writings, and so is the Christmas imagery, which, besides being self-derivative, is soft, sloppy, and obvious. On top of this, *The Mutilated* is performed in strictly routine fashion (though Margaret Leighton, with a Miriam Hopkins drawl, has affecting moments as the spinster); and it is directed horrendously, with a chorus of seedy tramps, whores, and sailors warbling Williams' purple lyrics with all the sticky harmoniousness of the Trapp family singers.

In his second playlet, *The Gnädiges Fraulein*, Williams treats similar material with more flair and humor, and a brave effort at novelty. A farce-fantasy in the absurdist manner, the work concerns a visit by the "Southernmost" gossip columnist in America to an old female crony, whose boarding house is being terrorized by "Cockaloony" birds. There she observes the desperate survival tactics of the title character, a battered European circus performer who must compete with these ferocious creatures for her board and keep ("Three fish a day keep eviction away"). The Gnädiges Fraulein has both her eyes pecked out as a result, but she continues to pursue her food, thus demonstrating something about the capacity of the human race to Endure and Prevail, I suppose. The play has undeniable weaknesses in tone and theme and doesn't run the stretch; but it also has a little daring, even a certain degree of charm, and it is directed and acted with some expertise. Alan Schneider, aided by his designer Ming Cho Lee, has this time found a congenial approach (he treats the play as a comic strip), and there is an especially bright performance by Zoe Caldwell, wearing clown white makeup and looking like Mammy Yokum, supported by

Kate Reid, looking like Maggie Jiggs, and Margaret
Leighton, looking like Olive Oyl.

William Inge's latest debacle shows an even more depressing failure of identity on the part of the American
playwright: it is a conscientious effort to reflect the received opinions of the Broadway audience, with results
that are square even by that body's limited geometric
standards. The main plot of *Where's Daddy* concerns a
young Bohemian couple who are trying to live according
to what Inge calls "contemporary thinking and philosophy." The girl is about to have a baby, but the boy—himself an orphan—does not think that he is "emotionally
prepared for parenthood," and so is planning to split the
moment the child is born. Various characters—including
the boy's guardian, the girl's mother, and a Negro couple
from next door—regard this impending desertion with
disapproval. When the boy's analyst also rejects him,
the play predictably closes with the hero cuddling his
baby and nuzzling his wife, amidst benevolent smiles
from the entire cast of characters.

The play, in short, simply dazzles you with its conventionality, but this is nothing to the conventionality of its
ideas: the plot is merely a springboard for the author's
homely reflections on several pressing questions that have
obviously been disturbing him. These include the sloppy
dress of the younger generation ("You all go around
looking like sexy rejects from a poor farm"), youth's
self-indulgent demands ("Don't you all get tired of being
true to yourselves?"), psychoanalytical concepts ("I never
call it neurosis—I simply say I'm having a bad day"),
modern hopelessness ("If life is empty and hopeless, there
is no reason why we shouldn't make our stay on earth as
pleasant as possible"), and avant-garde plays ("I suppose
you prefer those plays in which people come out of ash
cans and urinate on the floor"). All of this is so incredibly

ignorant, simplistic, and insulting to its subjects (who are permitted no reply) that I would not mention it were it not for the fact that, in each case, the author's mouthpiece is a university professor—and a homosexual at that! Pinky, as the hero's guardian is called, may very well be the first homosexual *raisonneur* in the history of the drama, but there is never any danger that he will say anything radical or daring: Inge is working too hard to show that despite his sexual proclivities, Pinky is precisely the same as everyone else. The climax of the play, in fact, occurs when Pinky and the heroine's mother (already identified as a typical suburban housewife) discover that they are in perfect accord on every subject: Pinky confesses that he adores *I Love Lucy* because "I can't sit around reading Milton all the time"; Mom goes into raptures upon learning that "men like you" are not "different" at all; and on this blissful conformist tableau, the curtain mercifully descends.

The entire plot of James Goldman's *The Lion in Winter* revolves around which of his sons will succeed Henry II on the throne of England—a matter of crashing indifference to the audience, and even, apparently, to the author, since he never bothers to resolve it in his play. Instead, Goldman uses his historical setting merely as a subterfuge for romantic comedy, and it is to romantic comedy that the audience responds, as the most elevated questions of state are reduced to domestic quarrels, witty asides, informal banter, and sexy situations. Obviously inspired by Robert Bolt's *A Man for All Seasons* (and directed by the same man, Noel Willman), *The Lion in Winter* has a much more conventional structure and much less historical relevance: it gives us medieval kings, queens, and princes only for the purpose of exposing their contemporary underwear. Thus, while the play possesses a modicum of wit, the wit is completely dependent upon a single

comic device: transforming royal personages into the
stock figures of situation comedy.

This device occasionally accounts for a funny line or
an energetic domestic battle; more often, it sells the play
short for cheap laughs. "Hush dear, Mother's fighting,"
says Eleanor of Aquitaine in the midst of a harangue with
her estranged husband, Henry—and adds, after she has
informed the king that she may have cuckolded him with
his father, "What family doesn't have its ups and downs."
There is a good deal of intriguing going on among the
three sons of Henry, and even a scene suggesting a homosexual affair between the oldest boy and the young French
king—but the major interest of the author is obviously
in the autumnal love-hate relationship between Henry
and Eleanor. Thus, the play ends with sentimental affirmations ("We have each other, and for all I know, that's
what hope is"), at the very same time that Henry is
banishing Eleanor from his kingdom, as though the emotions of the play were totally divorced from its exterior
action. As for the performances, Robert Preston is bushy,
chesty, and chuckly as Henry, Rosemary Harris twinkles
pleasantly as Eleanor of Aquitaine, and Christopher
Walken and James Rado are vigorous and interesting as
two of the young men—but the whole performance could
very well be transferred to a contemporary TV series, involving a business executive, his designing wife, and
their teenage sons. Goldman, in short, seems to know his
audience much better than either Tennessee Williams or
William Inge, and has written for it a convenient play—
but a play without historical insight, psychological depth,
or inner reality.

1966

The Unseriousness of Arthur Miller

THE PRICE
by Arthur Miller

If Arthur Miller seems old-fashioned today to many seriously interested in the theatre, it is not because he has failed to keep abreast of the latest techniques in playwriting—nobody expects him to compete with La Mama —it is rather because his concerns are so curiously insulated from the world in which we now live. The nation's cities are in total disarray, drowning in swill, torn by riots, seething with violence; our disgraceful involvement in the Vietnam conflict is making large numbers ashamed of being American; the administration has systematically destroyed our confidence in its credibility and good intentions, perhaps in the democratic process itself; our young are either apathetic and withdrawn or inflamed with fury and frustration; our sense of reality is disintegrating, our illusion of freedom faltering, our expectation of disaster increasing—yet, Arthur Miller, the most public-spirited of dramatists, continues to write social-psychological melodramas about Family Responsibility. I don't mean to imply it is just his subject matter that makes all this seem so crashingly irrelevant. After all, fathers and sons still exist in the world, and there are other issues for contemplation besides war and riot. But how can a new play fail to be affected, if only indirectly, by the events of its time? Even the atmosphere of a middle-class living room is charged with special tensions these days. Even conflicts within the family are inevitably informed by the frustrations that are driving the country mad.

As a citizen, Miller is deeply involved with these events; as a playwright, he is now choosing to ignore the life around us, and this explains his peculiar insularity of method. His new play, *The Price*, is designed to be a domestic drama in an Ibsenite vein—that is to say, it attempts, through a process of exhumation, to reveal the past and the present simultaneously. But while the play moves backward easily enough to a Depression period thirty years previous, it moves forward only a quarter of an inch; and all that is exhumed—after a great deal of jabbering and jawing and why, why, why—is an empty grave. Ibsen was interested in the effect of the past on the present, as a clue to how mankind got on the wrong track; Miller, on the other hand, is more concerned with the way the present reveals the past. As a result, he writes comfortably only about the thirties and forties, and describes the Depression more vividly, through conversation, than he represents, through action, the living events of his play.

The Price, in short, is more accurately called a memory play than a play about contemporary life: it is pulsing with nostalgia for another time. Some of this nostalgia is evoked in Boris Aronson's skillful rendering of an attic room crammed with old lamps, broken harps, armoires, chests, couches, tables, and gramophones; and the actors are at their most poignant when fingering these dusty objects. Something happened in this room—something Miller has written about three or four times already—involving a father who had a business failure and two sons torn between their concern for this failure and their impulse to lead their own lives. That Miller keeps returning to this situation suggests that he has not yet worked it out—nor does he work it out here. As a playwright, he seems in the grip of a repetition compulsion which makes *The Price* a composite of *Death of a Salesman*, *All My Sons*, and *After the Fall*, involving the same family, the same polarities between love and money, the same oblique references to the "system," the same clumsy effort to turn prosaic speech into heightened rhetoric. Even the dialogue seems lifted from earlier Miller plays: "The icebox was empty and the man was sitting there with his mouth open." "We were brought up to succeed. . . . Was there ever no love here?" "One day you're head of the house, head of the table, and the next day you're shit."

The rhetoric improves considerably, however, when-ever a second-hand furniture dealer named Solomon is on stage: although of only tangential importance to *The Price*, he is, by all odds, one of the most effective char-acters ever devised by this author. A descendant of the grandfather in Odets' *Awake and Sing*, and a close rela-tive of those Jewish clowns imported to Broadway from the Yiddish theatre by Menasha Skulnik, Solomon— though hardly original or profound—reveals an unex-pected comic streak in Miller's temperament which I hope he will cultivate. Aphoristic, ancient, a scrupulous bar-gainer and former acrobat, Solomon takes an infectious delight in doing business, and his sense of conviction pro-vides him with just about the only decent dialogue in the play ("The only thing you can do today without a license is go upstairs and jump out the window").

The other characters, however, seem like refugees from the golden age of television, and so, unfortunately, does the plot. Victor, a policeman, returns to the attic room in which he spent his young manhood; the house is con-demned, and the furniture—artifacts of once prosperous days—is up for sale. This sale brings about a crisis meet-ing with his brother Walter, a surgeon, whom he hasn't seen for sixteen years. A representative of empty Amer-ican success, Walter selfishly pursued his education and career while Victor sacrificed his opportunities in order to support their impoverished father (it is typical of the play's imperviousness to modern moods that Miller's in-tegrity figure is a cop!). Walter's success has not made him happy; he has recently suffered both from a divorce and a nervous breakdown. When he offers Victor an administrative job in his nursing home, Victor refuses to accept gratuities, just as he rejects a profitable tax saving that Victor has devised on the furniture. A series of (interminable) arguments reveal finally that Victor's sacrifice was in vain, and that Walter is not as selfish as everyone supposed. The brothers separate, their quarrel unreconciled, both affected deeply and irremediably by these furniture revelations.

There is a term used in acting to describe the externalizing of emotion called *indicating:* it is a term that accurately describes the writing of *The Price.* Everything is signaled, climaxes are superimposed, and exits are timed for applause rather than as natural departures. When the playwright indicates, it is difficult for actors to avoid indicating, and thus we find perfectly competent performers being routine and unconvincing. Harold Gary is excellent in the actor-proof part of Solomon, but the others are entrapped in a Kraft Theatre style of earnestness that finds them screaming at each other for no apparent reason, and expressing a great deal of anguish, desolation, and shame on grounds not supplied by the author.

The play, in short, is not serious. It is solemn, it is determined, but it is not serious. A serious play, in interpreting the lives of its characters, interprets the lives of the auditors, providing images that intensify awareness. But *The Price* is virtually divorced from concerns that any modern audience can recognize as its own. With the comic character of Solomon, Miller, for a moment, turns serious, thus proving that laughter can sometimes be a quicker road to reality than pathos. But the play as a whole gives us merely the appearance of significance, behind which nothing meaningful is happening—a propped-up façade which hides rather than reveals the known landscape—and the name of that game, gentlemen, is escapism.

1968

FROM ABROAD

The Theatre in London

THE NATIONAL THEATRE
at the Old Vic

There are theatrical treasures to be found in London this spring, but none have been mined in the West End. Apparently working the same exhausted vein as Broadway, the English commercial theatre is currently offering nothing but quartz and fool's gold: flatulent British revues; sleek musicals from America; and half-hearted comedy-dramas which will inevitably find their way across the ocean next season to expire on our doorstep. Of all the plays in the West End, only John Osborne's *Inadmissible Evidence* contains more than routine interest—it has a galvanic performance by the young actor Nicol Williamson, and a stunning first act; but the play eventually shatters into formless fragments as the author begins to indulge himself in rhetorical essays on subjects only remotely related to his theme. Nor can the commercial theatre lay claim even to this flawed pearl, since it was originally produced by a noncommercial resident group —the English Stage Company—and transferred to the West End only after a successful engagement at the Royal Court.

From all the appearances, the new English drama would seem to be stalled at present. No interesting playwrights have followed on the heels of Osborne, Pinter, Wesker, and Arden, and even these writers have not fully realized themselves. This promises a crisis—but I doubt if a crisis will come. For if English playwriting is in a slack period, English theatrical production is flourishing —the level of performance in this country must surely be at some kind of peak. What remains perpetually astonishing to foreigners like myself, conditioned by the spasmodic nature of American theatre, is the number of first-rate permanent theatre groups in England which do consistently excellent work. There are more distinguished companies in London alone than in the whole United States, and these represent but a small portion of the fine companies at large.

The most popular of these companies—and the one with the highest standards of acting—is the National Theatre, now temporarily housed at the Old Vic until its own new building can be financed and constructed. The National Theatre institutionalizes the concept of British repertory; it represents the logical culmination and development of the policies of the Old Vic. Although it has certain vague affinities with this defunct group, however, the National Theatre is a much more dynamic organism, and its personnel is almost completely new. Under the leadership of Sir Laurence Olivier—a dedicated artist never known to sink into the sedentary doze of past achievements—the company has recruited some of the most brilliant young actors and directors in the country, and is continually experimenting with adventurous production techniques on a very lavish scale.

Not since its beginnings at Chichester, however, has the National Theatre always proved equally adventurous in its choice of plays, and the program of this season must, I think, constitute a low point. I had the ill luck to arrive here while Olivier was making a film, and *Othello* and *The Master Builder* had been consequently removed from the program. These plays, along with *Mother Cour-*

age, which is just preparing to open, are certainly solid choices in any repertory season. But the five plays that remain, and that I was able to see, could have been done just as easily by a commercial management. I am told that the company directors thought they were taking quite a gamble in producing Peter Shaffer's *The Royal Hunt of the Sun,* but it is a huge popular success, and predictably so—there is nothing in the play itself to discourage West End producers except the enormous expense required to mount it. I have no doubt that Hollywood will be very attracted to this pseudo-epic on the Spanish conquest of Peru, because its bloated form, pretentious theme, mundane prose, and sentimental sermonizing are tailormade for CinemaScope. As for the four revivals in the program—*Much Ado About Nothing, Hay Fever, Hobson's Choice,* and *The Crucible*—they are all, in varying degrees, familiar enough chestnuts, and hardly in desperate need of warming over by a largely subsidized theatre.

The National Theatre, to be sure, is not an experimental troupe, but one does expect of it a little more daring, if only because Kenneth Tynan is its resident *Dramaturg.* Its timidity can be partly traced, I think, to the English audience, which, while made up of inveterate and enthusiastic theatregoers, is not composed of many eager for probing artistic experiences (the majority of Englishmen seem to me, if I can risk a huge generalization, seriously unsettled by—if not actually hostile to—expressions of the intellect, whether in art or elsewhere). Then, again, part of the blame can be attributed to that Board of Governors which has been appointed to pass on each play in the National Theatre repertory, for although this bureau has only exercised its veto once (in the case of Wedekind's *Spring's Awakening,* a play immediately produced, and very sensitively, by the more courageous English Stage Company), its very presence must act as a restraining influence. Whatever the reasons, the National Theatre seems a little reluctant to lead its public much beyond the demands of a sound middle-class taste.

Within the limitations of its program, however, the company functions admirably. As an ensemble, it manifests a continuing identity in everything it does, but each production enjoys a unique style of attack, and the performers are so versatile that they are virtually unrecognizable from play to play. Modeled on the approach of Olivier, who is probably the greatest character actor in the world, the technique of the company is to submerge personality entirely in the demands of each role. Costume, makeup, inflection, posture, gesture—these, rather than personal idiosyncrasies or egoistic self-indulgence, are the conspicuous elements on the National stage. The company constitutes such a brilliant ensemble, in fact, that it can almost change your mind about the quality of its plays, for it brings to each work a vital pulse and a new dimension.

This is most evident in the National Theatre production of *The Crucible*, a play I prepared to see without enthusiasm, having endured it many times and never with much pleasure. Under Olivier's muscular direction, however, what had always seemed to me a rather simplistic melodrama of ideas took on some of the proportions of Shakespearian tragedy—heroic, grandiose, and even rather dark. Most impressive of all was the transfiguration of Miller's dialogue. Spoken by the cast in English country accents, it developed such vigor and authority that I had to admit I had been underestimating the eloquence of the author's language in this work; and the final prison scene was acted so movingly (particularly by Joyce Redman) and staged so cruelly (with Proctor and his wife confronting each other in opaque gloom, haggard with fatigue and torture, their wrists crippled by manacles) that I was almost persuaded there were real emotional depths beneath all the self-righteous posturing.

Hobson's Choice and *Hay Fever* were equally impressive productions of extremely fragile plays, but in neither was the company, for all its felicity of style, able to sustain my interest through the full course of the evening. Harold Brighouse's Lancashire comedy of 1916 was included in the repertory, I assume, not only because it is popular with audiences but because it is generally thought to be the forerunner of recent regional English plays—but I found it much closer to the sentimental tradition of Barrie's *What Every Woman Knows.* Then, David Lean had already adapted a fine movie from this play, with an incomparable performance by Charles Laughton as a brawling, eructating Hobson, and this made the National Theatre production, though smart and sprightly, pale by comparison. Noel Coward's *Hay Fever,* wisely directed by the author as a period piece, displayed the company in a variety of blazers, flannels, cloche hats, bobbed hairdos, and John Held evening clothes, doing hilarious caricatures of upper-class idlers, changing partners for that incriminating kiss in the library. Most of the comedy here was to be found between the lines—in the reactions of Maggie Smith's bored vamp, of Robert Lang's sedate and blinking diplomat, of Robert Stephen's fatuously grinning playboy—but the crispness of the subtext could not sustain the slackness of the text for more than one act, and the play evaporated long before its end.

The company's fondness for playing subtext threatened to become really outrageous in *Much Ado About Nothing,* a play adjusted to a more contemporary idiom by Robert Graves, and directed by Franco Zeffirelli as if it had been written for a nineteenth-century Sicilian carnival. Zeffirelli's whole conception was based on the fact that Shakespeare had located the play in Messina. Encouraging his actors to speak in a variety of Italian accents (some continued to speak, unaccountably, in standard English), he introduced blaring brass bands, tinkling pianolas, street festivals, Italian tenors, brawling washerwomen in the style of Magnani, ice-cream vendors, espresso waiters, and

peanut-cracking villains obviously recruited from the
Mafia. This sort of hare-brained notion you either accept
or reject entirely, writhing over the violations to the play
and its poetry. My impulse was to accept it for the sake
of the fun it added to the comic portions of the play; but
I gradually grew tired of the director's perpetual interruption of the intrigue plots in order to introduce his
increasingly self-conscious and coy tricks. It is one thing
to have some actors, costumed like Neptune and his mer-
maids, impersonate a stone fountain as a means of
dressing the stage; it is quite another to have Benedick
shake hands with this "fountain" at the end of a scene.
On the other hand, the company performed with such
joyous spirits that one was willing to forgive many of
the excesses and inconsistencies of the production; and
Albert Finney, playing Don Pedro as a melancholy, cigar-
smoking aristocrat, and Frank Finlay, translating Dog-
berry into a swarthy leader of the *carabinieri*, with an
immigrant accent, Charlie Chaplin mustache, and trail-
ing Napoleonic cloak, executed the director's concept so
perfectly that it was almost redeemed from its own gim-
mickry.

The most colorful and opulent production of the National Theatre season, surely, was John Dexter's and
Desmond O'Donovan's staging of *The Royal Hunt of the
Sun*. I will wait for the New York presentation before
elaborating on my low opinion of the play; but whatever
his inadequacies in dramatizing them, Peter Shaffer has
certainly used materials that are eminently theatrical.
Antonin Artaud was also aware of the theatricality implicit in a Spanish-American conquest, and wrote a
scenario for his Theatre of Cruelty based on such an
event. One of the many advantages of the Artaud version
over the Shaffer is that it is a wordless spectacle, and
whenever the National Theatre company was permitted
to escape from Shaffer's long-winded pseudo-Lawrentian
mulings, it created a vibrant visual display that Artaud

would have adored. Performed on a wooden platform backed by a huge golden medallion (this opened later to become a raised inner stage), the action traversed continents, oceans, jungles, and mountains. By the use of ritualized mime, the Spanish troops arduously climbed the Andes in full armor, engaged the Incans in a swirling, tumultuous battle, looted the temple of its masses of gold, witnessed dances of harvest, death, and rebirth, and finally strangled the Incan king in one last act of vicious betrayal. It was a rich, stirring production which drew on all the possibilities of the stage and all the magnificence of an exotic Peruvian culture; and it had a performance of supreme incandescence by Robert Stephens as Atahuallpa, the Incan king-god—physically expressive, vocally bizarre, the closest thing to Kabuki acting I have seen on the Western stage.

This, like most of the company's productions, is splendid theatre, but much less satisfying as drama; and I, in my churlish way, would be happier if the company could serve the interests of both. The National Theatre, now only a few years old, has quickly established itself as perhaps the best acting ensemble in the English-speaking world, and has attracted a large and well-deserved following; but it remains to be seen whether it will use this advantage or be used by it, whether it will develop more boldness in its programing or continue to mount works that guarantee popular appeal. This decision, in turn, may help to decide whether England will continue to play a part in the advance of the drama or simply relax into a theatre of wholesome entertainment and pleasant civilized escape. But such is the excellence of the current English stage that even the latter alternative is hardly to be deplored.

1965

Peru in New York

THE ROYAL HUNT OF THE SUN
by Peter Shaffer

The Royal Hunt of the Sun has arrived from London with the same director, scenic designer, costumer, movement coordinator, and composer; every effort has been made to reproduce the effects of the brilliant National Theatre production; but because of the new cast and a more restricted stage, a good deal of its atmospheric pageantry has been lost. This is a shame because without spectacular theatricality, the play amounts to very little; it may be total theatre but it is strictly fractional drama; and being exposed to Peter Shaffer's meditations on religion, love, life, and death for three solid hours is rather like being trapped in a particularly active wind tunnel with no hope of egress. In the London production, there were always choreographed massacres, treks through the Andes, harvest dances, ritual gestures, and an extraordinary performance by Robert Stephens as the sovereign Inca, Atahuallpa, to distract one from the pretentiousness of Mr. Shaffer's theme, the conventionality of his characters, and the poetastrical quality of his dialogue ("Look into him," says one character of the hero, "you'll see a kind of death"). But in New York, with a more limited physical production and a more insecure cast, such distractions no longer work, and one finds escape from the play only in reflections on how the author has muffed his opportunities.

For the conquest of Peru by the Spanish invaders is a natural subject for the theatre; it is the kind of dark myth that fascinated Antonin Artaud as an alternative to the decaying subject matter of the Occidental stage. The idea for the play, as a matter of fact, was probably suggested to Mr. Shaffer by Artaud's first scenario for his projected Theatre of Cruelty, a tableau sequence called *The Conquest of Mexico*. In this unproduced spectacle, Artaud hoped to "contrast Christianity with much older religions" and correct "the false conceptions the Occident has somehow formed concerning paganism and certain natural religions," while dramatizing, in burning images, the destruction of Montezuma and his Aztecs by the armies of Cortez: "Space is stuffed with whirling gestures, horrible faces, dying eyes, clenched fists, manes, breastplates, and from all levels of the scene fall limbs, breastplates, heads, stomachs like a hailstorm bombarding the earth with supernatural explosions." Mr. Shaffer treats the annihilation of the Incas in a similar manner, and (having done his history homework carefully) occasionally engages in some speculative comparative anthropology. But at the same time that he is fashioning cruel Artaudian myths, he is mentalizing, psychologizing, and sentimentalizing these myths. Underneath the tumult and the swirl lie a very conventional set of liberal notions about the noble savage, the ignoble Catholic, and the way brotherly love can bridge the gulf that separates cultures. By the end of the play, in fact, the whole brutal struggle has degenerated into a fraternal romance between a lissome young redskin and an aging lonely paleface—a relationship which is illuminated less by Artaud than by Leslie Fiedler in his essay "Come Back to the Raft Again, Huck Honey."

What has been lost in the Broadway version of the work is what is lost in every reproduction: color, depth, precision, and line. John Dexter, the director, has done his best to communicate the secrets of the National Theatre to his New York actors, but you don't turn a pickup cast into a repertory company in six rehearsal weeks, and the performances, consequently, seem scattered and thin. (I was surprised to discover, upon comparing programs, that New York was using just as many actors as London—the National Theatre stage, though much larger than the ANTA, seemed infinitely more crammed with life and bustle). David Carradine is occasionally powerful as Atahuallpa and John Vernon is stalwart as De Soto, but George Rose, the narrator, is surprisingly mannered and vocally flat: this good actor's work has been in a continual state of decline ever since *A Man for All Seasons*. As for Christopher Plummer, playing Pizarro, he gives us all the trappings of the character with little of its inner life. Hobbling, balding, and bearded like the pard, he has the look, gait, rhythm, and accent of his part (though he seems, as Richard Gilman has noted, to have modeled his dialect on Anthony Quinn's)—what is missing is variety, development, true passion. Plummer has excellent histrionic equipment, but he has lately been satisfied with mere impersonation. What he needs desperately is a good play and a permanent home—why not the Repertory Theatre of Lincoln Center, where he would have made a fascinating Danton?

1965

Thoughts from Abroad

MOTHER COURAGE

by Bertolt Brecht;
National Theatre

HENRY V

by William Shakespeare

THE HOMECOMING

by Harold Pinter;
Royal Shakespeare Company

The English theatre, unlike the English climate, knows no season, and this is sufficient compensation for the weather on that damp isle. New productions were appearing two or three times a week throughout the late spring, and will continue to multiply during the coming summer months. Of all the offerings I saw before I left England, the National Theatre performance of *Mother Courage* was the greatest disappointment. Weakly acted, flatly directed, prosaic and lifeless, it became the occasion for another of those debates that rage, whenever a Brecht play is badly produced on either side of the Atlantic, over the author's credentials as a dramatist (the majority of English newspaper critics, though more literate than ours, are equally likely to blame a poor performance of a play on the play itself). With *Mother Courage*, however, Brecht was betrayed more by his partisans than by his enemies. Instead of finding a congenial English style for the work, William Gaskill, who directed, decided to model his production on that of the Berliner Ensemble, using Brecht's notes when his memory failed. This resulted in an extremely mechanical evening during which the play was less created than re-created, right down to Frau Helene Weigel's famous silent scream. Then, the English actors seemed bewildered by Gaskill's alienation theories, and floundered helplessly in an unfamiliar technique. Madge Ryan, especially imported into the company for the title role, proved completely inadequate to it, lacking toughness, resiliency, humor, and anguish, and trying to compensate by playing most of the part with her fists on her hips and her shoulders reared back. As for the National Theatre regulars, they tended to slip into the security of past characterizations—Frank Finlay, for example, endowed the Cook with a Lancashire dialect, squeezing out charm as if he were still doing Willie Mossop in *Hobson's Choice*. Finally, the songs were so caterwauled and the ironies so muffled that I almost began to remember the Broadway production—inadequate as it was—with something approaching affection.

As the National Theatre began to falter, however, the Royal Shakespeare Company began to sprint, opening its summer season at the Aldwych with a powerful performance of *Henry V*. John Bury's settings for this production, like Jocelyn Herbert's settings for *Mother Courage*, were obviously influenced by the starkness and simplicity practiced at the Berliner Ensemble (not least among the Brechtian influences on the English theatre has been a revolution in costume and scenic design). Bury's settings, composed of wire nets and heavy metal bands, removed the Shakespeare play from history and gave it a quality of dark metallic abstractness. This was in keeping with the production concept of the directors, John Barton and Trevor Nunn, who divested the action of panoply and presented instead an essay on the filth and squalor of war and the hollowness of military rhetoric. Rather than play Henry as a glorious warrior, achieving England's manifest destiny on French battlefields (Olivier's approach in the magnificent film version), Ian Holm chose to interpret the character as a frail, diminutive, sensitive youth who grows increasingly brutalized by senseless carnage. Holm's Henry is urged into battle by purely casuistical arguments, becomes an anguished participant in atrocities (in one scene, he cuts the throat of a French prisoner before the eyes of the audience), and suffers severely from shell shock and combat fatigue. When the battle of Agincourt is finally won, he is a shivering wreck, scarred inside and out, and crying like a baby. This concept obviously runs flat against the author's conscious intention, which was to glorify English heroism, and while it accounts for some terrifying battle scenes (murky panoramas bespattered by blood and smoke, and punctuated by the harrowing groans of the wounded), it is not fully sustained to the end of the play. On the other hand, it adds an interesting dimension which may even have been unconsciously put there by Shakespeare himself—how else can we explain the shaky morality of Henry's claim to France, his order to kill all French prisoners, his apparent indifference to the hanging of former comrades like Bardolph, and his personal stiffness and lack of scruples?

The second presentation at the Aldwych—which I saw in dress rehearsal the night before I departed England—was Harold Pinter's *The Homecoming,* his first long play since *The Caretaker.* The performance I witnessed was not finished, so I will withhold comment on it, except to say that Paul Rogers seemed to me miscast as a brutal father, or, perhaps, had not yet managed to eclipse the pleasantness of his own character under the unpleasantness of his role. The play also looked to me unfinished, but since it was soon released to the public unchanged, I can be less circumspect about criticizing it: *The Homecoming* adds no cubits to its author's stature. I have always been troubled by Pinter's reluctance to invest his works with anything more than atmosphere, but I have always admired his technical sureness and theatrical instinct—now even these have momentarily

failed him. The play is mutilated by an inconsistent tone
and a disunified style, as if the author were uncertain
whether to write a mysterious drama of menace like *The
Caretaker* or a drawing-room sex comedy with Pirandellian overtones like *The Lover* or *The Collection*. The
action is sometimes penumbral and sinister, sometimes
frothy and absurd; the authenticity of a naturalistic scene
is frequently shattered by laugh-pandering; and the whole
affair finally collapses in an unconvincing denouement.

The beginning of the play is promising: there Pinter
sets out to sketch the outlines of a petit-bourgeois family
nightmare. In a large peeling house, the dominant color
of which is black, live four men without women: a cruel,
spiteful father, his mild-mannered brother, and his two
sons. Pinter, as usual, creates suspense by withholding
all information about this family except for quotidian
facts, but he nonetheless manages to suggest their infinite loathing for one another, and to evoke harsh
comedy out of the cruelty of their hatreds. After the
electricity of the opening scene, however, the play short-
circuits. A third son arrives home—a Ph.D lecturing in
an American university—accompanied by his vague,
dreamy wife. Although the family has never met the
woman before, the father is instantly accusing her of
being a "stinking pox-ridden sculler" ("I've never had a
whore under this roof before, not since your mother died,
on my word of honor"), and the two sons are taking
turns making love to her. All this occurs before the husband's eyes, and as he watches bemusedly, pulling on his
pipe, the father and his sons decide to set her up as an
expensive prostitute and live off her earnings. She readily
agrees. The play ends with the husband leaving the
house, the uncle collapsing on the floor, the father having
a heart attack, and crawling toward his daughter-in-law
on all fours, begging for a kiss. The accumulated strokes,
fits, and coronaries that occur before the final curtain
give the ending a quality of unintentional farce, while—

for the first time in a Pinter work—the action escapes from probability altogether, and becomes mere exploitation of the bizarre.

1965

Seeing *The Homecoming* again a year and a half after its London production reinforces my respect for the British repertory system: the performance is brilliant. The spare setting has been somewhat redesigned by John Bury for a larger theatre so that now the upstage staircase may ascend forever, and the gray flats (black in London) underline the grayness of the characters. Peter Hall's direction is full of fascinating secular rituals. At the beginning of the second act, for example, four men in the act of lighting their cigars break away from the central match as if they were the opening petals of a carnivorous flower. Paul Rogers, who last year seemed too pleasant under his nastiness, is now convincingly churlish; Ian Holm remains full of cruel lithe grace; and Vivien Merchant retains her black, sphinx-like lethargy, though at the cost of some monotony.

I still don't like the play very much, though there is something in me that would like to join the crowd of theatregoers who have rallied to its support. I respect very much Pinter's efforts to extend his reach into the unexplored areas of human consciousness, and I recognize that *The Homecoming* is something of a new departure for him, but I still think the play tends to exploit the bizarre too much merely for its own sake. Pinter has the disturbing habit of establishing a convincing hypnotic atmosphere, only to break it with a strained stage effect, a *coup de théatre*, or an incompatible motivation. In *The Caretaker*, Aston's description of his sojourn in a mental institution rationalizes behavior that should have remained remote and inchoate, while in *The Homecoming,* a nicely formulated study of grotesque horror is compromised by a melodramatic conclusion in which everyone starts having coronaries all over the stage.

I won't attempt to interpret the work, since I don't think it is open to interpretation, but I do want to mention the interesting way in which Pinter brings to the surface the deepest sexual obsessions of family life. The wife of one son, a professor in an American university, becomes for his father, a butcher, and for his brothers, a pimp and a prizefighter, an object to be exploited erotically and economically, as a replacement for a dead mother (also described, by turns, as a saint and a whore). What all this means can be more easily experienced than explained—as the wife says, inadvertently describing Pinter's method, "Perhaps the fact that my lips move is more significant than the words that pass through them" —for like Antonioni, Pinter conveys a sense of the bleakness and coldness on our planet by violating conventional cause-and-effect patterns, and making verbal intercourse an obstacle rather than an aid to communication. All of this is highly suggestive, even important, but Pinter has not yet allowed himself to abandon a vaguely vulgar streak of theatricality or perfected the artistry necessary to support his explorations.

1967

The English Stage

An American visitor to London is dazzled by theatrical illuminations that shine even more brightly by contrast with our own darkling stage. America now has an ever-growing number of permanent companies, and some of them can boast of considerable achievements. But it will be a long time, I fear, before we can begin to match the adventurousness of the Royal Shakespeare Company at the Aldwych, the fine, fearless integrity of the English Stage Society at the Royal Court, or the expertise of the National Theatre at the Old Vic. There is something in the American character that has thus far proved resistant to collective artistic enterprise—something at the same time invigorating (an anarchic independence of will) and degenerate (a selfish opportunism)—with the result that our serious theatre has been continually engaged in an exhausting struggle with the frailties that are always threatening to destroy it, whether reflected in the actor's glory-lust, the producer's venality, the designer's self-indulgence, the director's careerism, or the spectator's fatigue and apathy.

That these frailties are also operative in the English theatre I have the word of some English theatre critics, but once away from the West End, they are not immediately visible to a visitor's naked eye—the quality, and even the quantity, of British permanent companies testify to a flourishing theatrical health. The new English drama, however, seems to me somewhat less robust at the moment. As a movement, it appears to be temporarily stalled, and it has yet to realize the promise of its auspicious beginnings. Osborne, Pinter, Wesker, Jellicoe, Arden, Delaney, Owen, and the rest of the "new realists" are continuing to turn out a substantial number of plays, some of which excite a good deal of interest; and there is no doubt that these plays are still much fresher and more energetic than the work of those who previously dominated the English stage—Coward, Rattigan, and Fry, for example. Furthermore, the new drama has engendered a breed of actors who, for sheer power, breadth, and truthfulness, are now unmatched in the English-speaking world, not to mention a company of designers who have brought a powerful abstract simplicity to costume and stage settings. Still, despite such achievements, few of these writers have proceeded very far beyond their initial phase of development, and none, to my mind, has turned into an artist of the first rank.

To substantiate this charge, and to find some reasons for it, one must turn to historical parallels, and there is an obvious analogy to be made between the English drama of the past decade and the American drama of the thirties. In each case, new playwrights emerged in significant numbers out of social-political ferment; and in each case, they found their identity less as inspired individuals than as members of a movement with specific social goals. The new English drama is, admittedly, superior to the American social drama of the thirties (which left nothing of lasting value, not even the works of Odets), but it has a similar coloration, being more impressive as a cultural phenomenon than as a unique artistic force. And it is equally restricted by the very conditions that originally gave it life. The revolution that recently swept across the English stage succeeded in clearing away the debris of artificial drawing-room comedies, sterile well-made plays, and vacant pseudo-Elizabethan poetic dramas, but like the social revolution in Depression America it created an ideological atmosphere in which many began to regard the drama as a weapon of class warfare. Fewer English than American playwrights have accepted these ideological roles with equanimity—some, notably Harold Pinter, have even vigorously repudiated them—but only one or two have managed to extricate themselves entirely from class interests and stand alone as free and independent artists.

The result is apparent in the new plays, many of which reek with sentimentality about the working class, excessive literalism, overinsistence on the grime and squalor of Midlands industrial cities, stale didacticism, and a kind of laziness about working out a theme in action. The result is also apparent in the writings of the critics, theorists, and polemicists who, like the Marxist critics of the thirties, have been exhorting the new drama since its beginnings. The latter company has been gathered in a recent volume called *The Encore Reader**—an anthology of articles from the influential little magazine of the theatre, *Encore*. Subtitled "A Chronicle of the New Drama," this volume embodies both the virtues and the failings of the movement it examines: it is bursting with energy, vigor, and excitement, and it is seriously lacking in balanced judgments or penetrating ideas.

One is struck, first and foremost, by a feeling of embattlement: each new article is a gauntlet, each new play a war game. The complicated issues of art tend to dissolve into simple oppositions: Socialism versus Toryism, the new versus the old, experiment versus tradition, the proletariat versus the upper classes, youth versus age—and everyone connected with the theatre is neatly catalogued. If an old lady expresses what to some would be an understandable indifference to a play of Arnold Wesker, then this, the writer speculates, is because Wesker "came too close to life, dealt with actual problems, felt strongly about them, and wanted to impel his audience to do something about them." Another writer, discussing Osborne's debacle *The World of Paul Slickey*, assumes without hesitation that its sour reception was motivated by hostility to the New Left, even though he

---

* *The Encore Reader*, edited by Charles Marowitz, Tom Milne, and Owen Hale (London: Methuen; 1965).

eventually forces himself to concede that the play is dismal.

Not all of the articles are so narrow, for the policy of the magazine is much less doctrinaire than some of its contributors. At the same time that Lindsay Anderson is demanding ideological rigidity, arguing that *Encore* should print not "every point of view," but only the "right one," John Whiting is questioning the intellectual and artistic value of socialist plays. And while some writers are advising modern dramatists to eliminate despair from their plays, accentuate the positive, and point the way toward utopian social goals (shades of Soviet realism!), others are extolling the virtues of such nonpolitical, non-affirming writers as Beckett, Genet, Ionesco, Artaud, and even such a disaffected comic anarchist as Lenny Bruce. When a gifted playwright or performer is being defended against the uncomprehending hostility of snobs and Philistines, or when artistic achievements are being examined in depth, then *The Encore Reader* performs a valuable critical function. But just as frequently the tenor of the anthology is cranky and contentious, while its tone tends to alternate between the shrill and the hoarse. Hospitality is extended to naïfs like Eli Wallach, discoursing inarticulately on the eloquence of the Method, and to egos from the film world like Joseph Losey, discussing Brecht's "influence on me" (and vice versa). Brecht himself is admired for what seem to me all the wrong reasons, and is, therefore, continually lumped together with a lesser writer like Arthur Miller, presumably because both deal in social-political problems. Familiar opinions on questions of race, sex, and society are paraded as advanced in a self-righteous manner recalling Roebuck Ramsden's liberalism; and finally, too much of the book is given over to garbled logic, ringing manifestoes, utilitarian demands, questionable motive hunting, fuzzy theories, and downright bad prose.

I make these complaints as a friend of the house, and

would in fact be less disturbed about these writers if I weren't so profoundly sympathetic with most of their aims. But their aims have now been largely achieved and, as so often happens with successful revolutionaries, their excesses now seem to be institutionalized, ossifying into postures that should be more supple and flexible. Chief among these is a certain indifference to poetry, imagination, form, and dialectic in the drama, and a partiality to plays that propagandize for change (this last demand, explicit in many articles in the anthology, is seconded by Kenneth Tynan in a long interview). What *The Encore Reader* finally lacks is a sense of critical disinterestedness. It does not advance dramatic art to defend bad plays because they support your prejudices, or to tolerate nitwittery for the sake of a Cause, or to reprimand playwrights for failing to deal with economic and political change. Overly permissive in one sense, the *Encore* critics have been overly restrictive in another, so that one comes away grateful for what they have accomplished in the way of supporting experimental playwrights, but dubious about their ultimate value to the movement of English drama as a whole.

This uncertainty increases when one looks at the movement itself. For while the new English playwrights have certainly proved less simplistic politically than most of their supporters (at least in their work), they nevertheless strike similar doctrinal postures. These, to be sure, are relatively implicit, being suggested less through direct appeals than through certain significant choices (thematic concerns, types of characters, theatrical style); but they are clearly responsible, in my opinion, for certain impediments to genuine advance. Despite an occasional leavening of epic technique from Brecht, for example, the dominant style of recent English drama has been social realism; and while this style may seem unusual to audiences conditioned by frothy commodities from Shaftesbury Avenue, it has long been exhausted as a medium for fresh dramatic insight and long been abandoned by the more adventurous dramatists of Europe. The English commitment to an old-fashioned style is accompanied by an infatuation with what one *Encore* writer calls "the gritty realities of working-class life." This also has its unfortunate side since, at the same time that it opens up an area of experience long ignored or patronized by English playwrights, it inspires another form of class consciousness—a species of inverted snobbery only slightly less offensive than the old.

Two English dramatists are relatively free of such limitations—Harold Pinter, who (perhaps in reaction against the sermonizing of his colleagues) excludes state- ment from his work altogether, and John Arden, who has managed to preserve a certain unpredictability. Both offer hope for future growth and development (though Pinter has recently been repeating himself). One cannot be entirely sanguine, however, about the other members of the movement. Take the case of Arnold Wesker, a writer who seems to exaggerate all its worst faults. Let us pass over his irrepressible impulse to indoctrinate the working classes with Higher Forms of Art, though this may some day constitute one of the most embarrassing episodes in recent English cultural history. His plays are a good deal more complicated about such missions than his behavior warrants, and when he deals—in the *Chicken Soup* trilogy and in *Chips with Everything*—with the intellec- tual's poignant failure to merge with the masses, he un- corks a theme which is both convincing and deeply felt. His writing, on the other hand, though full of sincerity, is almost completely wanting in art, being crude, zealous, garrulous, and naïve; his sense of style has not developed much beyond the gray, exacting realism of Galsworthy; and his relentless missionary temperament and perennial innocence frequently turn his characters into caricatures from agit-prop.

Or take the case of John Osborne, who originated the

new movement and who remains its most showy figure. Osborne is unquestionably a born dramatist, and his vocabulary of invective is simply stunning, but I think he has yet to write a work that will endure. Too much of his writing remains unformulated, and too much remains unfinished: his plays have the quality of electrical particles without a nucleus to hold them in orbit. Osborne's dramatic discipline since *Epitaph for George Dillon* has grown increasingly loose, and more and more he has begun to indulge a weakness for dramatic ventriloquism: *Inadmissible Evidence,* for example, after a brilliant first act, collapses completely into structural chaos, as the author introduces rhetorical essays on subjects only remotely related to his theme. The typical Osborne scene consists of one person orating and another listening—the monologues are inspired but they do not admit of true argument. And he is capable, I think, of writing only one character fully: the cruel, blistering protagonist who evokes the spectator's pity when he reveals himself to be collapsing under the burden of his own unpleasantness. This suggests that under the hard veneer of Osborne's style there lurks considerable sentimentality, and makes it understandable why he has been successful on Broadway when the more radical dramatists from France cannot make it through the back door. Until Osborne can put his wonderful eloquence at the service of consistently worked-out themes, he will remain a playwright of the second rank.

I realize that I have been extremely harsh toward writers who are now a source of considerable national pride. But the whole development of recent English drama inspires an American with a sense of *déjà vu.* What began for us in a similar way—as a radical theatre movement tied to a radical politics—eventually became the standard form of our commercial stage, and American drama ever since has been trying to break loose from this debilitating inheritance. I suspect that because

English audiences have been traditionally Tory, English playwrights have assumed a correspondence between a left-wing politics and an advanced drama; but Americans can testify, to their regret, that no such correspondence exists—quite the contrary, our own politically liberal drama has been responsible for glib affirmations, simpleminded melodramas, and self-congratulatory conventions.

What most of the modern dramatists have understood (and even Brecht and Shaw, I believe, understood this secretly) is that whatever his personal affiliations, the writer must remain independent in his art—that even political plays must be free from partisanship—for when the drama becomes an instrument of utility or the captive of a creed, it is condemned and sacrificed. Theatrical conditions are marvelous in England at present, the nation's recent dramatic achievement is substantial, and when it comes to raw playwriting talent, it can compete with any country in the world. But English drama is now in some danger of dissipating its possibilities in the service of causes unconnected with the free imagination. On most subjects, Americans can tell the English very little, but in this case we have been there before. It would be a pity if they could not build on our mistakes.

1965

Live Blossoms in Dead Soil

THE RESISTIBLE RISE OF ARTURO UI
by Bertolt Brecht

THE THREEPENNY OPERA
by Bertolt Brecht and Kurt Weill

CORIOLAN
*by William Shakespeare;
adapted by Bertolt Brecht;
the Berliner Ensemble*

To get there, you can either take the S-Bahn to Friedrichstrasse Station and endure bureaucratic torments at the other end, or you can enter through Checkpoint Charlie and submit yourself and your car to an exhausting search for contraband. Neither way is pleasant, but the latter is recommended because it gives you an invaluable opportunity to drive through East Berlin. This is certainly an eerie experience, rather like motoring under water. In West Berlin, where automobiles crowd the avenues, you have to use the aggressive ingenuity of a New York cabbie to navigate among them, but in the East you ride through completely deserted streets, past darkened traffic lights, feeling like Orpheus in the underworld.

Much of this territory, and especially the section adjacent to the Wall, is now less a living area than a punishment area. The Soviets, who are great memorializers, originally elected to preserve this part of their zone as an artifact of World War II, keeping the rubble intact, and topping the ruins with gigantic signs underlining the consequences of *Fascismus und Militarismus*—subtleties which are lost on the natives because nobody is around to read them. If you follow the Unter den Linden farther east, you eventually leave the bombed-out areas and come upon some new architecture of a depressing kind (all new German architecture, East *and* West, is depressing). This includes a Museum of German History which devotes whole floors to replicas of Nazi atrocities— but like the streets, the museum is empty of civilians. Only armed patrols walk with confidence in this area. If the East Berliners are suffering remorse of conscience, they are doing so behind closed doors.

There flourishes in this city of the dead, however, a theatre of extraordinary vitality, situated in a square recently named after the theatrical genius who formed it—the Berliner Ensemble in Bertolt Brecht Platz. The company has occupied its present headquarters since 1954, performing in a building which seems almost as incompatible with the theatre's nature as the forbidding environment which surrounds it. The exterior façade is curiously drab and characterless while the interior walls and ceilings have been adorned with extravagant curlicues and baroque cupidons. The stage events, on the other hand, are innocent either of grayness or of embellishment: simplicity is the watchword, a simplicity compounded of joy, vigor, and strength. These qualities are costly and have obviously been paid for generously. As a showpiece of the regime, the Ensemble has been endowed with an apparently bottomless subsidy. The costumes, for example, are without ornamentation, but they are made of genuine leather and wool, and the company is not only very large in itself, but is supported by enough stagehands to people a banana republic (I saw this army in action while seated in a high perch at one of the shows, and I can testify that it is both huge and extremely well trained).

What accounts for the vital spark of the Berliner Ensemble, however, is not money but rather an uncom-

promising visionary dedication: the company certainly
deserves its growing reputation as the most accomplished
theatre group in Europe. Where it surpasses the established theatres of England and France is in its powerful
identity, an identity formed out of association with the
plays and techniques of Brecht. This association has also
accounted for a certain narrowness of range in the
repertory, which is made up primarily of Brecht's plays
and secondarily of plays with a political bias; but if the
Berliner Ensemble does not have an eclectic program, it
certainly displays enough versatility in its theatrical
techniques. Of the three productions I saw on my visit
there—*The Resistible Rise of Arturo Ui, The Threepenny
Opera*, and Brecht's adaptation of Shakespeare's *Coriolanus*—all shared a certain unity of inspiration but
each also enjoyed its own special tone and attack. For
the company actors have been trained not only to change
character in their various roles, but also to change style
in a manner that makes them virtually unrecognizable
from play to play. This proteanism suggests that however
limiting the *Verfremdungseffekt* may seem in theory, in
actual practice it is the source of great variety.

The best way to describe the genius of the Berliner
Ensemble is to describe some of its productions, and
there is no more satisfying production to begin with than
the famous *Arturo Ui*. Brecht's black comedy of gangsterism, ward politics, and monopoly capital in Chicago
still seems to me feeble as an allegorical explanation for
the rise of Nazism, but the company uses the text as a
springboard for a spectacular and irresistible theatricality.
Something of its approach was suggested in the Broadway production of the play a few years back, for Tony
Richardson lifted many of his ideas from the Ensemble
version, directed by Manfred Wekwerth and Peter
Palitsch. But like the National Theatre's recent *Mother
Courage*, the New York *Arturo Ui* merely demonstrated
the pitfalls of pirated productions when original outlines

are borrowed without the original inspiration. What the Ensemble actors possess abundantly—and what English and American theatre artists signally lack—is a capacity for histrionic exaggeration verging on madness. There is a galvanic fury in these actors, a kind of demonic rage restrained by form, that seems partially native to the German character, and partially derived from American silent films.

The acting techniques of American silents are imaginatively employed in *Arturo Ui*; instead of building character, in the tradition of Stanislavsky, the German actors create distinctive comic masks, in the tradition of Chaplin, Buster Keaton, and Groucho Marx. The emphasis, in short, is less on psychological penetration than on gesture, mime, costume, and makeup, and while a sense of reality may occasionally intrude upon the events, it is always subordinate to an effect of extravagant distortion. The Ensemble *Arturo Ui* is played like an animated cartoon, punctuated by jazz, machine guns, and real blood. Arturo and his lieutenants are made up with green grease-paint masks which highlight their lips and eyes while the hoodlums wear enormous holsters on their hips and huge fedoras on their heads. Wolf Kaiser plays Giri (Goering) looking like a corrupt Alan Hale, his features fixed in a circus-clown leer; Gunter Naumann as Roma (Roehm) has a great bloody scar across his cheek and nose, and before each murder whistles the opening bars of Beethoven's Fifth; and Hilmar Thate as Givola (Goebbels) carries himself with the jerky awkwardness of a crippled marionette, hanging limply over a balcony, his wrists dangling, for the rendering of a song.

The best realization of this grotesque technique is to be seen in Ekkehard Schall's Arturo Ui. Schall, surely one of the most accomplished actors in Europe, is a small muscular man with the arrogant stalk of Jimmy Cagney and the capacity to shape his body into whatever form he pleases. As Arturo (Hitler), he manages to slough thirty pounds off his actual weight merely by pulling in his pelvis, hunching his shoulders, and thrusting his hands inside his seedy raincoat. When he first appears in the opening scenes—his red mustache thrust forward like a toothbrush, his hat in his hand, bowed with false humility before the door of the Stock Exchange —he communicates grimness, penury, unctuousness, melancholy, violence, and menace all at once; and thus having established all the values of his role in a trice, he proceeds to put the rest of his scenes at the service of pure comic virtuosity. Schall's manipulation of his voice is remarkable—he can shift without warning from wheedling whispers to screaming rages—but his use of his body is exceptional. He is dynamic even when slumped in a chair or prostrate over a pinball machine, but in movement he is audacious in the extreme. At the Mammoth Hotel (a scene created entirely out of a few props —carpet, plant, and men reading in plush chairs), he arbitrates a quarrel between Givola and Roma. Roma pulls a gun and Schall develops the shakes, shoving both hands entirely inside his mouth. Recovering his courage, he leaps onto a chair, topples over the back of it, lands on his feet, gives the Hitler salute, and looks back angrily at the chair—all without a pause in his speech. Later in the scene, when he is asked to betray Roma, he throws a fit of hysterics, lying down on the floor and eating the carpet, then somersaults to his feet, breaks an umbrella over his knee, and collapses into agreement. Athleticism and artistry perfectly conjoined.

The limitation of Schall's performance is the limitation of Brecht's character—Hitler emerges as less a psychopathic monster than a fascinating clown with considerable charm and appeal. Chaplin had a similar difficulty with a comic Hitler, suggesting that while ridicule may be sufficient to deflate the pomposity of Nazism, it is not sufficient to measure its evil. Still, if the play is unsuccessful as a political diagnosis, it is effective enough as a political cartoon, and it gives the company the chance to display the full range of its comic powers.

The Threepenny Opera is a more conventional production of a better work. Directed by Brecht's old friend and associate Erich Engel, this version lacks pace, integration, or coherence, and proves distinctly disappointing after the brilliance of *Arturo Ui;* but it is interesting to see the company performing in a totally different style. The style is relatively realistic, modified by vestigial alienation techniques (the orchestra, for example, is placed on an upstage platform behind a curtain which parts at the beginning of each song). Wolf Kaiser plays Mackie Messer, quite properly, as a suave, thickening, middle-aged Lothario—brutish and dapper, with the heavy grace of an aging dancer and the sad lethargy of a basset hound. Like all the Ensemble actors, he labors to suppress his charm, but the charm is there nevertheless, concealed like the sword in his walking stick. The performance itself is in a rather low key, occasionally tuned up by imaginative business. At Mackie's wedding to Polly, for example, he kicks his henchman in the behind at the same moment a champagne cork pops; implored by Polly to stay and make love to her, he curtly refuses—but stops for one searching look at her legs; when he sits down to his account books, he puts on the rimless glasses of a serious businessman. Engel's production is often inventive—especially arresting is a march across the stage of horribly deformed beggars—but too much of the invention is there for the sake of spectacle; the company acting is surprisingly weak (Peter Kalisch's Peachum is a grave bit of miscasting); and the singers often seem to be rushing the orchestra. To this company, *The Threepenny Opera* may be something of a chestnut by now, for it is acted out of the same listless sense of duty that certain Shakespeare companies perform *Romeo and Juliet* and *The Merchant of Venice.*

With *Coriolan,* however, the company recovers its enthusiasm and its inspiration: the production shows that
tragedies are performed as magnificently as comedies at
the Berliner Ensemble. Brecht's interest in this play was
probably stimulated by its political-economic aspects: it
features a conflict between the patrician and plebeian
classes which is partly motivated by the high price of
corn (Brecht wanted food and money to replace love and
power as the central motifs of the drama, and, in this
play, he must have felt Shakespeare to be moving in the
same direction). The class war and its economic motives
have not been particularly underscored by the Ensemble,
however, possibly because Brecht died before finishing
the adaptation. In its present form, completed and re-
arranged by other hands, the text seems like a fairly
straightforward translation of the original play, and what
is most striking about the evening is not so much its
political as its theatrical values. For the Berliner Ensemble performs the play in a highly ritualized modern
style, somewhat similar to the style with which Peter
Brook approached *King Lear* (though less arbitrary and
more relevant).

After a white muslin drop unravels to tell the story of
Coriolanus, we find ourselves in a grim barbarian city,
more savage than civilized, less Roman than primitive
German. The citizens are costumed in concentration-
camp grays, and even the garments of the patricians look
stained and worn. Gustav Hoffman's setting consists of
a single white arch, which later revolves to become a
wooden stockade for the battle scenes before the Volscian
camp. But the stage is essentially bare, dressed only with
occasional benches and props. One of the more remarkable things about this production is its spatial design.
Instead of directing the action from one side of the stage
to the other, as in conventional productions, Manfred
Wekwerth and Joachim Tenschert have given it a circular

movement, locating much of the action in the deep upstage area, and bringing it forward by means of a revolving track.

The revolving stage, in fact, is used here as a crucial theatrical device, functioning not only to change the scenery but to illustrate the values of a scene. When Coriolanus appears before the citizens to ask their voice for his consulship, wearing a red toga over his gown of humility, the stage brings him from plebe to plebe, as if he disdained to make the conciliatory gestures himself. And in the magnificent battle scenes, the moving stage helps to play on your nerves and emotions. When the armies of Coriolanus and Tullus Aufidius, the Volscian general, prepared to engage in battle, three sets of twin loudspeakers, arranged dimensionally toward the back of the stage, begin to sound with battle chants, consisting of the contrapuntal repetition of each leader's name: *Cai-us Mar-cius—Au-fidi-us*. When Coriolanus and Aufidius engage in battle, they first stalk each other like two visored soldiers from ancient statuary (both actors are of the same height); and as the stage revolves, their combat becomes a ritualized dance, performed to the sound of castanets. Helmets, armor, and swords fall from each warrior in turn; hand-to-hand combat follows; Aufidius' eye and nose are horribly bloodied; Coriolanus conquers and is borne aloft by his troops, down rows of dead soldiers and mangled helmets on pikes, his hands raised casually to acknowledge the general cries.

Makeup is used in the same imaginative way, as a symbolic aid to the action. After Coriolanus is banished from Rome, his golden hair turns darker and his face grows drawn; and after Menenius fails in his attempt to win Coriolanus back, he appears in the next scene totally white. Aufidius, similarly, grows into a gray and tortured little man, who seems to be eaten away with envy of Coriolanus as by an acid. At the end, when he hurls his sarcastic insult at Coriolanus—*Mutterkind!*—he speaks it as if it were a chewy savory. Coriolanus dies laughing as the entire Volscian army stomps on his body, and after Aufidius is carried over him in triumph, he is left alone on stage, his corpse composed in a hideous and grotesque death.

As for the acting, it is just as brilliant as the direction. Ekkehard Schall's golden Coriolanus is biting, contemptuous, and unsexed (he embraces his wife with his hands hanging by his side); Hilmar Thate's Aufidius is a seething cauldron of suppressed rage; and Helene Weigel's Volumnia is a fierce tyranny of mother love. Frau Weigel's performance was still unfinished when I saw it—she had just replaced another actress in preparation for the London tour of the Ensemble—but she was already doing some startling things. When she pleads with her son, for example, to return to Rome, she bows down before him and knocks her head against the ground—three times—with a sickening thud. But her performance seemed to me too isolated from the general proceedings—a fine bit of virtuoso acting which was nevertheless alien to the unity of the production.

And it is this collective strength that finally emerges as the most impressive quality of the Berliner Ensemble: the company constitutes a perfect artistic community within which each element functions with gaiety and dedication. It is the political version of this community that the Ensemble propagandizes for in its program notes and in some of its plays, but to judge by the leaden despondency of its surroundings in East Berlin, it will be a long time before the Ensemble sees in society what it has achieved in art. One wonders what underground springs account for the freshness and vitality of this group when the soil around it is so dry and full of clay. Still, art has blossomed in the most outlandish places and under the most oppressive regimes; it has flowered when the air around it was choked with vapors; it has flourished when the climate seemed inhospitable in the extreme. Whatever its political feelings, the Berliner Ensemble has found its nourishment within itself, and it is by feeding on such fertile artistic sources that it has continued to thrive.

1965

An Embarrassment of Riches

THE PERSECUTION AND ASSASSINATION
OF MARAT AS PERFORMED BY THE
INMATES OF THE ASYLUM OF
CHARENTON UNDER THE DIRECTION
OF THE MARQUIS DE SADE

by Peter Weiss;
Royal Shakespeare Company

This verse play, more popularly known by its short title, *Marat/Sade*, is a work about which I have my reservations, but it is full of marvelous incident and it forms the occasion for an intoxicating evening of theatre. Inspired by his unusual material, Peter Brook, the director, has fashioned one of the most spectacular stage events of recent times, while the author, Peter Weiss, has provided him with a cornucopia of complex theatrical ideas. The play is at odds with itself in a manner I hope shortly to illustrate, but first I would like to express my admiration for this playwright's image-making power: he has an uncanny instinct for seizing upon central modern obsessions and transforming them, through a process of symbolic compression, into visual art. Ultimately, the play proves too rich for its own blood and fails to realize its extraordinary promise, but not before the author has taken us on a daring invasion of hitherto forbidden dramatic territory.

Weiss has conceived an imaginary confrontation between two fascinating antagonists: the Marquis de Sade, a cold voluptuary who attempts to transcend the malignity of man and nature through the passionate enactment of crime ("In a criminal society I dug the criminal out of myself so I could understand him and so understand the times we live in"), and Jean-Paul Marat, a rabid proto-Marxist French revolutionary who wants to overcome the malignity of man and nature through radical social-political upheaval ("In the vast indifference, I invent a meaning . . . We can't begin to build till we've burnt the old building down"). The one is an extreme individualist, the other an extreme collectivist, and together they embody a number of crucial antitheses which extend beyond their historic functions: imagination versus action, poetry versus politics, stasis versus progress, anarchism versus communism, the yogi versus the commissar. Thus described the play sounds like a Shavio-Socratic dialogue on the order of Shaw's *Don Juan in Hell;* but the debate between these two men is actually underdeveloped and intermittent, and it is interrupted too frequently to gather momentum. One of the weaknesses of Weiss's design is that in stating and restating his two positions he never lets them engage each other fully. Both Sade and Marat are probably irreconcilable aspects of the author's character (though as a Marxist, he claims to have more sympathy with Marat), but if so, they exist in separate compartments of his brain, and never lock in significant combat.

Instead of developing his theme, Weiss concentrates on his spectacle—the intellectual debate tends to get swallowed up in theatrical delirium. For the confrontation of Sade and Marat takes place not in a tribunal designed for rational discourse but rather in the bath hall of a madhouse. There, Sade (institutionalized for his bizarre sexual proclivities) puts on plays for the entertainment of the director of the Charenton asylum and his family, the amusement of a fashionable audience, and the therapeutic advancement of the inmates, who function as Sade's acting company. Thus, Marat is not an actual historical personage but rather a figure invented by Sade and enacted by a maniac, while Sade himself functions both as the author-director of the play-within-the-play and as one of the characters in it. There are Pirandellian possibilities here which Weiss exploits by having the mad actors continually falling in and out of their roles; and at the same time that he is showing us the fantastical antics of melancholiacs, erotomaniacs, dribbling idiots, spastics, and paranoiacs, he is subtly suggesting (a suggestion which seems to invalidate his own politics) that human activity is insane, and that human history takes place in a madhouse.

The central event in Sade's play-within-the-play is the assassination of Marat by the young idealist from Caen, Charlotte Corday. Doomed by a painful skin disease to remain immobilized in his tub (an object shaped like a huge black club foot), Marat is visited three times by Corday before she plunges a knife into his side. Weiss frequently interrupts this action with imaginative tableaux and frenzied speeches, including the Sade-Marat debates, mimes of the revolution, execution scenes, musical history lessons, and surrealist episodes out of Marat's past, while at the close of the play the madmen get out of control, attack the guards, rape the nuns, trample the fallen, murder the helpless, and disperse through the audience. This conclusion is phantasmagoric in the extreme, but it leaves one with unanswered questions. For the theatrical effects have been insufficiently integrated with the intellectual dialogues, and the murder of Marat, while visually impressive, is hardly relevant as a climax to Weiss's thematic dialectics.

There are, in short, divisions in the play which leave one with a divided response to it; and these are nowhere better exemplified than in its mixture of styles. Most commentators have already observed how *Marat/Sade* is a compound of two radically different approaches to the stage—the cool alienation techniques of Brecht and the boiling "total theatre" of Artaud—and we may speculate that each approach proceeds from a different side of the author's nature. As a political animal committed to revolutionary change, Weiss is naturally attracted to the epic theatre as a medium of ironic disengagement, and he employs Brechtian conventions (a herald who announces the scenes and comments satirically upon them; a chorus of harlequins which provides exposition, historical bridges, and musical interludes) in order to indict the bourgeois spectator, and to awaken him intellectually to the social implications of the action. As an anarchistic theatre poet, however, Weiss is more attracted by the cruelty techniques of Artaud—fits, paroxysms, trances, hallucinations—and he is always tempted to subordinate coherent action to sensational spectacle, using language as a medium of incantation rather than of sense.

Weiss is a master of both theatrical traditions, but he is less masterly in combining them. What results is a double exposure with blurred edges in which the theatre of cruelty accounts for the stronger image. Sade's most important speech, for example—a melancholy diatribe about the withering of individual man under the mechanical uniformity of the state—is delivered while he is being whipped by Charlotte Corday; and since gesture is more arresting in this play than language, the flagellation distracts rather than illuminates. Weiss's conceptual intellect is strong and his visual imagination fertile, but these qualities are still disjunct in him, so that we are left with a scattering of sharp impressions but an artistic experience that fails to fuse.

Peter Brook has understandably elected to emphasize the Artaudian features of the play, and the results are stunning, brutal, galvanic. The action takes place on a raked stage dressed with movable wooden slats and pocked with deep pits; catatonic musicians in boxes above the stage contribute chamber music, cabaret background, and eerie sound effects; and perched on tiers downstage sit the complacent director of the institution, his timid daughter, and his smirking wife (a typical benefit-audience matron who throughout blinks and simpers at the audience without looking once at the stage). Though Brook keeps the stage in constant motion and the action at a level of frightening intensity, the most hair-raising moment of the evening is the first entrance of the madmen, for they represent a terrifyingly convincing bedlam, partly through makeup (gray faces, scarred skulls, suppurating wounds, elongated and distorted heads, electrified hair) and partly through the most carefully sustained delineation of insanity on the part of all the actors: one talking to herself with her hands held aloft, another staring fiercely at the audience, another suffering involuntary spasms, another continually slavering from mouth to chin. It is a chamber of horrors which would not be out of place in a Hammer film starring Peter Cushing, but the effects are always controlled and almost always organized toward ironic purposes. Brook, as a matter of fact, has chosen to subdue Weiss's cruelties, with the result that these cruelties are all the more harrowing and derisive (the text calls for Corday to scourge Sade with a whip but the production has her lash him with her hair; the text calls for a belly to be pierced and arms and legs to be sawn off, but the production offers a comic execution charade, climaxed with the pouring of blood from a bucket—red for the people, blue for the king, white for Marat).

As for acting, it is all of that impeccably high quality that we have come to expect from British repertory companies, and though it is unfair to single out individuals from a cast which endows the smallest roles with full imaginative life, I should like especially to praise Patrick Magee, frozen, disdainful, slightly effeminate as Sade, with a gentle caressing voice that conveys an infinite fatigue and despair; Ian Richardson as a sometimes vacant, sometimes fervent Marat; Glenda Jackson as Corday, with a piping delivery and a spastic, somnolent walk; and John Steiner as her admirer Duperret (played by an erotomaniac who takes every opportunity to paw her), stringy, licentious, stroking an enormous erection. The text, which has been translated by Geoffrey Skelton and versified by Adrian Mitchell, has bite, terseness, and color; the music by Richard Peaslee contains sharp Weill-like resonances; and the settings and costumes are beautifully conceived. All these elements account for an evening that makes us remember why we go to the theatre, and makes us want to return, for this is a play that touches on the borders of our secret being. If it doesn't touch our core, then this may be because Peter Weiss has not yet learned to marshal his abundant energies toward a consistent goal, to choose a single artistic commitment from a wealth of possibilities. But if this brilliantly theatrical play finally fails to achieve dramatic art, we can be grateful for once that its defects stem not from an author's poverty of imagination but rather from his excess of it.

1966

Osborne's
Elegiac Monody

INADMISSIBLE EVIDENCE

by John Osborne

Osborne's *Inadmissible Evidence* has three sources of strength—a blistering rhetoric of spite and disgust, a fascinating self-lacerating protagonist, and a superlative performance by Nicol Williamson. If a play could make it on eloquence and character alone, then this work would be home; but it contains little else in the way of dramatic values, neither discernible structure, coherent progression, variety of portraiture, nor thematic complication. Osborne's writing has always lacked a magnetic core around which particles of insight and feeling might collect—only his *Epitaph for George Dillon* (written with a collaborator) seems to me sufficiently formulated as a dramatic action—for he is much too concerned with composing single character sketches of a recurring figure, the caustic fire-eater who evokes sympathy when we discover that he is suffering more than the people he hurts. There is a thread of elegiac self-pity running through Osborne's work, a strain of pathos that frequently turns into sentimentality (consider the bear-and-squirrel sogginess of *Look Back in Anger*); and as his protagonists alternate between defiance and apology, his plays invariably close in on the divided self. In *Inadmissible Evidence*, Osborne withdraws even deeper into solipsism. Other characters appear on stage to stimulate the hero's lust, pity, vituperativeness, or self-hatred, but they are just as cardboard as the scenery and sometimes just as mute. And though the author introduces frequent editorials on Divorce, Adultery, Homosexuality, and Teenage Morals, these are not only largely irrelevant to the action, but wholly uninterrupted by the slightest hint of exception or opposition.

The play, in short, is a monodrama, a highly subjective form demanding a highly subjective approach. Osborne seems partly to realize this, for he begins the play with a dream sequence, showing his hero on trial for having published a "wicked, bawdy, and scandalous object" (i.e., his life). This prologue, however, is generically out of key with the scenes that follow, and is never used or referred to again; instead, the play turns realistic, though the realism is occasionally broken by equally inapposite devices (one actress, for example, plays all the female clients). What gives *Inadmissible Evidence* its only claim to unity is not its botched form but rather its one fully fleshed character—a middle-aged solicitor on the verge of breakdown named Bill Maitland. Sex-obsessed, nasty, unethical, hysterical, Maitland is a pulsing mass of infantile needs. He exploits everyone for love and understanding and betrays all who trust him; trying to keep afloat on a sea of impulse, he keeps his hand on the telephone to his patient mistress as if holding an umbilical lifeline to survival. But drown he must, and the only logical development in the play follows his self-destructive alienation of everyone he loves and respects. At the curtain, he is entombed in his office and spiritually dead, having evacuated his fury over everything from young lovers in cars ("flatulent, purblind, mating weasels") to the machine society ("Some mathematical clerk will feed all our petitions and depositions and statements and evidence into some clattering brute of a computer and the answer will come out guilty or not guilty"), and having revealed a good deal of helpless compassion for the agonized clients who file through his doors.

The New York production has severely reduced the

text along with some of the impact of the play; but it
has had the good sense to retain Anthony Page as director and Nicol Williamson as chief actor, surrounded
by a competent American cast. Williamson, whose features are a cross between the cragginess of Van Heflin
and the slyness of Alistair Sim, is a tall, graceful actor
of astonishing power. Slightly adenoidal, his brow con-
tracted with rage and woe, he chews his lines into a
mash and spits them out with brutal wit, then just as
quickly turns the invective into whining apology—his
transitions are extremely swift. Williamson has found
perfect emblematic gestures for Maitland—drawing his
hands to his aching temples to exile the outside world,
shaking his foot up and down with nervous contempt,
staring vaguely into the middle distance as if confronting
his involuntary cruel demon—it is the actor, even more
than the author, who manages to exonerate this character. His performance is brilliant, as brilliant as Robert
Stephens' George Dillon, Albert Finney's Martin Luther,
and Sir Laurence Olivier's Archie Rice; and it suggests
that if Osborne does not yet write coherent plays, he
continues to compose magnificent roles.

1966

Waiting for Hamlet

ROSENCRANTZ AND GUILDENSTERN ARE DEAD
by Tom Stoppard

Tom Stoppard's *Rosencrantz and Guildenstern Are Dead* is obviously giving considerable pleasure to large numbers of people, so I advance my own reservations feeling like a spoilsport and a churl: the play strikes me as a noble conception which has not been endowed with any real weight or texture. The author is clearly an intelligent man with a good instinct for the stage, and his premise is one that should suggest an endless series of possibilities. But he manipulates this premise instead of exploring it, and what results is merely an immensely shrewd exercise enlivened more by cunning than by conviction.

As is now generally known, *Rosencrantz and Guildenstern Are Dead* is a theatrical parasite, feeding off *Hamlet, Waiting for Godot,* and *Six Characters in Search of an Author*—Shakespeare provides the characters, Pirandello the technique, and Beckett the tone with which the Stoppard play proceeds. Like Pirandello, Stoppard tries to give extradramatic life to a group of already written characters, introducing elements of chance and spontaneity into a scene previously determined by an author. His object is to discover what happens to people whose lives are completely fixed and formalized when they are allowed to meditate, self-consciously, upon their own predestination.

To do this, he borrows a pair of secondary figures from *Hamlet,* and examines their behavior when they are not playing one of their seven written scenes. Summoned by a messenger to the court of Elsinore, Rosencrantz and

Guildenstern await the completion of their roles in an action whose outcome they cannot divine, passing the time in small talk, exits and entrances, verbal games, coin flipping, philosophical disputations, and various meetings with other characters from the play. Like Beckett's two tramps in *Waiting for Godot*, Rosencrantz and Guildenstern are baffled characters imprisoned in a timeless void where they alternate between brief vaudeville routines and ruminations on the vacancy of life in general and theirs in particular.

Rosencrantz and Guildenstern encounter the players who eventually enact the murder of Gonzago at Claudius' court; they catch glimpses of that larger drama being played out by Hamlet, Claudius, Gertrude, Polonius, and Ophelia; and after playing their own parts, they eventually wind up on the ship that is bringing Hamlet to England—presumably to his own death. Hamlet switches the letters; the pirates overwhelm the ship, and Rosencrantz and Guildenstern, having discovered that destiny cannot be cheated, resignedly accept their coming deaths at the hand of the English king. The curtain comes down on Horatio's dialogue with the English ambassadors in *Hamlet*, Act V, scene 2.

In outline, the idea is extremely ingenious; in execution, it is derivative and familiar, even prosaic. As an artist, Stoppard does not fight hard enough for his insights—they all seem to come to him, prefabricated, from other plays—with the result that his air of pessimism seems affected, and his philosophical meditations, while witty and urbane, never obtain the thickness of *felt* knowledge. Whenever the play turns metaphysical, which is frequently, it turns spurious, particularly in the author's recurrent discourses upon death: "Death is not romantic . . . and death is not a game which will soon be over . . . death is not anything . . . death is not. It's the absence of presence, nothing more . . . the endless time of never coming back." This sort of thing is squeezed out like toothpaste throughout the play, the gravity of the subject never quite overcoming the banality of its expression: "The only beginning is birth, and the only end is death— if you can't count on that, what can you count on?" Compare this with Pozzo's lines in *Godot:* "One day we were born, one day we shall die, the same day, the same second, is that not enough for you? They give birth astride a grave, the light gleams an instant, then it's night once more"—and you will see how much Stoppard's language lacks economy, compression, and ambiguity, how far short it falls of poetry.

There is, in short, something disturbingly voguish and available about this play, as well as a prevailing strain of cuteness which shakes one's faith in the author's serious intentions: "Eternity's a terrible thought," reflects one character, "I mean where's it going to end?" Hamlet spits into the wind, and receives his spittle back in his eye. There is a good deal of innuendo about the ambiguous sexual nature of the boy playing the Player Queen. And the two central figures are whimsical to the point of nausea.

It is, in fact, the characters of Rosencrantz and Guildenstern that account for a good deal of my queasiness about the play. In Shakespeare, these characters are time servers—cold, calculating opportunists who betray a friendship for the sake of a preferment—whose deaths, therefore, leave Hamlet without a pang of remorse. In Stoppard, they are garrulous, child-like, ingratiating simpletons, bewildered by the parts they must play— indeed, by the very notion of an evil action. It is for this reason, I think, that Stoppard omits their most crucial scene—the famous recorder scene where they are exposed as spies for Claudius—for it is here that their characterological inconsistency would be most quickly revealed. Since the author is presumably anxious to demonstrate the awful inevitability of a literary destiny ("We follow directions—there is no *choice* involved. The

bad end unhappily, the good unluckily. That is what
tragedy means"), it hardly serves his purpose to violate
the integrity of Shakespeare's original conception. But I
suspect the author has another purpose here—that of
amusing the audience with winning heroes—and the
necessity to be charming is not always easily reconciled
with the demands of art.

Derek Goldby's production services the play well, and
matches it exactly: it is theatrical, entertaining, energetic, ultimately without dimension. The actors playing
Rosencrantz and Guildenstern perform with a boyish
flippancy that links them less with Vladimir and Estragon
than with the pranksters in *The Knack;* always technically proficient, they never once startle us into an
arresting perception of reality. As for the actors playing
parts in Shakespeare's play, they are generally well-
spoken, but I cannot say they left me with any desire to
see them in a full-length version of *Hamlet*—after the
reforms introduced by the Royal Shakespeare Company,
it is tiresome to be brought back to the empty elocutionism
of Old Vic Shakespeare. Desmond Heeley's costumes—
pressed velvet garments that look like they're crumbling
to dust—and his settings—scrims and platforms behind
a peeling inner proscenium, tasseled in the manner of a
nineteenth-century playhouse—are extremely attractive,
and extremely well lit by Richard Pilbrow; but they do
not settle the problem of precisely where and when this
supposedly "Elizabethan" action is taking place.

Mr. Stoppard doesn't bother to settle the problem
either. Worse, he does not seem aware that it exists or
that he has a certain responsibility to work out the deeper
implications of his choices. We are left wondering why
this admittedly entertaining play has found such ready
acceptance on Broadway when *Waiting for Godot*—without which it would not exist—still awaits a sustained
New York production thirteen years after it was written.
I do not think it is too much to say that Stoppard is

benefiting from a *Zeitgeist* created by authors whose works nobody wants to see, and is achieving his success by offering a form of Beckett without tears. *Waiting for Godot* is the creation of a poet, *Rosencrantz and Guildenstern Are Dead* the product of a university wit. Will the poets ever have their day as well as the wags?

1967

COMPANIES

Consensus Theatre

SCHOOL FOR SCANDAL
by Richard Sheridan

RIGHT YOU ARE IF YOU THINK YOU ARE
by Luigi Pirandello;
APA Repertory Company

The Association of Producing Artists, accompanied by a guest producing artist named Helen Hayes, is now firmly ensconced at the Lyceum, after having collected a number of warm reviews from the New York newspapers and the mass magazines. Walter Kerr, for example, has called this group the finest repertory company in the country—a rather rash superlative for him, considering how little theatre he has visited outside of New York. Perhaps his new responsibilities on the *Times* will lead him to investigate more what is happening off the Great White Way—but even by our own inferior national standards, the APA hardly merits such unstinting praise. Compared with the Theatre of Living Arts in Philadelphia, the APA lacks radical daring and a sense of exploration; compared with the Minnesota Theatre Company at the Guthrie Theatre in Minneapolis, it lacks depth, energy, and range. I do not doubt the smoothness of its ensemble work, the technical facility of its individual actors, or the entertainment value of certain of its shows (particularly its light comedies), but I do not think the APA very often rises above the level of a provincial English rep.

Actually, the enthusiasm of Mr. Kerr and people like
him suggests what certain elements in our theatre are
demanding these days from permanent ensembles. The
APA's appeal is to those who grow nostalgic over Maurice
Evans–Judith Anderson–Margaret Webster Shakespeare,
Broadway revivals of Wilde and Shaw, and Theatre Guild
Pirandello. Mr. Kerr gives the show away when he praises
the APA for making the audience forget it is seeing an
old play, and for making the dialogue of Sheridan sound
indistinguishable from Broadway conversation. Classics
without tears! Polished, bland, effete, and harmless—
utterly immune to the tensions of life or art—the APA
is becoming a perfect candidate for an official American
consensus theatre. One is not surprised to read that the
company has been performing scenes for President Johnson at the White House or that Helen Hayes has been
named (with Charlton Heston!) to the National Council
for the Arts.

Just as Miss Hayes' appointment to this board suggests
that America's love of art is less intense than its appetite
for glamour, so her affiliation with the APA suggests that
this company's affection for plays is less intense than its
attraction to roles. To watch Miss Hayes come on in
School for Scandal, simpering like a Midwestern matron
on a New York shopping tour, or to watch her, in *Right
You Are*, transforming the tragic Signora Frola into a
mischievous Mrs. McThing, is to see an actress who never
for a moment loses sight (out of the corner of her eye) of
all those wonderful admirers in the audience. Miss Hayes
is clearly delighted with herself for having condescended
to play such relatively small parts; as compensation for
this sacrifice, she is invariably placed upstage center at
the apex of a triangle, and permitted a charming disregard for the values of the play, for the other performers,
and for the character she is playing. There are good
things in these productions, and occasional good per-

formances—Donald Moffat, for example, is by contrast to Miss Hayes a serious actor seriously probing a role—but my general impression of the APA is of empty expertise. One begins to wonder if it is enough—at this point of crisis in our theatre—simply to mount a series of plays without identifying some larger meaning or purpose.

1967

Bagatelles

JUDITH

by Jean Giraudoux;
APA Repertory Company

In *Judith,* the heroine perceives a blue vein throbbing in Holofernes' neck: that vein contains the only blood in the play. Giraudoux has a passion for such particulars, but his passion seems to stop there. Since he shows no inclination to probe below the subcutaneous areas of his characters, *Judith* is singularly stiff, inert, and cold. The play, to be sure, is an inferior work of its author's, but I should probably confess a prejudice here: even at his best—in *The Madwoman of Chaillot,* say, or *Intermezzo,* or *The Trojan War Will Not Take Place*—Giraudoux strikes me as an extremely fragile fantasist. There is something very artificial about his writings: they have the look of costume jewelry, bagatelles which sparkle and glitter without throwing off much light. This may be what is meant by Giraudoux's *préciosité:* the capacity to simulate the surface of art without ever engaging the depths of reality. In our own country, we have an over-worked term for such semi-serious art—*middlebrow*—and I have little doubt that, born in a different time and at a different place, Giraudoux could have been a kingpin in the American cultural revolution. Who among our dramatists so effectively combines such solemnity with such superficiality? Underneath the portentous exterior of Giraudoux's plays grinds a well-oiled Boulevard machine which is run by little more than gas and wind.

Take *Judith.* This, like most of Giraudoux's plays, is a reworking of an ancient story in modern terms. But whether the author gets his material from Greek mythology or (as in the case of *Judith*) from Old Testament Apochrypha, his purpose and motive remain the same—the purpose, to invent trivial motives for heroic actions; the motive, to make the legendary lives of saints, martyrs, and heroes conform to the domesticated experience of the local theatregoing bourgeoisie. Giraudoux's debater's platform reminds one of Shaw's, and *Judith* is somewhat influenced by *St. Joan;* but while both dramatists are inclined to please the crowd, Giraudoux is anxious to flatter it as well, and his ideas are usually scattered into a leaven of pure romance. The great "insight" of *Judith,* for example—which comes after three acts of exceedingly tedious wordplay—is that the famous virgin-heroine killed the Assyrian general, Holofernes, not to save the Jewish people, as legend has it, but rather to preserve the marvelous memory of her first night of love with him. This is the sort of thing usually dreamed up by reporters for *True Romances.* Giraudoux, to be sure, quickly introduces an archangel *ex machina* to inform Judith that she was unwittingly guided by the hand of the Almighty. But what really disturbs one about this dramatist is his apparent lack of interest in any of the subjects he debates so endlessly, whether God, sacrifice,

Jewish history, or (this least of all) female chastity. What really concerns him most, I fear, is that pulsing vein in Holofernes' neck.

At the APA, the production matches the play, being sumptuously appointed, closely detailed, well articulated, ultimately ersatz. This professional ensemble functions smoothly through long association with one another, but the performances lack any fire or subtlety. Rosemary Harris does not seem to me to have the right emotional bead on Judith: she plays the character as a charming, lively, rather lightheaded chatterbox, scanting Judith's modicum of visionary passion. As Holofernes, Paul Sparer is vaguely supercilious, rolling his eyes and resonating his vocal organs; I wish he would stop doing bits on John Barrymore and pay more attention to the heart of his roles. I liked Richard Jordan pretty well as John, and Nancy Marchand is good, especially in her opening scene, as Judith's anti-self, the prostitute Susanna. As for the rest of the company, it is solid, if uninspired, and Ellis Rabb's direction is sure, if flossy: there is a little too much chiffon on stage, too many oiled naked torsos, and the setting in Holofernes' tent is too reminiscent of Cecil B. DeMille's Judaea. But I do not wish to repeat myself about this ensemble. The APA remains, with all its high intentions, a kind of superior stock company, lacking not talent so much as identity, aspiration, vision. Its dedication is wholly to the theatre—but how can one love the theatre unless it functions as the instrument of some higher purpose? One might ask the same question of the playwright Jean Giraudoux.

1965

California Wine in New York Bottles

DANTON'S DEATH

by Georg Buechner; adapted by Herbert Blau;
Repertory Theatre of Lincoln Center

I will not attempt to mask my disappointment over the
first presentation this season by the Repertory Company
at the Vivian Beaumont Theatre. Not quite a disaster, it
is, nevertheless, the kind of failure that makes you grind
your teeth, for it demonstrates that the new Lincoln
Center company has limitations of a rather unexpected
kind. Some of these problems were observable in the old
company, and may very well be built into the architecture
of cultural complexes. Others are clearly the result of
specific miscalculations by the new directors, and since
these are the more easily corrected, it might be more
constructive to begin with them.

First of all, the play. When Herbert Blau and Jules
Irving announced their program last summer, I felt full
of exhilaration: the four plays selected for production
this year confirmed one's sense that these men, unlike
their predecessors, knew precisely what constituted a
sound and valuable repertory. I was, on the other hand,
a little uneasy about their decision to begin operations
with *Danton's Death*. For while Georg Buechner's doleful,
morbid study of the Reign of Terror is clearly a masterpiece, it is also one of the most difficult and elusive works
in all dramatic literature—thus, hardly a wise initial
choice for a company still in process of formation. The
play, for one thing, has no easy access, lacking horizontal
development or exterior conflict. Written in a compressed

epigrammatic style of harrowing intensity and divided into lightning episodes like those in Shakespeare's later Roman tragedies, it is primarily a mood study in which the author uses an historical crisis as a basis for metaphysical speculation—on nature, human character, the chaotic universe. Characters talk *past* each other, lost in their hallucinations and feverish thoughts, and though they are always reflecting intelligently on their fate, they are quite incapable of altering this fate through significant action. Danton himself is a thoroughly passive hero, "lazy," inert, nihilistic. He is in love with the grave from the very beginning, half out of guilt for his part in the September massacres, half out of genuine fatigue with life itself—his pursuit of pleasure hardly conceals a profound, irremediable despair. Behind Danton's despair lurks a horrible apprehension about human fatality. Convinced that man is no more than a marionette manipulated by unknown powers, and that human action is inevitably either futile or base, he chooses to suffer the guillotine rather than use it against others—Danton knows that Robespierre's "virtue" is merely the hypocritical mask of blood lust, ambition, revenge. *Danton's Death*, in short, has a protagonist who is dying before the curtain opens, and the whole play is actually a beautifully written death scene in four acts.

The last way to approach such a private, probing, intimate work is to treat it as an historical pageant or public spectacle; yet, pageantry and spectacle are basic elements in Blau's production. Instead of accepting the static nature of the action and letting the mournful arpeggios sound, the director chooses to inject activity, tumult, and clamor at every opportunity. He begins the play, for example, with an interpolated hunk of puzzling choreography, involving four whores, a dizzy revolutionary, and a symbolic loaf of bread; he is continually trying to fill the large stage with howling citizenry who grapple, grouse, roll on the floor, and grab each other's clothes; and nobody ever walks on this stage when he can fly on at top speed. Then, apparently fascinated by the mechanical gadgetry of his new theatre, Blau lets the play get swamped by technology. The music by Morton Subotnick is a whining electronic score that would be more appropriate as soundtrack for a science fiction thriller; the costumes are of such elegance that one wonders why the wearers are not guillotined for undermining revolutionary simplicity; and the neat perspective setting never suggests for a moment that this Paris is a slaughterhouse. Worst of all, Jo Mielzener has been permitted to indulge an obvious weakness for revolving trolleys, lateral tracks, movable screens, airborne balloons, and huge sliding set pieces (these include a convention hall, a revolutionary tribunal, and, finally, a full-scale guillotine, complete with scaffold and tumbril). I had the feeling, upon emerging from the theatre, that the production would have benefited enormously from the exertions of a good, dedicated machine wrecker.

For Blau seems so preoccupied with the technical aspects of his production that he has neglected to establish the values of individual scenes: the play is, at the same time, both overproduced and underdirected. One episode melts into another without having assumed its own tone, atmosphere, or meaning, and the entire play emerges as a little more than a chaotic sequence of undifferentiated tableaux. Some of the difficulty, no doubt, can be traced to the failure of the ensemble. As individuals, many of these performers are perfectly competent; as a company, they remain largely on the surface of the play. Roscoe Lee Browne as the cold demonic St. Just has a very telling moment in the first part when—with an ironic smile, rising inflection, and spasmodic gestures—he delivers a marvelous piece of demagoguery justifying murder as an act of Nature; Robert Symonds, looking like a malevolent Ben Franklin, frequently resonates with a strong, vibrant self-righteousness as Robespierre; and Robert Stattel, David J. Stewart, and Paul Mann have their moments in supporting roles. But these are only moments; the acting as a whole is rarely integrated; and, in the case of Alan Bergman as Danton, it is depressingly inadequate. I do not wish to be unkind to this actor, since the part of Danton would strain the powers of the finest performers in the world; but given the difficulties of the part, I fail to understand why it was entrusted to one who obviously has neither the physical, vocal, nor intellectual resources for a crucial, sustaining role. In Bergman's hands, Danton's cynical, febrile despair dissolves entirely into hollow intonations, graceless gestures, and theatrical guffaws, and without a Danton of stature and importance, the play is simply a long string of baffling scenes and pointless epigrams.

What are we to conclude from this first production by the new management of Lincoln Center? I think, at this early stage, the wisest thing would be to resist conclusions. I have seen the Blau-Irving troupe do brilliant work in San Francisco; it was occasionally erratic there, it will no doubt be occasionally erratic here; and we must refrain from applying our commercial hit-flop standards to a company that will assuredly develop from play to play. As far as the repertory ideal is concerned, there is a world of difference between failing a masterpiece and failing a work that should never have been produced; and if the choice of *Danton's Death* smacks a little of hubris, it also smacks of courage and ambitiousness, without which no permanent company would be worth a second thought.

Still, something troubles me. For the very qualities that distinguished the Actors Workshop in San Francisco—its vigor, healthiness, joy, informality, and exuberance—are notably lacking in this New York incarnation. Instead of assuming that good California wine doesn't travel, I am more inclined to think the fault lies with trying to turn wine into sparkling burgundy. Is there

something in the bubbly official atmosphere of Lincoln
Center that sours the hardiest grape? Certainly, the
directors of the company are already showing signs of
transformation. Their ads pronounce their theatre a
shrine; their program notes are full of inspirational
pieties about Civil Rights, the Human Spirit, and the
Advance of Culture; and they have now dedicated their
first season to the "still unfulfilled principles of the
Revolution which is the subject of our first play . . .
Liberty, Fraternity, and Exuberance among men."

Besides indicating what might have gone wrong in
the interpretation of *Danton's Death* (which is more
about bondage, alienation, and despair among men), a
statement like this suggests that a lot of creative energy
that might be more effectively channeled into a rigorous
confrontation of the plays is now being wasted in public
posturing. How easy it is for relaxed and carefree theatre
artists to harden into statues under pressure from a cultural mold. I have never been convinced that much of
consequence will issue from the plush theatre stadium at
Lincoln Center (I have much more hope for its small
experimental theatre), but I know the enterprise is
doomed entirely once it is hallowed and enshrined. If
anything is to be achieved there, the directors will have
to resist the temptation to become two more stone
columns in a stately facade, and loosen into their old
quiet work of producing good shows.

1965

Sartre, the Janus

THE CONDEMNED OF ALTONA

by Jean-Paul Sartre; adapted by Justin O'Brien;
Repertory Theatre of Lincoln Center

One of the most maddening things about Jean-Paul Sartre is how he continually promises, and continually fails, to be a poet of the stage. Buried somewhere deep inside of him there is an inventive theatre artist capable of fertile theatrical concepts, but while he thoroughly explores the philosophical implications of these concepts, he leaves their imaginative possibilities virtually untapped. What Sartre ultimately lacks is the artist's commitment to form: of all his dramatic works, only the short play *No Exit* seems to enjoy a structure congenial to its theme. As for the others, they all look like uneasy collaborations between a deft original thinker and a clumsy derivative playwright, for despite their intellectual vitality and suggestive scenic strategies, they invariably bog down into talky scenes, old-fashioned dramaturgy, and unconvincing character motivations that lessen the impact of their ideas.

That this is true of *The Condemned of Altona* is especially disappointing, since the work is potentially the most interesting of his full-length plays. The basic argument, certainly, is a corker: Frantz von Gerlach, a German officer reported dead after World War II, has been hiding in a secret room in his father's house for thirteen years, sequestered from the world and from all members of his family except his sister Leni (with whom he lives in incest). Convinced that Germany has been reduced to ashes by the vindictive Allied forces, and half mad with shame and self-justification, he is now pouring the history of his dismal century into a tape recorder for the benefit of some future tribunal, composed (he imagines man will then be extinct) entirely of crabs. What Frantz must eventually discover, of course, is that Germany has not only survived its crimes but has gone on to become the most powerful nation in Europe ("Today we have soldiers; tomorrow we have the Bomb"); and no longer able to use his country's supposed destruction as a cover for his own actual guilt (he has tortured Russian partisans), he can only attempt to atone a little by committing suicide.

Imagine what Beckett or Ionesco would make of those "masked inhabitants of the ceiling"—the crabs from the thirtieth century which scuttle over an earth barren of mankind—and imagine what Duerrenmatt or Weiss would do with the horrible irony of a German prosperity built on human bones. Sartre doesn't exactly bungle these possibilities but he certainly dissipates them with his unfortunate dramatic choices. *The Condemned of Altona* is fashioned in the form of a creaky bourgeois melodrama— one plot based on a vapid romantic triangle, the other on a conflict between father and son—which owes its basic techniques to the early family plays of Arthur Miller. Thus, we have a first act dedicated almost entirely to long-winded exposition in the Gerlach parlor; we have brief *Death of a Salesman* flashbacks during which Frantz, as a young man, wanders into the later action for background episodes; we have recriminations over the wartime activities of Frantz's father (a rich shipbuilder who once permitted his land to be used for a concentration camp) that recall the flap over Keller's faulty plane parts in *All My Sons;* we have the inevitable reconciliation scene between father and son following a moment of tearful embraces (*pace* Chris and Keller, and Biff and Willy); and we have the double suicide of Frantz and old Gerlach in an offstage Porsche, as we had Willy's suicide in his offstage Studebaker. Worst of all, the plot revolves around the revelation of a concealed secret (Frantz's activities as "the butcher of Smolensk") which, like Willy's adultery and Keller's involvement in the death of his son, seems overly contrived and insufficient to bear the weight of dramatic events.

Sartre makes every effort to enlarge the perspective seen from the family window, even to the point of allegorizing from a quibble on his hero's name (Frantz, the torturer, is homonymous with France and its torture policies in Algeria); and Frantz's addresses to his tape machine possess a sardonic eloquence that is fierce and arresting. Then, Sartre is able to evoke a certain concern for this cold Lutheran family even as its members are freezing each other to death, and he occasionally creates scenes of coarse-grained brutality that vibrate with ruthless energy. But despite the brilliance with which Sartre examines the consequences of the action, the action itself too often seems manipulated, with characters removing themselves from stage on flimsy pretexts, and important revelations (such as Germany's real condition) being made as a result of trivial motives (such as a lover's jealousy).

The Repertory Theatre's production suffers from similar difficulties: only intermittently does it find adequate theatrical images for its intellectual formulations. Robin Wagner's proscenium settings have a dour grandeur, the Council Room possessing the green moldy texture of an ancestral tomb, and Frantz's room an unearthly disarray that pulls it out of time, while Herbert Blau's direction has been carefully orchestrated for pace and rhythm. But too few of the scenes are cohesive and too much of the acting is pallid, as if the play had sapped the energies of its youthful cast. This is especially true in the first act, which seems interminable; later, when we move up to Frantz's room, something more exciting begins to happen, both to play and production. For Tom Rosqui, while hardly physically ideal for the part of Frantz (two women, after all, are supposed to be in love with him), handles the more important values of the role quite well: he gives us a rasping, feverish figure, petulant and disgusted amidst his champagne and oysters, who spits out his loathing with an eccentric, staccato delivery that contains elements of grisly humor and real daring. George Coulouris, as his father, lacks the requisite steeliness and strength, though he looks rather like General Jodl with his white hair and brush mustache, and the two ladies of the play, though handsome enough, do not have the histrionic means to disguise the machinery of the plot. Still, while this is not a brilliant production, it is faithful enough to show us what the play is, and in Justin O'Brien's lucid adaptation, it exposes us to both the virtues and the faults of Sartre's dramatic approach.

His virtues stem from an adventurous mind, his faults from an inability to be equally adventurous in his use of the stage. As a thinker, Sartre has no peers among contemporary playwrights, but he has not yet learned to forge his ideas into powerful myths. He is certainly a dramatist, but one who presently looks backward, even as he is pushing forward intellectually to the limits of human thought.

1966

Further Reflections on Lincoln Center

THE CAUCASIAN CHALK CIRCLE

*by Bertolt Brecht; English version by Eric Bentley;
Repertory Theatre of Lincoln Center*

The Repertory Theatre presentation of *The Caucasian
Chalk Circle* is just adequate, and this is what makes it
so very disappointing: surely something more than bor-
derline competence can now be expected of this company
after its fourth production at Lincoln Center. The play
itself poses no problem—it is absolutely irresistible—but
I must quarrel with the ponderous way it has been staged.
The essence of the work is simplicity; yet once again, the
treadmill rumbles loudly at the Vivian Beaumont, and
once again the mechanical spectacle overwhelms the
dramatic action. The set is a heavy piece of stone architecture that hampers the performance rather than aids
it, and while the costumes have a Persian-carpet gor-
geousness and the masks are cleverly designed, these
trappings provide little inspiration for the actors, who
discover no character clues in their masks, and who move
in their clothes as if they were borrowed. What should
be terse, precise, suggestive, and ritually graceful thus
becomes noisy, clumsy, busy, and agglutinated.

Still, the play is virtually production-proof and much
of it manages to seep through, bubbling with those holi-
day spirits that are so rare in Brecht's writing. *The
Caucasian Chalk Circle* is a masterpiece of the author's
later parable style. Offered as a moral lesson with deference to the techniques of Oriental theatre, the play is
actually singularly lacking in didacticism and owes more

to Elizabethan conventions: it looks like Shakespearian romance leavened with Jonsonian satire. The Prologue, for example, which introduces us to a group of peasants in Soviet Russia, functions like the Induction to *Taming of the Shrew;* the main plot is based on intrigue, misunderstanding, and suspense, like the plots of *As You Like It* and *Twelfth Night,* reaching its climax in a courtroom scene, like *The Merchant of Venice;* and the subplot revolves around a bustling comic rogue in the tradition of Falstaff, Toby Belch, and Autolycus. Then, Brecht's Storyteller has the same functions as Shakespeare's chorus figures; the songs, like Shakespeare's, are lyrical interludes with only a metaphorical relation to the action; and the conclusion reminds us of Shakespeare's method of tying off a romantic plot—with reunions, reconciliations, and a dance.

Brecht's plot construction, however, shows interesting deviations from the Elizabethan pattern. For where Shakespeare and his contemporaries build vertically, alternating the main plot with a subplot, Brecht builds horizontally, providing an uninterrupted presentation of the main plot in Part One, then suspending this in Part Two in order to return to the initial point of time for the subplot, then combining both plots at the end. Technically, this gives the impression of two separate actions converging on each other, and finding their moment of impact in the climactic scene of the chalk circle.

The main plot is a story of flight. Like the gentlewoman Rosalind, the peasant Grusha is forced to flee the city as a result of usurpation and revolt. Having saved the abandoned child of the dead Governor's wife, she risks her life for her maternal instinct, struggling with pursuing soldiers, passing over dangerous bridges, marrying a dying man who (like Dan Burke in Synge's *Shadow of the Glen*) immediately revives to plague her, and almost sacrificing her returning lover, Simon. Grusha Vashnadze, the sweetest and most generous of Brecht's child-loving heroines, is eclipsed as a character only by Azdak, one of the finest rascals in the whole of dramatic literature. Azdak functions as a Lord of Misrule—the Shakespearian rogue crossed with Charlie Chaplin and Groucho Marx. Drunken, corrupt, lazy, and lecherous, Azdak is nevertheless responsible for the only acts of justice in this primitive, strife-torn land. For once having been appointed magistrate as a consequence of a prank, he uses bourgeois legal chicanery in order to pass down anti-bourgeois legal decisions: "Statute and rule he broke like a loaf to feed the folk." Azdak, whose password is "I accept," is a monumental bribe taker, but he always manages to blunder into the most human decision, Brecht's ironic point being that in a corrupt world like our own, justice is served only through error or subterfuge. It is through such practices that Grusha is awarded the child and reunited with her lover in Brecht's charming final scene.

The Azdak episodes are the most brilliant in the play; they are also the most impressive in the current production, thanks to Robert Symonds. Symonds is, I think, essentially miscast in this role, which really belongs to a madcap like Zero Mostel or Jonathan Winters (or even a good burlesque top banana), but though he plays the part for character rather than for comedy, he does capture its appetitive aspect, and he has exciting moments during the scene of the chalk circle. Elizabeth Huddle seems better cast as Grusha, with her apple cheeks and peasant walk, but she lacks sufficient power or poignance and her voice is too monochromatic, while Brock Peters as the Storyteller adds a sanctimonious bass-baritone tedium to the proceedings, along with excessive hands-on-hips posturing. Ray Fry is very funny indeed as a horny monk, crossing Grusha before her marriage and letting his benediction conclude on her left breast, but most of the other actors would be more at home in Liggetts than the Caucasus, and rarely convince one they know anything about the death and pain of which they speak. Eric Bentley's version of the play is his best Brecht translation (though marred a little by American colloquialisms), but Morton Subotnick's tuneless music is enervating, and the all-girl trio that sits on stage to sing and play it would be better employed in some Balalaika nightclub.

Two final complaints, the first about the director's mishandling of certain key scenes. Grusha's flight across the rotten bridge, for example, was obviously written to be staged across the back of the theatre for maximum Pearl White thrills, but Jules Irving has staged it toward the audience with inevitable loss of excitement. Then, Irving also muffs the scene in which Grusha, having found Simon again, is asked by the Ironshirts whether she is the true mother of the child. This should be a moment of anguish for Grusha, since her answer will lead either to the loss of Simon (if she answers yes) or of the child (if she answers no); yet the actress makes her reply without a moment's hesitation. In this way, the separate scenes of the play lose their value and rhythm —lose, in short, the inspiration with which Brecht conceived them.

My final complaint is a more fundamental one, and concerns the acting company as a whole. There is something courageous in the refusal of Blau and Irving to alter substantially the group that came from San Francisco, but there is something foolhardy about it too: the old members of the company have failed to grow sufficiently, and the recently added members are not very good. I think it is time to admit that the spirit of the Actors Workshop is simply not transferrable to Lincoln Center, for what is exciting and adventurous in a small theatre functioning on a modest budget may only look sloppy and amateurish in a plush theatre provided with all available means, especially when those means are permitted to dominate. If we acknowledge this fact, only two alternatives are plausible for Blau and Irving: either to abandon the main stage of the Vivian Beaumont and continue work on its smaller experimental stage, or to abandon most of the present company and close up ranks with the finest available repertory-trained performers. A young exploratory company and an old establishment audience do not make ideal bedfellows, and so far neither theatrical advance nor official culture has been very well served by the results.

1966

Sepulchral Odors at Lincoln Center

THE ALCHEMIST

by Ben Jonson;
Repertory Theatre of Lincoln Center

Jules Irving had two possible alternatives when he decided to stage Ben Jonson's *The Alchemist*—either to find some modern equivalent for the action which might point its relevance to contemporary America or to choose a more traditional mode of presentation and offer the work frankly as a revival. Irving made the latter option, setting the play near its own time (the seventeenth century) and adopting a style common on the English stage about fifteen years ago: measured pace, lots of props, elocutionary delivery. The initial decision was honorable enough—it is a pleasure to see a work as brilliantly conceived as *The Alchemist* either in a new framework or an old—but within that option, the production is not successful. For all the farcical frenzy and frenetic activity on the stage of the Vivian Beaumont, there is no real speed in the performance, with the result that some inner vitality has been lost and one of the fastest works in the English language now seems like one of the slowest.

It is difficult to account for the longueurs of the evening: certainly the playwright is not at fault. The con games Jonson provided for his three central characters are still as fresh and inventive as the day they were conceived, and if alchemy is no longer exactly a popular hipster racket, why then politics and advertising can easily be substituted. Tribulation Wholesome and Ananias, those fanatical Puritan elders, have been replaced by more glib but no less dubious personalities like Oral Roberts and Billy Graham; the gigantic hedonism of Sir Epicure Mammon is now being realized by the kick-seeking Hollywood and Bohemian aristocracy; and open-mouthed suckers—like Jonson's gullible Dapper—are still looking for shortcuts to fortune with the horses or the numbers. Kastril, the angry boy who lives to quarrel, is personified today by those who try to prove their manhood through persistent violent encounters, and Abel Drugger, who wants his tobacco shop blessed with magical charms, is no more absurd than those who put religious icons in their automobiles. As for Jonson's amiable con artists, Subtle and Face, they have become as indigenous to American life as Mom and apple pie—indeed, Melville took the confidence man to be an archetypal national figure. Perhaps the ideal actors in these roles would have been W. C. Fields and Groucho Marx, perhaps the ideal epigraph of the play a common Americanism: never give a sucker an even break.

Then, Jonson's manipulation of his complex action is absolutely masterly: Coleridge was correct to call this one of the three most perfect plays in literature. The author keeps at least six distinct plots bustling simultaneously, not to mention countless secondary plots, and enormous energy is unleashed through this method—none of the strands allowed to touch until the conclusion, when they are rolled into a tight ball with the appearance of Face's master, Lovewit, returning to London.

Why then does the Repertory Theatre production seem so dull? The company is considerably more accomplished than previous casts at Lincoln Center, James Hart Stearn's setting captures the atmosphere of the Jacobean theatre without sacrificing the spaciousness or ingenuity of the modern one, and George Rochberg's brassy score has a fine dissonant, and occasionally electronic, raucousness. But the evening suffers from much too much production, as if the budget for the show were a large one and every penny had to be spent. Points which should be made through character are made through the use of expensive props; a huge steam-producing machine, with a female figurehead, is pumped for laughs whenever the action flags; the costumes, though handsome, do not look as if they had ever been worn by human beings; and none of the actors manages to make a vivid imprint on his part.

The failure of the actors to rise above the production is the most disappointing aspect of the evening, for most of these performers have been extremely impressive in previous roles. Perhaps they are hamstrung by the casting —I certainly found it strange. Epicure Mammon, for example, possibly the most extravagant and voluptuous figure in dramatic literature, is reduced, by George Voskovec, to a mincing courtier with nervous mannerisms and minor appetites. Mammon's desires are so immense that even his speech is a form of gorging: note how, in his description of the banquets and orgies he intends to give after achieving the philosopher's stone, the sibilant consonants make him sound as if he were slobbering over his words:

I myself will have
The beards of barbels served, instead of sallads:
Oil'd mushrooms; and the swelling unctuous paps
Of a fat pregnant sow, newly cut off,
Drest with an exquisite, and poignant sauce . . .

Mammon is a Marlovian figure who wishes not to conquer the world but to swallow it; Voskovec turns him into a hungry Middle European who would be perfectly satisfied with a few scraps in a restaurant not even endorsed by Michelin.

The actors playing Subtle and Face also seem to be miscast, since each would have been more effective in the other's role. Michael O'Sullivan—a galvanic actor with Beatle bangs and a marvelous dental smirk—is too light for the weighty Subtle, while Robert Symonds—a heavy presence with the sonorous chuckle of Frank Morgan—is too earthbound for the quicksilver Captain Face. Both Symonds and O'Sullivan are extremely inventive performers who are perfectly capable of managing the numerous impersonations called for by the text (*The Alchemist* is based on the varying of shapes), but since it is makeup and costume that is forced to do the job, one goes away remembering not so much alterations in character as changes in wigs, cloaks, and beards. Philip Bosco, an actor who looks like Redgrave and sounds like Gielgud, is solid and authoritative as Lovewit, and Nancy Marchand, as Dol Common, maintains a solid, vulgar, brawling quality which suggests more than anything the low-life character of the play. But the actors as a whole simply cannot hold one's attention for more than moments at a time, or wake one from a state of semi-somnambulism.

The production, finally, is without risk, and without the fine ensemble work that might divert attention from the lack of risk. Oh, there is one playful textual innovation—Tribulation Wholesome is played by a woman.

Aline MacMahon, who plays the part, is a charming, warmhearted actress, but charm and warmth are hardly appropriate qualities for this smooth, unctuous hypocrite, and considering what the Puritans thought about the "monstruous regement of woman," it is not very likely that a female preacher would have been accepted into the ranks of the Anabaptists. Ultimately, then, the production is the result neither of good antiquarian research nor of a new vision, and that may be why, for all its intermittent moments of vitality, it gives the impression of having entombed the play.

1966

Saturn Eats His Children

Repertory Theatre of Lincoln Center

I know nothing of the circumstances surrounding Herbert Blau's resignation from the Lincoln Center Repertory Company, but it is a melancholy decision for which we all bear some measure of responsibility. Blau's tenure with the company was far from distinguished; it is hard to think of a single play produced by him at the Vivian Beaumont that stimulated any real excitement, expectation, or sense of adventure. But given the quality of the man himself and of his past work, we must surely look to other causes than artistic inadequacy for some clue to his failure.

One fact is clear: something vital was drained from the Actors Workshop company after their movement east.

In San Francisco, these actors constituted a healthy, organic unit, proudly indifferent to audience pressures, developing each play for the sake of the next, so that a production of *Waiting for Godot,* for example, might be preparation for a new approach to *King Lear.* In New York, these same actors grew heavy limbed and leaden hearted, while the productions looked like a sequence of disconnected blunders, each being mounted as if everything depended on the individual success. Such a radical change can be largely attributed, I think, to the new conditions in which this young company was operating. The existence of a Lincoln Center Repertory Company implies the existence of an established American theatre, and this in turn suggests the existence of a rapprochement between two distinct kinds of theatregoers: those who wish to see a play and those who wish to be seen at one. Since this rapprochement is far from achieved (indeed may never be achieved), Blau and Irving were given the impossible task of unifying the disparate members of their audience during the very first season, and in trying to satisfy everybody, they succeeded in satisfying no one. The audiences began clamoring for hits. The critics—including myself—became impatient for results. And all the pressures usually surrounding commercial New York presentations were brought to bear on a situation that required relaxation, patience, and an opportunity for growth.

Even the physical theatre proved an obstacle to development. There is something seriously wrong with the spatial relationships at the Vivian Beaumont: a heavy curtain of air seems to divide the audience off from the actors. In order to penetrate this curtain, directors feel compelled to fill the stage with bustle and movement, designers are tempted to overproduce, and actors tend to stress their points more emphatically than necessary. John Hirsch's production of *Yerma,* which utilized the forefront of the stage, partly managed to overcome the sense of distance between the audience and the play, but most of the other productions made excessive use of machinery and concentrated primarily on external effects, with the result that the company—once noted for firmness of intelligence and simplicity of design—now seemed to be hiding artistic failings behind technology.

For a number of reasons, the eastward move of Blau and Irving was premature. Had they waited one more year, they might have functioned admirably in the recently opened Forum Theatre at Lincoln Center, since its smaller, more simplified stage would have freed them from existing economic and cultural handicaps, and released their bottled creative energies. Through the exercise of hindsight, one can now say that the Actors Workshop would never have been comfortable in the Vivian Beaumont Theatre—neither the company nor the audience really had anything to communicate to each other. There is not much to be hoped for from spectators who complain, as one did on television after the opening night of *Danton's Death,* "Everyone looked so beautiful and the gowns were so splendid—why do they want to depress us like that on the stage?" Given Blau's intelligence, it is hard to understand what kind of dialogue he expected to start with such theatregoers; it took a little arrogance to assume that an audience conditioned by *Hello Dolly* and *Barefoot in the Park* could be won over to the plays of Buechner, Sartre, and Wycherly, even if offered in good productions. But if Blau was guilty of hubris, he has certainly paid for it twice over through the dissolution of a creative partnership that had lasted more than ten years.

Thus, an institution presumably dedicated to fostering the theatre succeeded only in destroying one of the few genuine theatres in America, and this brings us to our moral: it is high time we stopped building culture centers before we have built a culture. Lincoln Center is now for all intents and purposes empty—and probably destined, for all intents and purposes, to remain empty, no matter what now tries to fill it. I have a vision of this building, along with all the other culture centers being built in the country, constituting a Stonehenge of the future, visited only by scholars engaged in vain speculation on what their function could possibly have been. For our theatre will not spring to life, fully grown, in the middle of a building. If it is to be reborn, it must begin like an infant, taking its first tentative steps before a very few interested observers; and only the shape of its growth will determine the shape of the building that grows around it. The American habit of creating architecture and then looking around for something to fill it signifies that our cultural explosion is still largely a manifestation of real estate. But until our love of art is at least equal to our passion for bricks and mortar, centers like Lincoln Center will continue, like Saturn, to chew up its children.

1967

III

observa-
tions

The Madison Avenue Villain

Throughout the history of American dissent—in order that the complex problems of a large and multivarious society may be more simply apprehended—political, social, and economic conflicts have been given the shape of an allegory, usually inaugurated on a stage of national grievance by a malevolent Mr. Badman from the East. In the past, dissident groups like the Jacksonians, Silverites, Populists, and Marxists generally identified this allegorical Vice as the grasping Wall Street financier who coldly victimized a wide-eyed American Everyman; but recent critics, while preserving the same hero, have changed the nature of the allegory by substituting a new villain. Today, Mr. Badman has softer features, a more subtle profession, and more centrally located New York headquarters: the Wall Street villain has yielded the stage to the villain from Madison Avenue. The old allegory, despite its simplistic character structure and hysterical climaxes, was a crude but viable dramatization of the economic motivation behind American social evils; the new one, though more sophisticated in approach, merely muddies the issues, weakens the power of dissent, and deflects attention from the true source of current abuses. Beginning with a comparison of the two allegorical villains, I intend to analyze the origins of the new allegory in order to show how it fosters and encourages serious evasions among certain groups of American spokesmen.

The Wall Street villain is today totally obsolete, surviving as an ominous *persona* only in the Communist press, but he was once a crucial figure in American plays, novels, movies, manifestoes, and newspapers of radical persuasion. There he was almost invariably characterized as a monster of greed and avarice, for, while originally inspired by such magnates as Morgan, Carnegie, and Rockefeller, he soon became less a portrait of a living person than a Marxist-Socialist symbol of capitalist abuse. Everyone over thirty can remember that porcine Banker, Oil Magnate, or War Profiteer who used to hover hungrily over exploited millions in his top hat and cutaway coat, his fat lips curled around a long black cigar, his chubby fingers groping money bags, his cruel eyes reflecting dollar signs. This was the Robber Baron of popular cartoons, the personification of the sweat shop, the trust, and the shady deal—self-made, vulgar, domineering, his empire constructed atop the prostrate bodies of the poor.

The Wall Street villain quietly expired as a national scapegoat some time during World War II, leaving the Madison Avenue villain as his only heir. But while the latter is now accused of practices just as shadowy as the Robber Baron's, he is a figure of much greater depth and complexity, and comes equipped with a personal life of substantial pathos. The reasons for this can be found in his origins: the Madison Avenue villain was first created not by angry radicals to symbolize economic abuse but by unimpassioned social scientists as an image of social-psychological behavior. Thus, the Madison Avenue villain is an evolutionary figure (still in the process of evolving) who starts out quite harmlessly as an object of sociological study, and who retains many of these earlier characteristics to the present day. In this guise, he is clearly no match for his fearful predecessor. His individual powers, for example, are not very strong, for he is less a business executive than an account executive, less a self-made man than a man without a self. Rather than being marked by physical blemishes, he is natty to the point of narcissism—sleek and feline in his Ivy League suit, Brooks Brothers shirt, and Oppenheimer haircut. And as for his education, instead of being unread, he might almost be called an intellectual *manqué*—the college-bred son of wealthy parents who begins his career, perhaps, with ambitions toward the *Kenyon Review* before settling down in the "creative department" of Kenyon and Eckhardt.

Seen through the neutralizing haze of the social sciences, in other words, he may not be an attractive figure, but he is hardly a threatening ogre like his Wall Street counterpart. Rather, he seems the confused victim of the complexities of modern life, and it is in this role that he first comes to public attention in dozens of best-selling works of popular and high sociology. Through these, it has been revealed how intensely he depends on the opinions of others, how desperately he seeks security and a sense of belonging, how anxiously he desires a "home" with his firm. Mountains of statistics record the incidence of his weekly sexual activity, the average price of his ranch house, the mean number of his TV sets, automobiles, and freezers, the rate of delinquency in his child-centered suburb, and the extent of his debts when his salary is $40,000 a year. Tons of descriptive material identify him as a Status Seeker, an Organization Man, an Exurbanite, an Expense Account Aristocrat, a Waist-high Culturist, a citizen in The Genial Society, and a member of The Lonely Crowd, for he has been so carefully analyzed that there is hardly a private corner of his life left to be examined.

This detached exploration of his anxious personality, however, is now being accompanied by a scorching critique of his professional activities, where he is held accountable not as a social victim but as a cultural victimizer. In the press, in the pulpit, in publishing, and on political platforms, the Madison Avenue villain is frequently identified, at least in his *function*, as the Machiavelli of modern life. Since his Machiavellian activities have been so well rehearsed over the past few years, they require little elaboration here. I shall only suggest the bare outlines of the mystique which the mere phrase "Madison Avenue" is now sufficient to invoke: the manipulation of consumer and voter opinion by commercial repetition; the false, misleading, and fatuous quality of modern advertising; the invidious control by the ad and talent agencies over the mass media; the vacuity and violence pervasive in TV; the slavish deference of networks and advertisers to rating reports; and the general defeat of truth and spontaneity by blandness and uniformity. Every day, in fact, a new charge is added to a burgeoning list of indictments—the latest by Newton Minow, chairman of the FCC, who stigmatizes the networks and the agencies for their baleful influence on the Young. In short, the various institutions lining Madison Avenue have finally become the targets for frustrations and resentments which, in other forms, were once aimed at Wall Street. Or, put into the language of allegory: the Madison Avenue villain today holds the American Everyman as tightly in his sweaty palm as the Wall Street villain once held him in his powerful fist, only now the methods of control are considered even more crafty, cunning, and subliminal.

There is one significant alteration in the substance of the new allegory: it now has hardly any politico-economic resonance at all. The Wall Street villain—whose critics were attacking the nature of free enterprise itself—was considered the incarnation of a flawed system which permitted men to exploit America's resources for their own profit. The Madison Avenue villain, on the other hand, embodies no reflections on the system; his chicanery is thought to be mainly psychological and cultural, consisting in the manipulation or corruption of men's minds for sinister, and often unnamed, motives. The switch from the politico-economic to the cultural-psychological emphasis is partially dictated by the nature of the new problem. It is not the evils of unequal wealth but rather the evils of the mass media which are now thought to be among our most serious domestic afflictions. Despite the special nature of this new evil, however, it would seem perfectly logical to suspect an economic basis for it, especially when the media representatives refer so frequently to the demands of their sponsors. Yet, most critics have been reluctant to concede such motives, preferring—like Newton Minow*—to assign the blame for media deterioration to cynical broadcasters who persistently undervalue the level of public taste. In short, public disapprobation lights on the person of the Madison Avenue villain; and thus, instead of urging political reform, critics of the media recommend palliatives for the "improvement" of the mass arts—apparently satisfied that if the Madison Avenue villain would only mend his ways, the major abuses of the media would somehow magically disappear. It is more likely that the media would collapse altogether, since they are based on these abuses. But before elaborating this point, let me demonstrate why I find the new allegory so inadequate as an explanation of the sources of these problems and so useless as a path to a solution.

First of all, it should be obvious that the Madison Avenue villain, whatever his importance to the prosperity of our economy, is simply not equal to his assigned role. One has only to glance at the work he actually performs to see that his allegorical significance has been over-inflated. Prototypically, of course, the Madison Avenue villain is an adman—but he also works in a variety of positions created by advertising and the media over the past twenty years. To mention but a few of these, he can be an editor or publisher of mass-circulation books and magazines, a book-club organizer, a network executive, a producer or packager of TV shows, a network continuity

---

* "I do not accept the idea that the present over-all programming is aimed accurately at the public taste. . . . A rating, at best, is an indication of how many people saw what you gave them." Speech before the National Association of Broadcasters, May 9, 1961.

man, a quiz contestant, a casting director, a story editor, a script editor, a market researcher, a motivation expert, a public relations man, an agency representative, and a press or actor's agent. None of these jobs is essential to anyone's health, balance, or sense of fulfillment. But if the Wall Street villain was always an exploiter, the worst thing to be said about the Madison Avenue villain is that he is unnecessary, for he markets something that he has not made and that people do not need. The greedy financier could be stigmatized for his accumulation of wealth in a time of poverty and want, but the man in the gray flannel suit is only a superfluous man in a culture of abundance—a *mittelmensch* in his function, taste, and class.

It is this mediocre quality that makes it so inappropriate to identify him with a radical evil—he almost always works in a subordinate capacity. The Wall Street villain was the undisputed boss of a large business empire, solely responsible for decisions which he alone could make. But the Madison Avenue villain, no matter how exalted his title, is only a salesman—which probably accounts for his anxious and overaffable manner. One may wonder how such a cipher came to be the personification of Madison Avenue treachery; yet, there is really nobody else to blame. The Madison Avenue organization seems to have no boss—no Ford or Gould or Vanderbilt to invest the firm with a strong human identity. Run by hordes of faceless, trembling vice-presidents, the typical agency or network has the quality of an anonymous oligarchy. Policies seem to develop almost organically, rather than being initiated by individuals, and in place of decisions, changes are made through "expressions of feeling." This notorious lack of individual responsibility in policy making* can no doubt be explained by the com-

* Demonstrated by the agility with which Madison Avenue can pass the buck. After Minow's "wasteland" speech, for example, the ad agencies expressed, in private, their resentment that the FCC chairman

plicated corporate structure of modern organizations, but
it is more likely explained by the fact that the Madison
Avenue organization has no real autonomy. For if the
Madison Avenue villain is only an agent or a salesman,
in this he typifies his entire firm. Both the communications and advertising industries are basically sales organizations—clients' middlemen whose major function is
to market goods in the most profitable manner possible.
To criticize the techniques of Madison Avenue is, therefore, only to badger the salesman for policies approved by
the company and necessary to its survival. Yet, even
some of the most severe indictments of the mass media
stop short of this simple perception, choosing to probe a
rotten branch of the tree without examining its cankered
roots. To account for the obtuseness of these critics, one
must understand the conditions under which the new
allegory found its form.

The demise of the Wall Street villain is easy enough to
understand. It is difficult to work up much indignation
against a symbol of corpulent and inequitable wealth
when multitudes of obese Americans now spend their
leisure clipping coupons. Prosperity, full employment,
and social insurance had eradicated conspicuous poverty;
the old tycoons and their sons had softened their unpleasant image by becoming statesmen and foundation
philanthropists; the autocracy of family empire had been
replaced by the pseudo-democracy of big profit-sharing
corporations, making every stockholder a self-interested
defender of capitalism; and trade unionism had triumphed, developing its own forms of gangsterism and
exploitation.

The founders of the old allegory, the radical intellectuals, had changed also. By the time the Cold War and

---

was meddling in areas that concerned only the advertisers, their
agencies, and the networks. But in public, they praised the speech for
"touching all the bases" and being "right on target"—and promptly
blamed everything on the networks.

Stalinist Russia fixed the nation's attention on an enemy beyond its walls rather than its own domestic problems, the most influential dissenters had already abandoned Marxism. Socialism was losing most of its frustrated supporters. And when McCarthyism made any criticism of the American system a trifle dangerous, all organized radical activity appeared abruptly to cease. Anxious to dissociate themselves from a discredited or ineffectual political position, many of these old radicals turned rigid and defensive—"frozen," according to William Barrett, "into some publicly correct attitude of anti-communism whose political content was allowed to degenerate into variations on the chant that communism was bad." Thus, the energies of ex-radicals were now poured into defending the system, rather than changing it; and, in the fifties, the eagerness of some to find a substitute affirmation even resulted in an enthusiastic embrace of "Our Country and Our Culture" (as a prophetic *Partisan Review* symposium was called), which consisted of repudiating the old attitudes of dissent in favor of a more positive attitude toward American middle-class values.

In line with this, many intellectuals became interested in American popular culture, initiating cautious investigations into the significance of movies, TV, comic strips, Broadway, Tin Pan Alley, and the mass magazines. Except for a small group which attacked these expressions for their malign effect on the brains and nerves of the American people, observers were generally quite sanguine in their conclusions, and some even professed to find optimistic signs of intelligence and maturity in the mass media (the jukebox, for example, was hailed by one as an important twentieth-century innovation). But even when it ignored popular culture, intellectual activity seemed heavily influenced by the methods of the social sciences. Investigation became cool, objective, statistical. Analyses were qualified, moderate, and restrained. Conclusions were brimming with complications. The "end of ideology" was rather prematurely celebrated. Freudian and neo-Freudian insights became the vogue, and Riesman and Kinsey replaced Marx and Trotsky as the most influential writers of the period.

In short, where the tone of intellectuals was once primarily political and indignant, it soon became sociological, psychological, and complacent; where critics were once concerned over economic self-interest, they soon became involved with mass communications; where attention once focused on the Robber Baron and social injustice, it soon centered on the Organization Man and social behavior. As a result, the intellectuals, once alienated from society, were now being absorbed into it, a process of assimilation said to reflect their new sense of purpose, responsibility, and maturity. And American society, grateful for relief from these gadflies, was quick to provide its rewards: the media began to beckon invitingly; the mass magazines became more hospitable to highbrow writers; psychologists, sociologists, and economists by the hundreds left the university to take up lucrative "advisory" positions with industry and research organizations; and the Democratic Party even ran an egghead candidate twice. In this benevolent climate, liberal consensus completely triumphed over radical nonconformity, and the old allegory went up in smoke. The epitaph of the fifties might have been the First Player's smug reply to Hamlet: "We have reformed that indifferently with us."

It was during these transitional years that the personality of the Madison Avenue villain was most rigorously explored, the bland personification of a period of cultural narcissism during which America stopped to examine its image in a statistical looking glass. This period of cultural normalcy—so similar to the years presided over by President Harding—lasted through the doldrums of the Eisenhower administration, but even toward the end of that dreary interregnum one could sense that normalcy was coming to an end. A series of scandalous exposures, chief among them the TV scandals, began to usher out the era with a chorus of raspberries. As a result of these scandals, a limited form of muckraking came back into fashion, focusing attention mainly on the villainies of Madison Avenue. The nation's uneasiness over Madison Avenue techniques had already been exposed after the subliminal advertising scare. Now it was exacerbated by revelations that the mass media were rigged: quiz shows were fixed, commercials were fraudulent, TV incomes were supplemented by gifts, plugs, and bribes, and the FCC—designed to regulate the industry—was itself hamstrung by corrupt officials and the political power of the networks. The Teapot Dome affair had called attention to illegal business practices; the media revelations, though unimportant in themselves, fixed our eyes on the corruption of our communications.

But although these scandals suggested that the pickings in communications were just as big as those in oil, munitions, or government contracts, they provoked little criticism of the profit system which had caused them—partly because the voice of radicalism had been muted, partly because many critics were now involved in this system themselves and feared endangering their interests, but mainly because the corruption in the media was never traced to its source. Congressional committees are notoriously reluctant to push their investigations too far, but the Senate unit investigating the quiz scandals was even more reticent than usual. After throwing Charles Van Doren and a few TV producers to a public hungry for scapegoats, it closed up its investigations as quickly as a surgeon sews up the body of a patient when his exploratory reveals cancer in the entire system—and turned to more harmless matters like disc-jockey payola. As a result of the little that was revealed, only the contestants suffered any real damage (they are still being mercilessly hounded in the courts), though the networks and agencies, despite their readiness to betray their employees,* could not escape without tarnished reputations. As for the sponsors—who had profited the most and who undoubtedly controlled the fix—they remained completely unscathed. Left to stew over perjured TV idols and dishonest organization men, the public satisfied itself with blaming the whole affair on "Madison Avenue"—whose policies, nevertheless, remained substantially unchanged.

The case against the Madison Avenue villain was further strengthened by other developments: former admen began to produce best-selling *mea culpas,* promising sensational disclosures about waste making and hidden persuasion; the Ford Foundation issued a report publicizing the stringent censorial powers exercised by the agencies over writers for the media; and educators, TV reviewers, editorialists, and politicians discovered in Madison Avenue a convenient lapel on which to pin juvenile delinquency, public immorality, manipulated elections, mass conformity, national illiteracy, planned obsolescence, and the unfortunate image Americans enjoy abroad. Most of these charges contained germs of truth as far as they went, but not one of them took into account the vassalage of Madison Avenue to the American business economy. It was now bad taste to mention the profit motive. Instead of demanding to know how our communications had fallen into the hands of business, critics were content to dramatize a gratuitous conspiracy perpetrated against the public by dark-intentioned hucksters.

This situation of a year ago remains unchanged today —if anything, it has been intensified by the election of the Kennedy administration with its promise (until the

* It is now a fixed practice to let the organization men take the rap for the actions of the company (cf. the recent electrical equipment scandals). When the heat is off, however, the employees generally return to the company, quite often in their old positions. Many of the quiz show producers, for example, are now back in television—some of them again producing quiz shows.

air leaked out of the tire) of a Galbraithian neo-radical-ism. The Madison Avenue allegory now has strong support in official government circles, mostly among consensus liberals with middlebrow tastes, but it is precisely there, against the background of political power, that its inadequacy as an explanation of our cultural deterioration is most depressingly revealed. For if the responsibility for the condition of the media rests only on the agencies, the producers, and the broadcasters, why have they not reformed in the face of mounting criticism of their actions? If the manipulators of TV are merely lazy or stupid or cynical men who misjudge public taste, why do they always fail to obtain sponsors and audiences for works of art, educational programs, and public-affairs offerings? Why has Mr. Minow been unable to achieve even minor changes in the structure of the FCC? And why have congressmen of both parties refused to support his reforms? The answers to these questions suggest that the problems of the media have not been sufficiently analyzed, and the pressure groups blocking a solution are a much more formidable lobby than an anxious coterie of Madison Avenue organization men.

One suspects that the entire free enterprise system is lobbying against reform. For not only are the abuses of the media absolutely essential to their survival as commercial enterprises, but the survival of the economy is, in turn, largely contingent on the media. Whatever their avowed function, TV, radio, movies, mass magazines, most publishing, and a majority of newspapers are now primarily dedicated to the marketing of unnecessary goods (either their own or their sponsors'), and without these mass markets the present system would probably flop. Thus, the question posed by Newton Minow to the National Association of Broadcasters—"Is there a person in this room who claims that broadcasting can't do better?"—has an air of crashing irrelevancy. Since the main purpose of the media is to sell the largest number of goods to the largest number of people, the standardization or debasement of the product, whatever the personal attitudes of the producers, is the almost mechanically logical outcome.

For, despite the pained protestation of liberal critics, the present condition of the media is one of the inevitabilities of popular democracy when the will of the compact majority invades the field of culture. One would like to have faith in the instinctual good taste of the masses, but there is absolutely no evidence to confute the findings of media experts like Leo Rosten of *Look,* who writes: "When the public is free to choose among various products, it chooses—again and again and again—the frivolous as against the serious, 'escape' as against reality, the lurid as against the tragic, the trivial as against the serious, fiction as against fact, the diverting as against the significant."* Correlate this with the following statement by Frank Stanton of CBS and you will see why liberal analyses of these problems in terms of Madison Avenue villains are so fearfully inadequate: "A mass medium survives when it maintains a satisfactory batting average on affirmative responses, and it goes down when negative responses are too numerous or too frequent." Taken together, these two propositions coalesce to form an indisputable logic—the logic of profit—which will never be contravened as long as the media must pay their way through mass appeal. For the logic of profit compels the media to manufacture trash, treacle, and triviality as mechanically as the assembly line manufactures cheap and shoddy goods, the difference being that in the media there is no room for a luxury market. Under these condi-

* In short, Westerns and gangster programs have not been forced on the people—they have been demanded by them. The reasons for these demands are too complicated to pursue here. Suffice it to say, mass culture is the inevitable result of mass industrial society, and inevitably accompanies it. I suspect that when the networks develop methods by which to measure public taste more accurately, the programs will get even worse.

tions, an honest reply by Madison Avenue to Mr. Minow's question might sound very much like the plaint of Brechtian man: *Wir waren gut—anstatt so roh/ Doch die Verhaltnisse, sie sind nicht so* ("We would be good— not coarse and crude/ But rigid circumstance won't have it so").

To speak, then, of improving mass culture without developing a much more radical vision of what is wrong with it is to lose sight of the most obvious economic realities. The media will never reform because they survive by selling to the agencies; the agencies will never reform because they survive by selling to the masses; and the masses will never reform because they are always being brutalized by the media—a vicious circle which promises only to revolve more ferociously in the future. As for pay TV, which some envision as an alternative solution, this plan will merely eliminate the Madison Avenue villain without eliminating the need for a mass market. There will probably be no reform at all without some action of an extreme kind to recover the media from those who control them for profit, but this would mean a radical revision of the whole economic system.* Since it is doubtful if our liberal critics are willing to contemplate such action, we are left with a static situation in which American communications, which should be the instrument of free expression, remain the instrument of "free" enterprise, resisting all efforts at change. The inevitable inference is this: while we all were happily harmonizing with American life, the system was tightening its grip. For the Wall Street villain has not disap-

* Even this might not prove enough. The only alternative to commercial sponsorship of the media is government sponsorship, but under our present system this would simply mean handing the media over to politicians who, having their own products to sell, would be just as subject to mass demand. A truly representative democracy might develop levels of programing along the lines of the British system. But this involves distinctions of cultural classes which American egalitarianism would never countenance.

peared. He has merely had his face lifted. And if that face is now unseen, it is because he hides behind the anxious figure of the villain from Madison Avenue.

It is, in short, not a group of cynical broadcasters but the economic system itself which accounts for the abuses of the media, the greatest of which is, indeed, reminiscent of the old perfidy of Wall Street: regulated by business interests, the media have turned into near monopolies, holding dire consequences for the future of free speech. For just as the means of production were once controlled by a few special-interest groups, so this control is presently exercised over the means of communication. The communications monopoly, of course, is not a prosecutable fact, since the media are actually divided among a number of competing corporations. But since the motive of each is maximum profits, the end result is the same as if all the media were in the hands of a cartel. Here we touch upon the worst evil of the system—not simply its effect on the mass mind but its threat to the function of the intelligentsia, for the victim of this is anyone with something to communicate. As Paul Goodman has described it: "In American society, we have perfected a remarkable form of censorship: to allow everyone his political right to say what he believes, but to swamp his little boat with literally thousands of millions of newspapers, mass-circulation magazines, best-selling books, broadcasts, and public pronouncements that disregard what he says and give the official way of looking at things." This species of censorship embodies a new and subtle menace which is extremely difficult to combat— instead of the suppression of ideas, rigid control over the free dissemination of ideas. At present, there is no way for unofficial or unpopular expressions to reach a substantial public without first being processed by the media.* A wall is descending in front of the intelligentsia,

* This is another problem peculiar to mass society. In a tiny country like Ireland, where an unpublished student paper by Joyce was within

as thick and impenetrable as a wall of steel, which soon may ghettoize all thought that cannot promise quick profits. In Soviet Russia, this impediment was built under government supervision. In democratic America, it is being fumblingly constructed not through conspiracy but through financial expediency. Despite its recurrent affirmations about freedom of speech, our system is inexorably reducing the avenues of choice until the future could be little more than an endless, unwinding road of uniformity and carefully engineered consent.

What, then, is the true nature of the Madison Avenue villain? We must conclude that he is no villain at all. He is an agent of this system, not its founder, and though he profits by the present system, he cannot be held ultimately responsible for it. If we condemn him, then his ranks must be expanded to include not just the adman and the broadcaster but anyone who accommodates for the sake of a platform, anyone who compromises his basic convictions for the sake of media status. If we regard him as the hired middleman between the profiteer and the masses, then he is all the bought intellects of our society, and all the salesmen, even those marketing art, culture, and thought. He is, in fact, most of us at some time in our lives, some of us at all times; as we proceed to lose our natural antipathy to this kind of collaboration through frustration, ambition, or financial want, he multiplies among us every day. In substantiation, I should like to conclude by distinguishing two broad types of intellectual middlemen in order to show how the Wall Street villain is presently threatening to implicate us all.

The first type is, paradoxically, often one of the most vigorous critics of Madison Avenue, apparently unaware

---

a week being discussed all over Dublin, oral communication is still effective. In a country the size of America, the loudest and most barbaric yawp remains unheard unless it is of interest to public relations groups.

that he is himself an Intellectual in a Gray Flannel Suit. By taste or design, he is invariably a middlebrow, described by Hannah Arendt as "often well read and well informed, whose sole function is to change cultural objects to make them palatable to those who want to be entertained—and this is worse—to be 'educated,' that is, to acquire as cheaply as possible some kind of cultural knowledge to improve their social status." This intellectual is quite often a network hack. But, quite often, he is a well-known personality, hired by the media to lend some authority to their vulgarization of high culture: a college president, a university lecturer, a symphony conductor, a novelist, a poet, a psychologist, a theologian, a TV journalist, a cultural critic. His activities are many and varied, but whether he moderates panel discussions, teaches TV cram courses, dispenses superficial psychological advice, popularizes Shakespeare, bowdlerizes dramatic and literary classics, simplifies the problems of music, or formulates quiz questions, his function remains the same: to convert the objects of the intellect into commodities which can be sold across the counter like a bar of soap.

The justification with which this artist or intellectual tries to distinguish his media activities from those of a commercial salesman is familiar to us all—it has to do with "raising the level of popular taste." This oft-repeated formula stubbornly maintains its popularity, despite the obvious and continuing decline in popular taste, precisely because it permits the middlebrow to flourish in a commodity system while still proclaiming his belief in liberalism and progress.* Ibsen demonstrated long ago that there is no restriction on the human capacity for self-

* This rationalization was unintentionally parodied by the quiz show producers who affirmed, in testimony, that they were developing a new respect for the intellect, and by the producers of TV Westerns who contended that their programs gave Americans an educational glimpse into their historic past. Parodied or not, the name for this is middle-class hypocrisy.

delusion when fame, money, and power are at stake; and these pseudo-altruistic affirmations cannot disguise the fact that, like the Madison Avenue villain, the media intellectual is, in actuality, the volunteer of a system where there is no room for high standards. As such, he is to be pitied, for he has achieved his popularity by suppressing his true identity. One thinks of Mitchell Miller, once a gifted oboist with a promising future as an interpreter of Cimarosa and Vaughan Williams, who now—replete with an arty beard, a grotesque smile, and a fatuous media personality—cavorts in front of the home screen enjoining the spectator to "Sing Along with Mitch"; or of Groucho Marx, blunting his barbs on a quiz show (his brother Harpo is selling motor oil on TV); or of Alistair Cooke and William Saroyan, on *Omnibus*, patronizing the avant-garde drama; or of David Susskind passionately gesticulating against Madison Avenue before unctuously introducing a commercial. These men help to dignify the media's debauching of culture, but only through a corresponding loss in their own dignity, exchanging their talent or humanity for a well-tailored gray flannel suit.

The second group of intellectual middlemen includes many highbrows, for some of our most distinguished intellectuals are now purchasing gray flannel cloth for their wardrobes which they wear during occasional excursions into the world of Madison Avenue. Some of these junkets are admittedly made for extra funds; some to advance reputations in the nonintellectual world; others are justified as an attempt to reach that great untapped soul of America which has hitherto been inaccessible to genuine art or real ideas. But whatever the motive, hundreds now work as part-time or full-time commercial salesmen, promoting book clubs, sponsoring record clubs, endorsing syntopicons, writing for movies and TV, advising industry and the media, guesting on panel and interview shows, and writing popular articles for mass magazines. Most of them, of course, continue to pursue their legitimate work at the same time, so these activities are not of great significance when contrasted with their other contributions. Nevertheless, one feels that some unspoken covenant has been broken, which helps to shake our resistance to whatever is pernicious in the culture.

The recent increase in these activities can probably be explained by the intellectual's recent rapprochement with the American middle class, and possibly even by his repudiation of the political in favor of the social-scientific discipline. For, like the sociologist hero of George P. Elliott's *Parktilden Village,* who begins by studying the "social significance" of comic strips and ends by producing a successful strip himself, one can be tripped by purely analytical and descriptive procedures into abandoning one's ethical values (when you begin to ask "What is it?" instead of "Is it good?" you are already on the way to joining "it"). At any rate, many intellectuals now openly flout their association with business enterprises, adding—when they admit to selling their reputations—that nothing could be better sold to America than the intellectual life. But the logic of profit always proves stronger than the best of motives, and the ends of intellect are almost never served. The book clubs, if originated for discriminating readers, soon run out of quality books, or, forced to seek a wider membership, soon lower their standards, with the result that the critic starts writing inflated blurbs for second-rate literature. The record clubs usually offer inferior recordings which are not moving fast enough in the stores. The movies and TV scripts, if at all out of the ordinary in draft, are quickly rewritten to formula. The mass-magazine articles are either pure hackwork or an embarrassment to the writer, or suffer from the glossy vulgarity of the surrounding material. As for the panel and interview shows, harmless enough in themselves, they are always dominated by such soupy-minded moderators or long-winded guest "personalities" that the isolated highbrow must join the discussion on the lowest possible level. I do not wish to sound prissy or self-righteous about these activities; the needs of intellectuals are no different from those of someone else. On the other hand, we should be conscious of what we are exchanging for these tantalizing rewards. In accepting them, we all become Madison Avenue villains, inadvertently serving as front men for the media monopolists whose strategy it is to absorb what they cannot defeat, silencing critics by making them partners in the general debasement of standards for profit.

To sum up, then, the allegory of American life remains substantially the same as ever, even though its *dramatis personae* have lifted their faces to suit the demands of the time. The American Everyman is no longer an exploited farmer, laborer, or miner; he is the modern consumer, brutalized by the persuasive vapidity of the mass media. The Wall Street villain is no longer twirling his mustaches, but he is still exploiting American resources: controlling communications, degrading culture, and muffling opponents by impounding their organs of expression. If this new exploitation masquerades under the name of "entertainment," and if it is largely responsible for our present affluence, it is no less enfeebling to the health of the nation, for there are other forms of starvation besides the physical. As for the Madison Avenue villain, he is not the source of this spiritual famine, but merely its agent—in a special sense, its victim. In our commodity society, where fame, love, wealth, and power accrue to the most questionable enterprises, he has attained these rewards by thwarting and stunting his true potential. In helping to undermine culture, he has actually undermined his own spontaneity and creative life.

What can we do in the face of these conditions, which now seem so fixed and irremediable? Here one runs the risk of sounding visionary, or, what is worse, impudent and hortatory, for we are so far from solutions that even a beginning requires a tremendous effort of the moral will. As an immediate objective, one might work toward restoring the lost values of the intellectual community— honor, dignity, integrity—by returning to the traditional intellectual attitudes of alienation and dissent. If this means the isolation of thought in places where thought is still free (the academy, the little magazine, the scholarly journal, and listener-supported FM radio), then this is still more honorable, if less profitable, than that "worldliness" where the intellectual is tempted to soften or suppress what he knows for the sake of an expanded pocketbook; and, at least, we will no longer be giving our sanction to the mutilation of culture. The ultimate objective—the wresting of the organs of communication from the persuaders and the profiteers—demands more utopian solutions, for it will not be accomplished without renewed radical debate leading to the complete transformation of society. As a start, we must first readopt the negative side of the Wall Street allegory—its insights into the motives of the villain, not its sentimentalization of the hero—stripping it of totalitarian ideological components and introducing changes appropriate to our time and problems: a cultural radicalism designed to preserve a pocket of America where truth and art may still survive. I realize this defines an attitude rather than a program, but we may have reached the point where an honorable act of resistance is the best we can do. If this seems too little, consider the alternative: truth and art on the market block, everyone in a gray flannel suit.

1961

America's
New Culture Hero

In the last eight or ten years Americans have been charmed by a new culture hero, with far-reaching effects upon the quality of our spoken arts. In a persistent effort to find a voice for America, to find a language, vocabulary, and intonation peculiarly our own, we have come temporarily to settle for no voice at all. The stage, motion pictures, television, and even popular music are now exalting an inarticulate hero, who—for all the dependence of these media on language—cannot talk.

Of medium height and usually of lower-class birth, his most familiar physical characteristic is his surly and discontented expression. His eyes peer out at the world from under beetling brows; his uncombed hair falls carelessly over his forehead; his right hand rests casually on his right hip. He is extremely muscular and walks with a slouching, shuffling gait. He scratches himself often, slumps in chairs, and almost never smiles. He is also identified by the sounds which issue from his mouth. He squeezes, he grunts, he passes his hand over his eyes and forehead, he stares steadily, he turns away, he scratches, then again faces his adversary, and finally speaks. What he says is rarely important but he has mesmerized his auditor by the effort he takes to say it. He has communicated not information but feeling; he has revealed an inner life of unspecified anguish and torment.

From this description it should be clear that I am talking about a character familiar not through any particular work of art but rather through association with the many actors who impersonate it—Marlon Brando, James Dean,

Ben Gazzara, John Cassavetes, Montgomery Clift, and the countless others whose identification with sex, violence, and incoherency unites them as a school. What endears this peculiar creature to the general public? Where does he come from, what is his significance, and what has been his effect on present-day dramatic writing?

The inarticulate hero of today clearly finds his immediate origin in Tennessee Williams' Stanley Kowalski as interpreted by Marlon Brando. His tradition, however, goes further back than *A Streetcar Named Desire*. Ever since Eugene O'Neill created Yank in *The Hairy Ape* (1922), American playwrights have been trying to find dramatic expression for the man of lower birth—of Northern urban or Southern rural origin—who was denied the language and manners of his more cultured countrymen. Quite often, in spite of superior physical strength, this man was pictured as a victim. O'Neill's stoker Yank has the power to make the ship go, but once on land, in the clutch of the cold concrete city, he is overcome by pushing crowds, political complexity, and the ridicule of a highborn woman, and finally is crushed to death while trying to embrace an ape, the only animal with whom he finds intellectual communion. The sharecroppers, migrant workers, and tramps of John Steinbeck are victims too, but since his heroes are more unqualifiedly noble than Yank (for Steinbeck virtue and poverty are almost always equated) their defeat is political rather than personal and implies an indictment of society. In the early works of Clifford Odets, the political note is struck even harder. O'Neill's and Steinbeck's proletarian heroes are often characterized by their lack of verbal coherence, but Odets' heroes are singular for their extreme verbosity. Rather than being speechless in the face of their dilemma, they never stop talking about it.

The unspoken assumption of the Group Theatre, the company that produced most of the proletarian dramas of the thirties, was that sensitivity, fire, intensity, and sexual potency were primarily the properties of the underprivileged and the uneducated. Using the acting techniques of Stanislavsky in forms altered to suit American needs, the Group Theatre created a style with which to impart the supercharged mood of these plays and an acting company to impersonate the underprivileged heroes. The most representative actors in this company, John Garfield and Luther Adler, rather than being stammerers, were highly articulate; rather than being enmeshed in a world too complex for their intelligence, they were extremely precise about the forces leading them to ruin.

The Group Theatre was dissolved in the early forties, but some of its functions were taken over by the Actors Studio, organized in the late forties by former members. Unlike the Group Theatre, the Actors Studio was designed not as a production unit but primarily as a workshop where actors could perfect their craft. And yet, because of the widely publicized popular success of some of its members, the Actors Studio has managed to wield more influence on acting styles and playwriting than any other single organization, even those dedicated to the actual production of plays. It is in the Actors Studio that most of today's proletarian heroes are being spawned.

Although much (if not all) of the acting that emerges from the Actors Studio would seem to indicate that the proletarian is still considered more interesting, more electric, and capable of deeper feelings than the owner of a store or the manager of a bank, this assumption seems no longer accompanied by a political conviction. The proletarian hero of the fifties has lost his political flavor and, even more important, his power of speech. He combines the inarticulateness of the Hairy Ape with the dynamism (now adjusted from a boil to a simmer) of the Odets hero, and adds to these certain qualities which neither Odets nor O'Neill had endowed him with. Stanley Kowalski is the first character in American drama to unite most of the identifying characteristics of this hero, but it is difficult to determine how much the actor, Marlon Brando, and the director, Eliza Kazan, both Actors Studio associates at the time or soon after, contributed to his formation. All drama is a collaboration, and dramatists find their characters subtly changing coloration in the playing. Stanley Kowalski, as he became known to the general public in the original New York production and the excellent movie made from it, was probably the collaborative product of Williams, Brando, and Kazan. Stanley, as written by Williams, is a highly complex and ambiguous character, one who can be taken either as hero or as villain. As a social or cultural figure, Stanley is a villain, in mindless opposition to civilization and culture—the "new man" of the modern world whom Williams seems to find responsible for the present-day decline in art, language, decorum, and culture. As a psychological or sexual figure, however, Stanley exists on a somewhat more heroic moral plane. He is akin to those silent, sullen gamekeepers and grooms of D. H. Lawrence (an early influence on Williams) whose sexuality, though violent, is unmental, unspiritual, and, therefore, in some way free from taint. The conflict between Blanche and Stanley allegorizes the struggle between effeminate culture and masculine libido. It is no accident that Stanley, in the climax of the play, subdues Blanche by a brutal sexual assault. One assumption of the play is plain: culture and tradition are desirable, but breed effeteness and perversity (Blanche is a nymphomaniac) and make one an easy prey to the unenlightened.

It should be clear, even from this brief analysis, that with Stanley, Williams wrought significant changes in the proletarian hero. If one sympathizes with Stanley it is not because he is underprivileged or exploited or victimized—Stanley is at all times an active character, one who manipulates each situation in which he appears. Rather than expressing dissatisfaction with the grubby conditions in which he lives, he exults in them, and he does not indicate any desire to better himself. More important, Stanley, as brute force incarnate, has no poetry or sensitivity or nobility in him—neither John Garfield nor Luther Adler could ever have played this role. His intelligence is mostly animal cunning and his power of speech limited to expressing basic desires.

And yet, if Williams created an ignoble rather than a noble savage, how do we explain the spectacular success of Brando and the extensive influence his playing of Stanley has had on acting ever since? The answer, I think, lies in the personal values Brando contributed to the role. As played by Brando, Stanley Kowalski somehow emerged as a more appealing, a more sympathetic, and (most important) a more sensitive character than Williams created, and the play became a conflict between two protagonists, one less noble but no less interesting than the other. When Anthony Quinn, taking over the part, played it more like the thick-headed antagonist Williams intended, the focus of the play shifted back to Blanche. There is irony in the fact that, although *Streetcar* is Blanche's tragedy, the villain of the piece became the prototype for a hero, the inarticulate hero of popular culture. After Stanley, the brutal proletarian was rarely to be seen again. As he emerged from the Actors Studio and the pens of the writers who began creating parts for these actors, he had once again acquired a helpless attitude in a hostile world. And although he inherited Stanley Kowalski's speechlessness, his animality, and his violent behavior, these qualities were now seen as marks of profundity of character.

Thus in a period of prosperity and political conformity, the proletarian hero has managed, paradoxically, to accomplish something he failed to do in a period of depression and political radicalism—he has made the audience take notice of him. At a time when America has the largest middle-class population in the world (when, in one sense, it sees itself as entirely middle class), one of its most conspicuous dramatic heroes is poor and un-educated. Although the Broadway audience is predominantly from the cultured, leisured classes, the typical Broadway product is peopled with dock workers, drug addicts, juvenile delinquents, prostitutes, pimps, butchers, Southern farmers, seamen, machine shop workers, and drifters. By finding "reality" and "truth" (though not necessarily virtue) in the outcasts of society, playwrights have created a problem they did not have to face in the thirties: they have estranged their audience from the difficulties of their heroes. I do not wish to repeat the charges made against realism in the drama; its smallness of vision, its prosaicness, and its pedantic re-creation of the least penetrating aspects of life have become all too apparent. I do want to add, however, that when the drama centers on the proletarian and faithfully records his speech, it often becomes mindless, almost anti-intellectual. Ideas and subtle emotions are communicated primarily through speech and even the bluntest emotion loses its meaning if it is not reflected upon. How empty would be the suffering of Lear or Oedipus were it not followed by an illumination of the heart and the mind. In limiting the expression of their heroes, playwrights have limited their heroes' understanding of their suffering. The difficulties of the modern proletarian hero end on an unresolved question—Why?

That the tongue-tied emotionalism of many modern plays is partly the result of directing and acting techniques is indicated by the fact that even in relatively literate plays, inarticulateness is sometimes imposed by the production. In the recent Broadway showing of *Compulsion*, for example, the two actors called upon to play boys of superior mental capacities and wealthy backgrounds brought the same verbal hesitation to their roles they might have used in playing a couple of hoodlums. Broadway apparently has still not devised a technique

to communicate intelligence. The paradox of the estranged audience applies to acting as well; although the
Broadway audience is relatively coherent and literate,
the emphasis on our stage has fallen off the spoken word.
The actor uses language only as a secondary instrument.
His main purpose is to convey the mute feelings within
his soul. The effect is admittedly quite explosive. The
struggle within an incoherent individual trying to express
his feelings can be extremely powerful, for one often
has the sense that the character's stammers, mumbles,
and grunts will, like those of Billy Budd, erupt into violence if they continue to frustrate speech. (Much of
O'Neill's power as a playwright stems from his inability
to say precisely what he means and his tortuous way of
talking round and round a subject.) The consequence of
this style of acting, however, is that we presently have
an actor's theatre. The actor has taken precedence over
the playwright; the play has receded before the performance. One becomes more conscious of the personal problems of the actor than of the character he is playing. In
some cases, the actor's and the character's problems
become inextricably confused.

The general uninterest in the classics demonstrated
by many of today's actors and directors (a recent Equity
symposium had the title: "The Classics: Are They Avant-
Garde?") is closely related to this problem, for most of
the classics of dramatic literature depend to a large extent on words. It is significant that one of America's most
able theatre and movie directors, Elia Kazan, has directed
only contemporary works. When asked if he would
ever produce Shakespeare, he replied: "I never have and
I never will. I am interested in the life that is around
me . . ."* This is an extraordinary statement, all the more
so because so few people in the theater consider it extraordinary. Apart from the intimation that contemporary

* Seven years after these lines were written, Mr. Kazan made his
first attempt to direct a noncontemporary, non-American play with his

playwrights probe more deeply into "the life around me"
than Shakespeare (or is Kazan concerned only with environmental truth?), these words yield very interesting
considerations. Imagine the conductor of the Philhar-
monic refusing to interpret Mozart and Beethoven on
the same grounds. Considering the appalling ignorance
most actors have of the works in their field, try to imagine
even the most benighted tenor, violinist, or ballerina in
a similar state of ignorance. One would look in vain for
the same paucity of classical works on the musical, ballet,
or operatic stage as one finds on Broadway. In refusing
Ibsen, Strindberg, and Yeats a hearing, the interpreters
of the drama have usurped the prerogatives of the creative artist, one of whose permissible functions is to be in
revolt against the techniques of the past.

Mr. Kazan goes on to express his admiration for
Chekhov (the one classical writer known and cherished
by most members of the Actors Studio) and this gives
us a clue why traditional drama holds no fascination for
him. Although Chekhov was a master of language (the
language, be it remembered, of the cultured, leisured
classes), it is not always the word that communicates
his meaning. More often, the action is revealed slowly
in fragments of discourse, and seemingly commonplace
statements conceal the intense desires and anguish of
the characters. Chekhov thus offers relative liberation
to the actor and director; he offers a freedom of interpretation not granted by Shakespeare or Shaw. The in-
direct techniques of Stanislavsky become a possible
method of conveying Chekhov's fragments and impressions (although Chekhov complained most of his life
that Stanislavsky had misinterpreted his plays) because
the subtext, or the feeling behind the word, has gained
more importance than the word itself. In less impression-

Lincoln Center Repertory Theatre production of *The Changeling*. It
was a very badly fumbled effort, showing how difficult it is to reverse
the habits of a lifetime career when the decision comes too late.

istic plays than Chekhov's, however, the subtext can be a stratagem by which the actor ignores the playwright's meaning, substituting the feeling he himself finds to be more compelling. The actor becomes a creator rather than an interpreter, seeking the clue to his performance in his own experience instead of in the experience of the character he is supposed to be playing.

Granted the power of a school of acting and production techniques to impose a special kind of theatre on the Broadway audience, is this school's power operative in the movies as well? I think not. Broadway audiences are notoriously pliable and faddist, while the more intransigent mass audiences respond primarily to that which moves or speaks for them. Furthermore, although on Broadway the literate play can be roughed up by the performance, in Hollywood parts are tailored to fit personalities. What personality did the inarticulate hero assume in the movies? It is obvious that when Brando went to Hollywood he took Stanley Kowalski with him. With very little adjustment, Brando's Stanley became the paraplegic war veteran of *The Men,* the ex-prize-fighter dock worker of *On the Waterfront,* the leather-jacketed delinquent of *The Wild One,* the peasant leader of *Viva Zapata!* and even Antony in the filmed version of *Julius Caesar* (to capitalize on Brando's box-office personality, Antony was changed into a sullen, beetle-browed muscleman). Although the hero maintained, in almost every case, his identification with sexuality and violence, he could no longer be accused of cruelty or brutality.

Was it merely to the magnetism of Brando's personality that the mass audience responded, as they had responded in the past to Clark Gable, Cary Grant, and Gary Cooper? Again, I think not. Brando's personality, as he never tires of telling the press, has little in common with that of the character he plays: one of his first Broadway roles was the sensitive poet Marchbanks in *Candida* and he has lately been attempting roles of a more articulate nature. Furthermore, those actors who have imitated Brando's inarticulate style have achieved almost as much success as he.

I do not think we can escape the conclusion that Brando's spectacular film success rests to a large extent on his being one of the images (he was the original image) of the inarticulate hero. It is, in other words, to the inarticulate hero that the mass audience responds.

The most conspicuous thing about the inarticulate hero as a movie figure is that he is invariably an outcast or a rebel, isolated from friends, from parents, from teachers, from society. This is emphasized by his shabby, careless appearance; in a world of suits and ties, the leather jacket and open collar are symbols of alienation and rebellion. The main character in *On the Waterfront* is, until he is beaten up by labor hoodlums, befriended by neither police nor peers and finds consolation only in homing pigeons. Although the hero of *The Wild One* begins as the leader of a group of cyclists who terrorize a small town, he repudiates his vicious companions and is, in turn, assaulted by the furious townspeople. The young boy (James Dean) of *Rebel Without a Cause* cannot gain acceptance by his adolescent contemporaries nor can he come to terms with his family until he is attacked by a juvenile gang revenging themselves for the death of their leader. The son in *East of Eden* is a pariah, doomed like Cain (with whom he is identified) to be despised by his father and rejected by the town in which he lives. The hero of *Edge of the City*, on the run from the police and alone until befriended by a paternal Negro dock worker, gets involved in a vicious hook fight with a sadistic dockyard foreman. The schoolboy in *Careless Years*, anxious to marry before he is old enough, isolates himself from everybody's love and friendship until he is soundly whipped in a fist fight with his father. The oil worker of *Giant* lives alone in a dilapidated shack, building a fortune so that he can revenge himself on the smug and settled families of the area. In *Jailhouse Rock*, the hero spends a year in jail for manslaughter, where he learns to play the guitar; upon being released, he becomes rich as a rock-and-roll singer, alienating his closest friends until he is beaten up by his best friend. In each case, although the hero is a rebel against established authority, he is not necessarily identified with the lawless elements of society. He is in the middle, isolated and alone, a victim of forces he cannot understand. Frequently involved with the police, he is often in jail. Society itself is viewed as the outside of a prison, mechanical, forbidding, inhibitive, and repressive, but curiously enough, the hero is trying to enter this prison, for it offers warmth and security on the inside. The obstacle is his own rebellion and before he can enter he must get involved in violence, as if in expiation for some sin. Before he can become a member of society, he must first be beaten up. In order to win— to be accepted—he first must lose.

The pattern of all these films, then, is the same: although the hero starts off on the wrong side, he is almost always converted to righteousness before the end. This is usually accomplished with the aid of his one ally in society, the girl who loves him. The girl (her face is that of Julie Harris, Natalie Wood, Eva Marie Saint, or Elizabeth Taylor, but her character doesn't vary) is frequently an adolescent and invariably virtuous and understanding. Unlike the boy, she speaks coherently (and interminably), attends school regularly, gets good grades, and is accepted from the outset by her family and friends. Most significant, she exhibits a maternal protectiveness that belies her adolescent appearance and tends to make the hero extremely dependent on her (a situation reflected in much of our popular music where the recurring motif is "I want you, I need you, I love you"). The boy's actual mother has little personality, little influence on his life, and even less of a role, while the girl friend is the only one who can control him. The disguised family

romance usually found in these movies becomes, in
Giant, more explicit. One of the main objects of dispute
between Rock Hudson and James Dean is Hudson's wife,
Elizabeth Taylor. Only she offers the boy understanding
and tenderness, and it is primarily for frustrated love of
her that the boy fashions his revenge on the moneyed
families of the town.

The antagonism which the boy feels toward society,
convention, law and order is, of course, merely an extension of hostility toward his father. While Brando's
films are not concerned much with family life (the isolation of the character he plays is complete), most of
James Dean's films center on the family situation, a fact
which accounts for a good deal of his posthumous popularity. In *East of Eden, Rebel Without a Cause,* and
Giant, Dean is found in violent combat with his father
or father figure. In *Rebel Without a Cause,* for example,
the crucial scene occurs when the boy lashes his father
for his weakness and for having no effective advice to
offer him in time of trouble. In *East of Eden,* the boy is
alienated by his father's indifference to him and his
inability to see that his best son is not Abel, the conventional good boy, but Cain, the unconventional rebel. The
boy's feelings toward his father, however, are, as we
might expect, ambivalent. In one scene in *East of Eden,*
the boy, whipped to indignation by his father's coldness,
begins to pummel and ends by embracing him. The boy's
acceptance by society at the end of these films is usually
a symbol of filial reconciliation. The greatest reward
the hero can achieve is acceptance by the group and the
love of his father. And here we have a glimpse into the
meaning of the hero's inarticulateness, for we are led to
believe that his original alienation arose out of misunderstanding. Conflict is caused by a failure in communication; the boy cannot express his true feelings and therefore the father thinks him hostile. In the final scene of
East of Eden, the father has suffered a paralytic stroke

and is dying. He lies mutely on his bed (the camera shooting from above emphasizes his helplessness), his arms and lips paralyzed, able to signify assent or denial only with his eyes. Only then, when the parental authoritative voice of the father is quiet, when there can be no interruptions from him, when the fear he has instilled has been dispelled by his powerlessness, only then can the boy speak truly, coherently, and clearly, and effect understanding and reconciliation.

Ambiguous feelings toward the father (leading to hostility toward society in general) is, of course, a classic juvenile dilemma, and there can be little doubt that the inarticulate hero is fostered and cherished by the juvenile elements of our society. The striking thing to note is how effectively adolescents have been able to persuade our culture today to conform with their views of it (a recent ad for *Look* magazine promises the life of Jesus as seen "through the troubled eyes of a teen-ager"). It is significant that not only Marlon Brando and James Dean have become spokesmen for the adolescent generation, but Elvis Presley as well; for Presley is the musical counterpart of the inarticulate hero. In Elvis Presley, the testament of Stanley Kowalski is being realized, for, besides the physical resemblances and the explicit sexuality they share, both prophesy the ruin of culture. It is no accident that the costume of the inarticulate hero (blue jeans, T-shirts, sneakers) is primarily the same as that of the proletarian hero. The burden of protest has been handed down, as a heritage, from the one to the other. Denied the social and political outlets rebellion once was permitted to take, the adolescent is now seeing dramatized, in his music and in the movies and TV, the only rebellion left him, the Freudian protest. Although this rebellion often has an apparently happy ending with the hero securely ensconced in the bosom of his family, in reality nothing has been resolved: the hero is never seen in a mature action. The adolescent rebel never grows up;

when James Dean grows to middle age, in *Giant*, he merely has some powder added to his hair.

These films, then, give the hero an appearance of growth but derive their success from catering to the anarchic impulses of the young. Inarticulateness is a symptom of this anarchy because speech is an instrument of control. To teach children to speak is to teach them to frustrate their sexual and aggressive desires. To accept this speech is to accept all the difficulties as well as all the glories that speech entails: the teachings of the father, the complexity of the world, the discipline of a developing intelligence, the gifts of tradition, history, science, and art. To reject it is to find consolation in raw feeling, in mindlessness, and in self-indulgence, to seek escape in sex and violence. In the hero's inarticulateness, we find represented the young American's fears of maturity, for to speak out—to be a speaker—is to be a man. It is to replace his father, to take the consequences of his hostility toward him, symbolically to kill him. The unnamed sin for which the hero is beaten, at the end of most of these films, is the sin against the father. When this is expiated by physical punishment, then the hero finds his way home, not to independent manhood but to the kind of security which breeds conformity and complacency.

We can see how much of the acting and the writing of the inarticulate hero is not only neurotic but conformist. The need today is not for a hero who seems to be a rebel while really conforming to an established pattern, but for a hero who, without rejecting language, tradition, education, and art—without finding consolation in the impulsive anarchy of Stanley Kowalski—can express the nonconformism which stems from a long, hard, individualistic look at the world.

1957

Reflections
on Horror Movies

Horror movies, perennial supporting features among Grade B and C fare, have recently been enjoying a vogue, a fact in which I shamelessly rejoice. I have been hopelessly addicted to them since the age of eight when my mother, with great anxiety lest I be traumatized for life, accompanied me to see Frederic March in *Dr. Jekyll and Mr. Hyde*. Since then, I guess I have seen about two hundred horror films but, although my mother had a couple of bad nights, I have always remained impervious to the inviting promise of their advertising ("Will Give You Nightmares FOREVER"). My satisfactions are more simple. Horror films give me pleasure by their very faults: the woodenness of the acting, the inevitability of the plot, the obstinate refusal to make any but the most basic demand on my mind. I can suggest nothing more remedial after a night of agony at the theatre than a late horror show at a 42nd Street flea pit.

It may seem a little graceless of me, in view of the enjoyment I have derived from these films, to analyze their "cultural significance" and run the risk of stifling any pleasure you (or I) might seek from them in future. But it has occurred to me over the years that, aside from modest shock motives, horror films always try to involve us in certain underground assumptions. They have been serving up a mess of cultural pottage whose seasoning gives science (and sometimes even all knowledge) a bad taste. Since I attended these films with childlike innocence, I consider these added motives an impudence, and I retaliate by pointing out to you what the hidden images are.

The horror movies I am mainly concerned with I have divided into three major categories: Mad Doctor, Atomic Beast, and Interplanetary Monster. They do not exhaust all the types but they each contain two essential characters, the Scientist and the Monster, toward whom the attitudes of the movies are in a revealing state of change.

The Mad Doctor series is by far the most long lived of the three. It suffered a temporary decline in the forties when Frankenstein, Dracula, and the Wolf Man (along with their countless offspring) were first loaned out as straight men to Abbott and Costello and then set out to graze in the parched pastures of the cheap all-night movie houses, but it has recently demonstrated its durability in a group of English remakes and a Teenage Monster craze. These films find their roots in certain European folk myths. Dracula was inspired by an ancient Balkan superstition about vampires, the werewolf is a Middle European folk myth recorded, among other places, in the Breton *lais* of Marie de France, and even Frankenstein, though out of Mary Shelley by the Gothic tradition, has a medieval prototype in the Golem, a monster the Jews fashioned from clay and earth to free them from oppression. The spirit of these films is still medieval, combining a vulgar religiosity with folk superstitions. Superstition now, however, has been crudely transferred from magic and alchemy to creative science, itself a form of magic to the untutored mind. The devil of the vampire and werewolf myths, who turned human beings into baser animals, today has become a scientist, and the metamorphosis is given a technical name—it is a "regression" into an earlier state of evolution. The alchemist and devil-conjuring scholar Dr. Faustus gives way to Dr. Frankenstein the research physician, while the magic circle, the tetragrammaton, and the full moon are replaced by test tubes, complicated electrical apparati, and bunsen burners.

Frankenstein, like Faustus, defies God by exploring

areas where humans are not meant to trespass. In Mary Shelley's book (it is subtitled "A Modern Prometheus"), Frankenstein is a latter-day Faustus, a superhuman creature whose aspiration embodies the expansiveness of his age. In the movies, however, Frankenstein loses his heroic quality and becomes a lunatic monomaniac, so obsessed with the value of his work that he no longer cares whether his discovery proves a boon or a curse to mankind. When the mad doctor, his eyes wild and inflamed, bends over his intricate equipment, pouring in a little of this and a little of that, the spectator is confronted with an immoral being whose mental superiority is only a measure of his madness. Like the popular image of the theoretical scientist engaged in basic research ("Basic research," says Charles Wilson, "is science's attempt to prove that grass is green"), he succeeds only in creating something badly which nature has already made well. The Frankenstein monster is a parody of man. Ghastly in appearance, clumsy in movement, criminal in behavior, imbecilic of mind, it is superior only in physical strength and resistance to destruction. The scientist has fashioned it in the face of divine disapproval (the heavens disgorge at its birth)—not to mention the disapproval of friends and frightened townspeople—and it can lead only to trouble.

For Dr. Frankenstein, however, the monster symbolizes the triumph of his intellect over the blind morality of his enemies and it confirms him in the ultimate soundness of his thought ("They thought I was mad, but this proves I am the superior being"). When it becomes clear that his countrymen are unimpressed by his achievement and regard him as a menace to society, the monster becomes the agent of his revenge. As it ravages the countryside and terrorizes the inhabitants, it embodies and expresses the scientist's own lust and violence. It is an extension of his own mad soul, come to life not in a weak and ineffectual body but in a body of formidable physical power.

(In a movie like *Dr. Jekyll and Mr. Hyde,* the identity of monster and doctor is even clearer; Mr. Hyde, the monster, is the aggressive and libidinous element in the benevolent Dr. Jekyll's personality.) The rampage of the monster is the rampage of mad, unrestrained science which inevitably turns on the scientist, destroying him too. As the lava bubbles over the sinking head of the monster, the crude moral of the film frees itself from the horror and is asserted. Experimental science (and by extension knowledge itself) is superfluous, dangerous, and unlawful, for, in exploring the unknown, it leads man to usurp God's creative power. Each of these films is a victory for obscurantism, flattering the spectator into believing that his intellectual inferiority is a sign that he is loved by God.

The Teenage Monster films, a very recent phenomenon, amend the assumptions of these horror movies in a startling manner. Their titles—*I Was a Teenage Werewolf, I Was a Teenage Frankenstein, Blood of Dracula,* and *Teenage Monster*—(some wit awaits one called *I Had a Teenage Monkey on My Back*)—suggest a Hollywood prank but they are deadly serious, mixing the conventions of early horror movies with the ingredients of adolescent culture. The doctor, significantly enough, is no longer a fringe character whose madness can be inferred from the rings around his eyes and his wild hair, but a respected member of society, a high school chemistry teacher (*Blood of Dracula*) or a psychoanalyst (*Teenage Werewolf*) or a visiting lecturer from Britain (*Teenage Frankenstein*). Although he gives the appearance of benevolence—he pretends to help teenagers with their problems—behind this façade he hides evil experimental designs. The monster, on the other hand, takes on a more fully developed personality. He is a victim who begins inauspiciously as an average, though emotionally troubled, adolescent and ends, through the influence of the doctor, as a voracious animal. The monster as teenager becomes the central character in the film and the teenage audience is expected to identify and sympathize with him.

In *I Was a Teenage Werewolf*, the hero is characterized as brilliant but erratic in his studies and something of a delinquent. At the suggestion of his principal, he agrees to accept therapy from an analyst helping maladjusted students. The analyst gets the boy under his control and, after injecting him with a secret drug, turns him into a werewolf. Against his will he murders a number of his contemporaries. When the doctor refuses to free him from his curse, he kills him and is himself killed by the police. In death, his features relax into the harmless countenance of an adolescent.

The crimes of the adolescent are invariably committed against other youths (the doctor has it in for teenagers) and are always connected with those staples of juvenile culture, sex and violence. The advertising displays show the male monsters, dressed in leather jackets and blue jeans, bending ambiguously over the diaphanously draped body of a luscious young girl, while the female teenage vampire of *Blood of Dracula*, her nails long and her fangs dripping, is herself half dressed and lying on top of a struggling male (whether to rape or murder him it is not clear). The identification of sex and violence is further underlined by the promotion blurbs: "In her eyes DE-SIRE! In her veins—the blood of a MONSTER!" (*Blood of Dracula*); "A Teenage Titan on a Lustful Binge That Paralyzed a Town with Fear" (*Teenage Monster*). It is probable that these crimes are performed less reluctantly than is suggested and that the adolescent spectator is more thrilled than appalled by this "lustful binge" which captures the attention of the adult community. The acquisition of power and prestige through delinquent sexual and aggressive activity is a familiar juvenile fantasy (the same distributors exploit it more openly in films like *Re-*

form School Girl and *Drag-Strip Girl*), one which we can see frequently acted out by delinquents in our city schools. In the Teenage Monster films, however, the hero is absolved of his aggressive and libidinous impulses. Although he both feels and acts on them, he can attribute the responsibility to the mad scientist who controls his behavior. What these films seem to be saying, in their underground manner, is that behind the harmless face of the high school chemistry teacher and the intellectual countenance of the psychoanalyst lies the warped authority responsible for teenage violence. The adolescent feels victimized by society—turned into a monster by society—and if he behaves in a delinquent manner, society and not he is to blame. Thus, we can see one direction in which the hostility for experimental research, explicit in the Mad Doctor films, can go—it can be transmuted into hatred of adult authority itself.

Or it can go underground, as in the Atomic Beast movies. The Mad Doctor movies, in exploiting the supernatural, usually locate their action in Europe (often a remote Bavarian village), where wild fens, spectral castles, and ominous graveyards provide the proper eerie background. The Atomic Beast movies depend for their effect on the contemporary and familiar and there is a corresponding change in locale. The monster (or *thing*, as it is more often called) appears now in a busy American city—usually Los Angeles to save the producer money—where average men walk about in business suits. The thing terrorizes not only the hero, the heroine, and a few anonymous (and expendable) characters in Tyrolean costumes, but the entire world. Furthermore, it has lost all resemblance to anything human. It appears as a giant ant (*Them!*), a prehistoric animal (*Beast from Twenty Thousand Fathoms*), an outsized grasshopper (*Beginning of the End*), or a monstrous spider (*Tarantula*). Although these films, in their deference to science fiction, seem to smile more benignly on scientific endeavor, they are unconsciously closer to the antitheoretical biases of the Mad Doctor series than would first appear.

All these films are similarly plotted, so the plot of *Beginning of the End* will serve as an example of the whole genre. The scene opens on a pair of adolescents necking in their car off a desert road. Their attention is caught by a weird clicking sound, the boy looks up in horror, the girl screams, the music stings, and the scene fades. In the next scene, we learn that the car has been completely demolished and its occupants have disappeared. The police, totally baffled, are conducting fruitless investigations when word comes that a small town nearby has been destroyed in the same mysterious way. Enter the young scientist-hero. Examining the wreckage of the town, he discovers a strange fluid which when analyzed proves to have been manufactured by a giant grasshopper. The police ridicule his conclusions and are instantly attacked by a fleet of these grasshoppers, each fifteen feet high, which wipe out the entire local force and a few state troopers. Interrupting a perfunctory romance with the heroine, the scientist flies to Washington to alert the nation. He describes the potential danger to a group of bored politicians and yawning big brass but they remain skeptical until word comes that the things have reached Chicago and are crushing buildings and eating the occupants. The scientist is then put in charge of the army and air force. Although the military men want to evacuate the city and drop an atom bomb on it, the scientist devises a safer method of destroying the creatures and proceeds to do so through exemplary physical courage and superior knowledge of their behavior. The movie ends on a note of foreboding: Have the things been completely exterminated?

Externally, there seem to be very significant changes indeed, especially in the character of the scientist. No longer fang toothed, long haired, and subject to delirious ravings (Bela Lugosi, John Carradine, Basil Rathbone), the doctor is now a highly admired member of society, muscular, handsome, and heroic (John Agar). He is invariably wiser, more reasonable, and more humane than the boneheaded bureaucrats and trigger-happy brass who compose the members of his "team," and he even has sexual appeal, a quality which Hollywood's eggheads have never enjoyed before. The scientist-hero, however, is not a very convincing intellectual. Although he may use technical, polysyllabic language when discussing his findings, he always yields gracefully to the admonition to "tell us in our own words, Doc" and proves that he can speak as simply as you or I; in the crisis, in fact, he is almost monosyllabic. When the chips are down, he loses his glasses (a symbol of his intellectualism) and begins to look like everyone else. The hero's intellect is part of his costume and makeup, easily shed when heroic action is demanded. That he is always called upon not only to outwit the thing but to wrestle with it as well (in order to save the heroine) indicates that he is in constant danger of tripping over the thin boundary between specialist and average Joe.

The fact remains that there is a new separation between the scientist and the monster. Rather than being an extension of the doctor's evil will, the monster functions completely on its own, creating havoc through its predatory nature. We learn through charts, biological films, and the scientist's patient explanations that ants and grasshoppers are not the harmless little beasties they appear but actually voracious insects who need only the excuse of size to prey upon humanity. The doctor, rather than allying himself with the monster in its rampage against our cities, is in strong opposition to it, and reverses the pattern of the Mad Doctor films by destroying it.

And yet, if the individual scientist is absolved of all responsibility for the thing, science somehow is not.

These films suggest an uneasiness about science which, though subtle and unpremeditated, reflects unconscious American attitudes. These attitudes are sharpened when we examine the genesis of the thing, for, though it seems to rise out of nowhere, it is invariably caused by a scientific blunder. The giant ants of *Them!*, for example, result from a nuclear explosion which caused a mutation in the species; another fission test has awakened, in *Beast from Twenty Thousand Fathoms*, a dinosaur encrusted in polar icecaps; the spider of *Tarantula* grows in size after having been injected with radioactive isotopes, and escapes during a fight in the lab between two scientists; the grasshoppers of *Beginning of the End* enlarge after crawling into some radioactive dust carelessly left about by a researcher. We are left with a puzzling substatement: science destroys the thing, but scientific experimentation has created it.

I think we can explain this equivocal attitude when we acknowledge that the thing "which is too horrible to name," which owes its birth to an atomic or nuclear explosion, which begins in a desert or frozen waste and moves from there to cities, and which promises ultimately to destroy the world, is probably a crude symbol for the bomb itself. The scientists we see represented in these films are unlike the Mad Doctors in another, more fundamental respect: they are never engaged in basic research. The scientist uses his knowledge in a purely defensive manner, like a specialist working on rocket interception or a physician trying to cure a disease. The isolated theoretician who tinkers curiously in his lab (and who invented the atom bomb) is never shown, only the practical working scientist who strives to undo the harm. The thing's destructive rampage against cities, like the rampage of the Frankenstein monster, is the result of too much cleverness, and the consequences for all the world are only too apparent.

These consequences are driven home more powerfully

in movies like *The Incredible Shrinking Man* and *The Amazing Colossal Man*, where the audience gets the opportunity to identify closely with the victims of science's reckless experimentation. The hero of the first movie is an average man who, through contact with fallout while on his honeymoon, begins to shrink away to nothing. As he proceeds to grow smaller, he finds himself in much the same dilemma as the other heroes of the Atomic Beast series—he must do battle with (now) gigantic insects in order to survive. Scientists can do nothing to save him—after a while they can't even find him—so as he dwindles into an atomic particle he finally turns to God, for whom "there is no zero." The inevitable sequel, *The Amazing Colossal Man*, reverses the dilemma. The hero grows to enormous size through the premature explosion of a plutonium bomb. Size carries with it the luxury of power but the hero cannot enjoy his new stature. He feels like a freak and his body is proceeding to outgrow his brain and heart. Although the scientists labor to help him and even succeed in reducing an elephant to the size of a cat, it is too late; the hero has gone mad, demolished Las Vegas, and fallen over Boulder Dam. The victimization of man by theoretical science has become, in these two movies, less of a suggestion and more of a fact.

In the Interplanetary Monster movies, Hollywood handles the public's ambivalence toward science in a more obvious way, by splitting the scientist in two. Most of these movies feature both a practical scientist who wishes to destroy the invader and a theoretical scientist who wants to communicate with it. In *The Thing*, for example, we find billeted among a group of more altruistic average-Joe colleagues with crew cuts an academic long-haired scientist of the Dr. Frankenstein type. When the evil thing (a highly evolved vegetable which, by multiplying itself, threatens to take over the world) descends in a flying saucer, this scientist tries to perpetuate its life in order "to find out what it knows." He is violently opposed in this by the others, who take the occasion to tell him that such amoral investigation produced the atom bomb. But he cannot be reasoned with and almost wrecks the entire party. After both he and the thing are destroyed, the others congratulate themselves on remaining safe, though in the dark. In *Forbidden Planet* (a sophisticated thriller inspired in part by Shakespeare's *Tempest*), the good and evil elements in science are represented, as in *Dr. Jekyll and Mr. Hyde*, by the split personality of the scientist. He is urbane and benevolent (Walter Pidgeon plays the role) and is trying to realize an ideal community on the far-off planet he has discovered. Although he has invented a robot (Ariel) who cheerfully performs man's baser tasks, we learn that he is also responsible, though unwittingly, for a terrible invisible force (Caliban) overwhelming in its destructiveness. While he sleeps, the aggressive forces in his libido activate a dynamo he has been tinkering with which gives enormous power to kill those the doctor unconsciously resents. Thus, Freudian psychology is evoked to endow the scientist with guilt. At the end, he accepts his guilt and sacrifices his life in order to combat the being he has created.

The Interplanetary Monster series sometimes reverses the central situation of most horror films. We often find the monster controlling the scientist and forcing him to do its evil will. In *It Conquered the World* (the first film to capitalize on Sputnik and Explorer), the projection of a space satellite proves to be a mistake, for it results in the invasion of America by a monster from Venus. It takes control of the scientist who, embittered by the indifference of the masses toward his ideas, mistakenly thinks the monster will free men from stupidity. This muddled egghead finally discovers the true intentions of the monster and destroys it, dying himself in the process. In *The Brain from Planet Arous*, a hideous brain inhabits the mind of a nuclear physicist with the intention of controlling the universe. As the physical incarnation of the monster, the scientist is at the mercy of its will until he can free himself of its influence. The monster's intellect, like the intellect of the Mad Doctor, is invariably superior, signified by its large head and small body (in the last film named it is nothing but brain). Like the Mad Doctor, its superior intelligence is always accompanied by moral depravity and an unconscionable lust for power. If the monster is to be destroyed at all, it will not be done by matching wits with it but by finding some chink in its armor. This chink quite often is a physical imperfection: in *War of the Worlds*, the invading Martians are stopped, at the height of their victory, by their vulnerability to the disease germs of earth. Before this Achilles heel is discovered, however, the scientist is controlled to do evil, and with the monster and the doctor in collaboration again, even in this qualified sense, the wheel has come full circle.

The terror of most of these films, then, stems from the matching of knowledge with power, always a source of fear for Americans—when Nietzsche's Superman enters comic-book culture he loses his intellectual and spiritual qualities and becomes a muscleman. The muscleman, even with X-ray vision, poses no threat to the will, but muscle in collaboration with mind is generally thought to have a profound effect on individual destinies. The tendency to attribute everything that happens in the heavens, from flying saucers to Florida's cold wave, to science and the bomb ("Why don't they stop," said an old lady on the bus behind me the other day, "they don't know what they're doing") accounts for the extreme ways in which the scientist is regarded in our culture: either as a protective savior or as a destructive blunderer. It is little wonder that America exalts the physician (and the football player) and ignores the physicist. These issues, the issues of the great debate over scientific education and basic research, assert themselves crudely through the unwieldy monster and the Mad Doctor. The films suggest that the academic scientist, in exploring new areas, has laid the human race open to devastation by either human or interplanetary enemies—the doctor's madness, then, is merely a suitable way of expressing a conviction that the scientist's idle curiosity has shaken itself loose from prudency or principle. There is obviously a sensitive moral problem involved here, one which needs more articulate treatment than the covert and superstitious way it is handled in horror movies. That the problem is touched there at all is evidence of how profoundly it has stirred the American psyche.

1958

A Comedy of Disaster

DR. STRANGELOVE, OR
HOW I LEARNED TO STOP WORRYING
AND LOVE THE BOMB

*produced and directed by Stanley Kubrick;
screenplay by Stanley Kubrick,
Terry Southern, and Peter George*

Dr. Strangelove possesses a great many distinctions as a work of the imagination, but I should like to cite it, first and foremost, for valor: I think it may well be the most courageous movie ever made. It is certainly one of the funniest. A nightmare farce which proceeds from horror to horror, culminating in the annihilation of the human race after an American hydrogen bomb has been dropped on Russia, it is, despite its cataclysmic conclusion, a peculiarly heady, exhilarating experience. I can account for this partially by the fact that the movie pays absolutely no deference at all to the expectations of its audience. Artistic courage always soothes the spirit and makes glad the heart, but when this quality enters as craven a medium as the American film one feels curiously exalted, ineffably happy. Then, too, there is something extraordinarily liberating in the nature of the movie itself. It is the kind of total theatre that Antonin Artaud would have admired, with its dark humor, its physical and anarchic dissociation. *Dr. Strangelove* is a plague experienced in the nerves and the funny bone—a delirium, a conflagration, a social disaster.

What Stanley Kubrick has done is to break completely with all existing traditions of moviemaking, both foreign and domestic. While the European art film seems to be inexorably closing in on the spiritual lassitude of certain melancholy French or Italian aristocrats, *Dr. Strangelove* invests the film medium with a new exuberance, expansiveness, and broadness of vision; compared with the sweep of this masterpiece, the weary meanderings of Resnais, Fellini, and Antonioni seem solipsistic and self-indulgent. Moreover, Kubrick's film is fun—this is its one debt to Hollywood. It is enjoyable for the way it exploits the exciting narrative conventions of the Hollywood war movie—say, *Air Force* or *Thirty Seconds over Tokyo*—and even more, for the way it turns these conventions upside down, and cruelly scourges them. This is what is arrestingly new about the film: its wry, mordant, destructive, and, at the same time, cheerful, unmoralistic tone. We have heard this sound emanating from our comic novels, cabaret acts, satiric revues, living rooms, and dreams, but, although it rumbled a little bit under the conventional noises of *The Manchurian Candidate*, it has never before fully entered the mass media. With *Dr. Strangelove*, a subterranean vibration becomes a series of earthquakes, shattering cultural platitudes, political pieties, and patriotic ideals with fierce, joyous shocks. If the picture manages to remain open, it will knock the block off every ideologue in the country: even now, I suspect, Sidney Hook is preparing the first of fifteen volumes in rebuttal.

To avoid a repetition of Mr. Hook's embarrassing performance on behalf of *Fail-Safe*, where he involved us in a closely reasoned, technical argumentation to refute the premise of a cheap, best-selling fantasy, let me announce that *Dr. Strangelove* is frankly offered to the audience as a cinematic sick joke, and that it is based less on verifiable facts than on unconscious terrors. The film's source, a prototype for *Fail-Safe*, is Peter George's *Red Alert*, but the film writers have employed the novel very loosely, and the director has imposed on the finished screenplay his own style and purpose. This style is Juvenalian satire; this purpose, the evacuation of fear and anger through the acting out of frightful fantasies. Kubrick has flushed a monster from its psychic lair—the universal fear of nuclear accident—and then proceeded to feed and nourish it, letting it perform its worst before your eyes. The consequence of this spectacle is, as the subtitle suggests, a temporary purgation: to witness the end of the world as a comic event is, indeed, to stop worrying and to love the Bomb.

The outline of the film is this: A psychotic right-wing general, convinced that the Communists are poisoning Americans through fluoridation, exercises emergency powers and sends a wing command to bomb the Soviet Union. The President, trying to recall these bombers, learns that the Russians have perfected a deterrent, a Doomsday machine, which is automatically triggered to explode the moment a bomb is dropped on Soviet soil, spreading a shroud of fallout over the earth for a hundred years. After the general's base has been destroyed by American forces, and the recall code has been found, both nations cooperate to bring the bombers back or shoot them down. One damaged plane, however, its radio inoperative, manages to continue on to target. Through the invincible doggedness of the pilot and his crew, a hydrogen bomb is dropped on a Soviet missile complex—and apocalypse follows.

Kubrick handles this external action with ruthless documentary realism. The battle scenes, for example, which show Americans slaughtering Americans, are photographed through a gray morning mist (the same smoky tones so effectively used in Kubrick's *Paths of Glory*) with a hand camera shaken by artillery explosions, and the flight of the bomber over Arctic wastes is a terrifying journey into the frozen unknown. At the same time, however, Kubrick is evoking savage ironies through the conjunction of unexpected images and sounds: the bomber, for example, proceeds to its destination (and to the destruction of the world) over a chorus of male voices humming "When Johnny Comes Marching Home."

The same blend of farce and nightmare is found in other scenes. During the credits, a B-52 bomber is fueled in the air through a phallic hose while the sound track plays "Try a Little Tenderness." A looming shot of two monstrous hydrogen bombs, triggered and ready to go, reveals two scrawled messages on them: "Hi There!" and "Dear John." And the epilogue is composed of a series of nuclear explosions (a sequence borrowed, I suspect, from a similar filmed skit used in *The Establishment*), which flower soundlessly while a female voice croons "We'll meet again (don't know where, don't know when)."

What these images suggest is that our heroic postures and patriotic reflexes have become hideously inappropriate to modern weaponry—the same thing is illustrated by the conduct of the crew on the lethal bomber. Kubrick has sardonically included among these crew members the various ethnic stereotypes of Hollywood war moves: a Negro bombardier, a Jewish radio operator, a Texas pilot, etc., all of whom behave, in crisis, according to preconditioned movie patterns—they engage in sexual banter, become comradely, grow steely grim and fighting mad. When the order is received to proceed over enemy territory and drop the bomb, the Texas pilot, Major "King" Kong, takes off his helmet, puts on a ten-gallon hat, assumes an unctuous leader-of-men speaking style, and delivers an inspirational lecture to the crew about their duty to "the folks back home," while promising them all decorations, "regardless of your race, color, or creed." When the plane is hit by a missile, he keeps it in action, flying low over jutting peaks, and when the bomb doors stick, he courageously climbs into the bomb bay, determined to fix the short circuit and complete his mission.

Kong finally clears the doors, and goes sailing down to target on the back of a bomb, waving his hat and whooping like a rebel. American heroism has become completely identified with American lunacy. So has American know-how—it is almost a structural principle of this film that our technology is wholly mad. Inside the bomber, for example, the camera peeks into complicated equipment and technical apparati—the instrument panel, the radar, the navigator's gear, the auto-destruct mechanism—all efficiently manipulated by this trained crew to create havoc and mass slaughter. The President's War Room, similarly, with its huge locating charts, is a model of gleaming competence and quiet decorum ("You can't fight in here," says the President to two dissidents, "this is the War Room"). Even the telephone works as an obstacle to survival. In one hilarous sequence, a British officer—having discovered the recall code—is trying to phone Washington with only minutes to go; but he lacks the necessary change, and the Pentagon will not accept collect calls.

If our technology is mad, however, then so are the technicians who create, control, and operate it. *Dr. Strangelove* is a satire not only on nuclear war and warriors, but also on scientists, militarists, military intellectuals, diplomats, statesmen—all those, in short, whose profession it is to think about the unthinkable. Thus, the movie contains a large number of superb caricatures, all treated either as knaves or fools, but still recognizable as familiar American types.

These include two sharp profiles of General Walker-like military men: General Jack D. Ripper, played by Sterling Hayden in another of his stiff, interesting non-performances—his eyes fanatically narrowed, his teeth clenched on a huge cigar as he drawls to an aide about how he confines himself to pure alcohol and rain water and refrains from orgasm to protect his natural essences against the Communist conspiracy; and General Buck Turgidson, Air Force Chief of Staff, played by George C. Scott in a fine frenzy of muscle-flexing pugnacity—stuffing his mouth with wads of chewing gum, and flashing an evil smile as he outlines his plan to obliterate the

"Commie punks" entirely ("I'm not saying we wouldn't get our hair mussed, Mr. President, but I do say not more than ten to twenty million dead depending on the breaks").

Then, there are three magnificent satiric sketches by Peter Sellers: Group Captain Mandrake, Ripper's befuddled British aide; President Merkin Muffley, a bald, bland, liberal Chief Executive, educated and slightly effeminate (a *merkin,* according to the *OED,* is a "female pudendum," while *muffley* is an obsolete word for a pubic wig); and, finally, that eerie figure from the Bland Corporation, the German scientist Dr. Strangelove.

Strangelove (formerly Merkwuerdigichliebe) is the most masterly character in the film, a composite portrait of Edward Teller, Werner von Braun, and Herman Kahn, played by Sellers with an excess of mischief, and conceived by Kubrick in an excess of fury. Imprisoned in a wheelchair, his mechanical hand gloved in black, his face fixed in a perpetual smile, he stares through dark glasses and sibilates through false teeth, suggesting emotion only through a slight emphasis on certain phrases, the word *human* being particularly distasteful to him. Strangelove is the perfect synthetic man, and he comes to us by courtesy of a Universal horror movie. In his person, the Mad Doctor and the State Scientist merge—Boris Karloff with a computer, calculating the proper use of deterrents and the halflife of cobalt-thorium-G.

This is extravagant enough, but toward the end, Strangelove goes completely haywire. So does the movie, as if Kubrick, having breathed the air of the outer limits for the first time, were suffering from stratospheric drunkenness. The bomb has been dropped; the Doomsday shroud is beginning to smother all life on earth; and Strangelove is outlining his plan for preserving "a nucleus of human specimens" at the bottom of mine shafts. His explanation is disarmingly rational, but his mechanical hand has gone out of control. It shoots up in a Nazi salute, it punches him on the jaw, it strangles him, and finally it propels him right out of his wheelchair—whereupon he screams at the President, "Mein Fuhrer, I can walk!" The lunatic inappropriateness of the remark somehow sums up all the lunatic inappropriateness of the theatrics and celluloid heroics that have preceded it; and it makes the devastation that follows seem singularly fitting and just.

Dr. Strangelove is a work of comic anarchy, fashioned by a totally disaffected and disaffiliated imagination: it is thus the first American movie to speak truly for our generation. Kubrick has managed to explode the right-wing position without making a single left-wing affirmation: the odor of the thirties, which clung even to the best work of Chaplin, Welles, and Huston, has finally been disinfected here. Disinfected, in fact, is the stink of all ideological thinking. For although *Dr. Strangelove* is about a political subject, its only politics is outrage against the malevolence of officialdom. Conservatives will find it subversive, liberals will find it irresponsible, utopians will find it bleak, humanitarians will find it inhuman—*Dr. Strangelove* is all these things. But it also releases, through comic poetry, those feelings of impotence and frustration that are consuming us all; and I can't think of anything more important for an imaginative work to do.

1964

The Memory of
Heroism

Like most monuments of the past in an America obsessed
with its present and future, the extant plays of the three
Attic tragic dramatists are works for which everyone expresses reverence, but which few read without compulsion. It is a commonplace that fifth-century Athens, along
with seventeenth-century Europe, produced the most sublime drama the world has ever known; yet, stage performances of Greek tragedy are extremely rare, casual
reading of the plays is almost unheard of, and, even in
the colleges—where the spirit of the past is kept fitfully
alive—the *Oresteia* is sometimes taught primarily as an
introduction to *Mourning Becomes Electra*. All things
conspire to keep Aeschylus, Sophocles, and Euripides at
a respectful distance. Present-day scholarship, when it
employs the (often valuable) archetypal critical techniques, tends to analyze the tragedies as mosaics of
mythical patterns rather than immediate, sensual experiences; and, on Broadway, the techniques of Greek
drama are exploited only to give dignity to dramatic
enterprises which have little importance by themselves.

Of the two major reasons for contemporary distance
from these works, the more obvious one has to do with
the technical problem of translation. For years, if we
ignore occasional renderings of individual plays by qualified poets, the only way those of us without a classical
education could see the whole of Greek tragedy was
through the frozen optics of Victorian poetasters. T. S.
Eliot has already described how Gilbert Murray did violence to Euripides by transforming his delicate lyrics into
ponderous and archaic pre-Raphaelite patterns; someone

has yet to document the well-intentioned damage done to Aeschylus and Sophocles by E. D. A. Morshead and R. C. Jebb. Afflicted less with indifference to the past than too much piety toward it, most of the translators of the last generation paid homage to the flower of Greek drama by turning it into a wilted bouquet. Since one could not even open the Oates and O'Neill edition without finding rotten blossoms like "Hast thou a front so bold," "Abate nought of thy intent," and "Teem the kine in double measure" decaying on the page, the reader formerly had no choice but to abandon the project for a good detective story or to retranslate each translation into acceptable English.

The Complete Greek Tragedies, previously called the Chicago translations and edited by Richmond Lattimore and David Grene, go a long way toward rescuing these imprisoned masterpieces from the gray walls of Victorian dullness. The thirty-three plays in the canon have been newly Englished by fifteen translators with Grene, Lattimore, and William Arrowsmith sharing the major burden. As we might expect from writers who combine careful scholarship with a sensitivity to language (some of them are accomplished poets), the verse is usually accurate, spare, and precise, yet rich with images, and, in one case (Fitzgerald's translation of *Oedipus at Colonus*), it rises to pinnacles of brilliance. Not all of these renderings, however, are ideal. Some of them, in laudably avoiding archaisms, fall into infelicitous colloquialisms (in one play, the chorus advises the heroine "Necessity's hot on your trail"); and, more often than not, the Chicago versions seem designed for the study rather than the stage, for the reader rather than the actor. Of the twelve translators of Euripides, in whose works characterization is so often paramount, only Arrowsmith successfully distinguishes the speech of one personage from another, while none of these writers possesses the metrical gifts of Edith Hamilton—oddly not represented in these volumes even though she, more than any modern translator, has managed to suggest the exciting rhythms of choral, dance, song, and speech.

But the plays have now been rendered into a heightened modern English not very remote from our own, and so, if some of the translations are not for all time, they are all very much for our time. And if, unlike Yeats' abridged, often inaccurate, but overpowering version of *Oedipus*, they may not inspire a flurry of Greek revivals on the stage, they will certainly enlarge substantially that small circle of admirers who find in Greek tragedy one of the major compensations for being alive. The authoritative Chicago translations consign all other complete collections to the wastebasket, and the common reader now has an invaluable opportunity to examine the whole corpus of Greek tragedy aided by informative and sometimes profound critical introductions.

By keeping these works available in readable form, the Chicago translations will undoubtedly eliminate the technical reason for contemporary indifference to Greek tragedy. They may even help to temper a more profound cause of this indifference—our distrustful attitude toward tragedy and tragic heroes. It should be clear that, in the last half-century, Greek drama has been subjected to a relentless process of minification, of making the mighty mean. Today, we prefer to reach the great tragic figures primarily through their complexes, for we are tolerant of them only when they are like ourselves—and that generally means ourselves as reflected in a psychoanalytical mirror. Oedipus, as a dramatic character involved in an action, groans and dwindles under the heavy psychological burden he has been made to bear for all mankind, and Philoctetes, through the critical exertions of Edmund Wilson, is now remembered less as a tragic figure of a specific time and place than as a universal symbol of the neurotically wounded but uniquely gifted modern artist. In contemporary drama, where the Greeks have been acceptable only when clothed in modern personalities, the tragic function becomes even more limited. Cocteau, Sartre, Anouilh, and Giraudoux, in France, have all invented actions for Greek heroes which any modern man might play; while Eugene O'Neill's Orestes is a gloomy suicidal introvert with a fierce fixation on his mother and sister; Robinson Jeffers' Medea is a ganster's moll; and T. S. Eliot's Heracles is a Christian mystic doubling as a psychiatrist.

Some of the changes have been introduced to satirize the inadequacies of the spectator, some to inflate the spectator beyond his proper dimensions, but, whether designed for parody or flattery, these are the tricks of a theoretical, self-conscious, and ironic age. As devices, they are, of course, hardly new. Euripides himself—the first of the debunkers—sometimes belittled the Greek heroes through clinical insights into their personal lives, and, like the dramatists of our age, he was writing for an audience grown exhausted with the Dionysian ecstasy. In the time of the inside dopester, the private elements in personality assume more importance than the public actions of character, while motives are examined more closely than deeds. We are anxious to uncover familiar guilty secrets like aggression, neurosis, and sexual deviation, for we are fond of the average, and, anyway, great heroes make us uncomfortable. Confronting us with the meagerness of our ambitions, highlighting our compromises, underlining our deficiencies of feeling and mind, they awaken in us a terrible suspicion: that the happy, adjusted life we seek may not be the most bright, ennobling, or even ultimately human one. The risks and rashness of the Greek tragic heroes stand as an implicit rebuke to our own drive toward security, and we revenge ourselves by chopping away at their pediments, by rationalizing their myths.

Sometimes, with the Greek rebuke gnawing at our consciousness, we may even try to erase the memory of heroism from history. It is not enough to minify the myths by placing them in new contexts; we even attempt to redefine tragedy to fit our preconceived social-democratic ideals. Thus, we exchange what is unique and ecstatic for what is common and humdrum, and congratulate ourselves on the superiority of our choice. Arthur Miller, for example, constructing a definition of tragedy for "we who are without kings," seeks it in the "heart and spirit of the average man":

> I believe that the common man is as apt a subject for tragedy in its highest sense as kings were. On the face of it this ought to be obvious in the light of modern psychiatry, which bases its analyses upon classic formulations, such as the Oedipus and Orestes complexes, for instances, which were enacted by royal beings, but which apply to everyone in similar emotional situations.

Of course, to conclude, by ignoring Oedipus' responsibility for the whole state of Thebes, that the "common man" is capable of Oedipus' greatness because he shares with him a psychological complex, which is not even operative in the play, is to forfeit logic altogether. But Mr. Miller is determined to make tragedy conform to American liberal dogma. In a later essay, he declares the theories of Aristotle, like those of the scientists Euclid and Hippocrates, out of date, because Aristotle constructed his image of the highborn hero while living in a slave state: "Things do change, and even a genius is limited by his time and the nature of his society." O wondrous progress that can forge Willy Loman out of Oedipus the King.

Opinions like these could be dismissed as personal eccentricities if we were all not so deeply implicated in them; Mr. Miller is the product of a world to which, in one way or another, we are all committed. It is a world where tragic actions turn into "emotional situations," a world where cant terms like "rightful status" and "stable environment" are invoked to cope with human experience —a world, in other words, where tragedy must suffocate while the social sciences flourish. The sociological world view, with its fervent belief in social progress, has helped to ameliorate physical suffering, but it is hardly a philosophy with which to define the qualities of the tragic life. To the social worker, busily combating inequality, poverty, and disease, "tragedy" is distasteful because it is synonomous with the human suffering he seeks to destroy.

Arthur Miller's affinities with the social worker are amply demonstrated not only by his language, but by his concept of the tragic situation as something to be illustrated primarily in order to be corrected: "Tragic right," he affirms, is a "condition in which the human personality is able to flower and realize itself," and "tragic wrong" a condition which "suppresses man, perverts the flowing out of his love and creative instinct." Considering the impulse toward reform which lies behind these statements, it is no surprise that he finally rejects the pessimistic basis of tragedy, asserting that in tragedies alone "lies the belief—optimistic, if you will, in the perfectability of man."

Mr. Miller sometimes writes effective modern plays (not tragedies). And, although it is a little horrifying to contemplate an ideal society that sounds so much like a progressive school (where "personalities" are also supposed to "flower and realize" their "love and creative instincts"), there is no reason why social or political reform should not be one of the implicit or explicit functions of his drama. But to think this a function of tragedy is to contribute to that fund of confusion which presently prevents Americans not only from producing tragic works but from responding to them. This confusion is similar to that perpetuated by the newspapers, where the word "tragedy" generally refers to pathetic accidents which should have been avoided, and which may, through the publicity, be avoided in the future. The "tragic accidents" caused by plastic bags resulted in public clamor for new plastic research; similarly, through the emotional effect of *Death of a Salesman* on its audiences, attention may be paid to people like Willy Loman, as his wife at one point demands. On the other hand, we would hardly conclude, after watching the action of Oedipus, that he needs attention. Since his fate has been preordained, attention would be useless; and since he is a hero of great stature, something of an impertinence. In short, the tragic for us is an accident we seek to avoid because it makes our lives poorer; for the Greeks it is an inevitability they do not hesitate to confront because it ultimately gives dignity to life and enlarges the possibilities of man.

It is this essential difference that separates the Greeks from ourselves. Aeschylus, constructing monolithic religious dramas, Sophocles, exalting the man both blessed and cursed, and Euripides, warring on Greek polytheism and the savagery of excessive civilization, did not share a single tragic vision; but they are alike, in their best works, in their commitment to the tragic condition. If only for the memory that this commitment was once possible, we need Greek drama. If we are no longer capable of responding to Nietzsche's exhortation—"Dare to be tragic men, for ye shall be redeemed!"—we must never stop responding to those who once *did* dare. Though drunk with progress, we may still learn from the tragic hero's act of daring that the terror of life can never be ignored, or legislated out of existence, or softened with progressive education, psychiatric clinics, housing developments, socialized medicine, or universal suffrage. Not the best will in the world can alter it because it exists independently of good will, independently of man, of society, even of the heavenly gods. For this omnipresent terror is what the Greeks called *ananke*, necessity, and, in a general sense, it is a metaphor for death itself. It is a terror we all share, and, since it is something for which progress provides no panacea, our culture tries to suppress all thought of it through the mass hypnosis of the communications media. Yet, in the contemplation of the hero's struggle with necessity, in the tragic action itself, we, the passive spectators, can still achieve our greatest comfort—not the comfort of the drugged stupor, but that metaphysical consolation which comes from the aesthetic representation of a courageous confrontation of the terrible.

In that sense, Greek tragedy, which is never optimistic, and which betrays not a hint of belief in the "perfectability of man," is—despite its transcendent pessimism—ultimately a source of strength and endurance. No matter how gloomy its themes or hopeless its actions, it can transfigure the spectator with a feeling similar to joy. The prevailing motif in so much of this drama—a motif attributed by Nietzsche to Silenus, the satyr, and by scholarly commentators to Solon, the archon—is the futility of action in the face of death. Yet, the very expression of this theme carries with it a sense of the sublime:

> Though he has watched a decent age pass by
> A man will sometimes desire the world.
> I swear I see no wisdom in that man.
> The endless hours pile up in a drift of pain
> More unrelieved each day; and as for pleasure,
> When he is sunken in excessive age,
> You will not see his pleasure anywhere.
> The last attendant is the same for all,
> Old men and young alike, as in its season
> Man's heritage of underworld appears:

There being then no epithalamion,
No music and no dance. Death is the finish.

Not to be born beats all philosophy.
The second beat is to have seen the light
And then go back quickly whence we came.

Here given its fullest range in the third choral poem from *Oedipus at Colonus,* it is not a theme which encourages happiness, but there is happiness in the courage and beauty with which it is expressed, and it is a conclusion of which Freud would probably have approved. In its unflinching acceptance of the human condition, it is the kind of wisdom which comes out of a deeply conservative view of life.

And yet, if the final Greek wisdom is conservative, the action of Greek tragedy is, of necessity, radical and romantic, for wisdom without action is not drama but philosophy. The stoical wise man, with his ready-made view of life, is incapable of tragic action: Tiresias, seeing further, experiences less than Oedipus, just as Horatio and Kent, though more balanced, are smaller men than Hamlet and Lear. Since the tragic hero begins as a rebel, he is not one who accepts wisdom or moderation easily; it is, in fact, his immoderate revolt against wisdom that often constitutes the core of his action. We should remember that Prometheus (himself a great tragic hero and the archetypal rebel) gave man not only the intelligence with which to think about his life but *blind hopes.* Through the attempt to fulfill these impossible hopes, the tragic hero develops a vision deeper than that of his choral commentators—deeper and more piercing because it has been reached through frenzy and suffering. Daring to transcend philosophy, daring to outface necessity, the hero stretches the outer boundaries of his limitations to their uttermost, and, in the consequent rending and tearing, establishes new boundaries toward which men may strive. Greek tragedy, at the same time that it contains some of the most profound wisdom, is the noblest act of resistance in literature.

Today, however, in our flatulent times, when moderation is hailed as a way of life for young and old alike rather than a difficult conclusion reached through travail, our alternatives have become more circumscribed. We prefer wisdom without suffering, insight without agony, calm without frenzy—or we settle for self-conscious rebellion, institutionalized revolt, and pseudo-Dionysian orgies of sex and violence. Whether committed to Suburbia or Bohemia, our humanity is becoming a paltry thing, and we are now a simmering, uneasy people with only routine wisdom to sustain us. Yet, Greek tragedy remains an enduring memory of heroism, and one of the best defenses against our own lack of conviction is to keep that memory perpetually green.

1960

Who's Killing the Novel?

A recent special edition of *Book Week* suggests that the novel is dying and inadvertently plunges the knife in further. Two hundred "prominent authors, critics, and editors" were polled to discover what books of fiction out of 10,000 titles published in the last twenty years "were most artful, most truthful, most memorable," and which writers have "created the most substantial body of work during that period." The result of these apparently earnest inquiries is another version of that parlor game invented some years back by *Esquire*, picked up by the women's fashion magazines, perpetuated weekly in the *New York* magazine, and reintroduced each time some editor needs new copy—the ritual listing of the "ins" and the "outs." I suppose it is uncharitable to begrudge the public their celebrities, the intellectuals their diversions, and the editors their space filler, but one can finally have too much of a bad thing: the man who first conceived this hot center approach to culture should be sentenced to an eternity of literary cocktail parties. *Book Week*'s version of the culture charade is more restrained and dignified than most, but it demonstrates just as dramatically how much time and talent can be wasted in meaningless pursuits. And it demonstrates, too, how some of the very people who seem most concerned over the current health of fiction really have very little interest in literature at all.

Consider the paradox of this special issue. Inside the cover of the magazine, which features the faces of contemporary American novelists juxtaposed with photographs of presidents, senators, astronauts, and movie stars, one comes upon brief bios and evaluations of the twenty most frequently cited authors, along with a list of the twenty most frequently cited books. The whole enterprise promises some glowing testimony to the robust condition of fiction; yet, most of the critics discussing their choices are upset by the declining state of the novel and the absence of many novelists of great stature. Among the reasons offered for this dearth are the Cold War, the Bomb, pornography, and the absence of style, but the explanation suggested most frequently is that the more important work is being done in nonfiction. This last argument, as a matter of fact, is picked up by Norman Podhoretz and made the occasion for a long essay called "Bringing the News." There he tries to prove, through a series of etymological contortions, that since the "primary role" of the novel in its original meaning was that of "bringing the news," and since the primary function of the novelist, therefore, is that of "news carrier," few creative writers are working as well today in their fiction as in their essays and reportage. Mr. Podhoretz asks himself: "Is it possible that some other literary form is taking over the job that the novel used to do?"

If one accepts Mr. Podhoretz's premise, then his question is rhetorical—as a medium for "sheer information," fiction cannot possibly compete with nonfiction, and the novelist must yield to the journalist, the sociologist, the psychoanalyst. But the premise is ridiculous. Who can accept a definition of the novel which ignores the elements of storytelling, character development, narrative flow, imagination, dialogue, pleasurable form? Why should we be asked to measure literature by the values of entirely different disciplines? I do not wish to be unfair to Mr. Podhoretz's argument. By "news," of course, he means a good deal more than topical happenings, and there is certainly truth in the assumption that *some* of the novel's functions have been pre-empted by the social sciences. But the writers Mr. Podhoretz admires have not tried their hands at sociology or psychology; they have, rather, been working in a mode of popular journalism; and it is the *novelist as journalist* that he would have us embrace and encourage. This I simply cannot accept. Even in its vaguest meaning, Mr. Podhoretz's definition embodies a secret hostility toward the essence of fiction, an open competitiveness with the artist, and a fallacious assumption that the chief value of literature is to be found in its discursive ideas.

Mr. Podhoretz has been developing this position for a long while now, though he has hitherto been more tentative about it. In the introduction to his recent collection of essays, for example, he confessed that fiction was important to him primarily because it raised "important issues," and that "it was the issues rather than the book itself that I really cared about." At the time, Mr. Podhoretz suspected that his admission was damaging. As a matter of fact, it immediately disqualified him as a critic of literature (though not as a social critic, a role in which he has done valuable work). For while nobody would deny the importance of literary ideas, it is absurd to argue for the predominance of ideas over all other literary values, for who would look to literature for issues that could be much more clearly formulated in rational discourse? Mr. Podhoretz naturally became disappointed in novels, as anyone would be upon eating lamb chops and thinking they were eggs.

The confusion seems willed, for, after all, Mr. Podhoretz is an intelligent man. Behind it, one can detect an effort to capture for the journalist some of the novelist's prestige. Many of Mr. Podhoretz's essays, in fact, express his annoyance at the notion that "novel-writing is the only 'real' writing there is," and, as far back as 1958, in a piece called "The Article as Art," he was already pleading that magazine articles should be considered just as imaginative and aesthetically pleasing as works of fiction. I suppose I should be grateful to Mr. Podhoretz for in-

251 / Who's Killing the Novel?

flating a form I use into an art form, but I can't help
noting that *he* uses it too; and it begins to look like special
pleading when, after belaboring contemporary novelists
for falling below the standards of their form, he goes on
to adulate a number of contemporary essayists, most of
whom could not hold a candle to Hazlitt, DeQuincey,
Lamb, or Arnold. One's worst suspicions are confirmed in
another recent Podhoretz article called "In Defense of
Editing." There the author bears witness to the importance of editors, announcing, with a perfectly straight
face, that "the editorial process is a necessity if standards
are to be preserved and if the intellectual life in America
is not to become wholly compartmentalized and ultimately sterile in spirit" (Mr. Podhoretz is chief editor of
Commentary). There is something poignant about this
writer's effort to elevate whatever profession he happens
to be pursuing at the moment, but there is something
solipsistic about it too. I am certain that if Mr. Podhoretz ever went into the plumbing business, we would
soon have an essay on how the toilet bowl is replacing
the book.

I concentrate on Mr. Podhoretz for two reasons: his
ideas are shared by a surprising number of like-minded
critics, and they can ultimately prove injurious to literary
art. His conclusion that novelists "are able to move
around so much more freely, intelligently, imaginatively,
creatively when they are not called upon to tell what they
know through the medium of an invented story" shows
his own prejudice against the inventive faculty or fancy;
but more than that, it is a siren song to writers, an invitation to concentrate on journalism. The majority of
fiction writers will undoubtedly remain deaf to the implications of such statements and continue with their
creative work. But there are also those who will be
tempted to channel off a considerable part of their
energies into essays, speeches, reviews, memoirs, and
reportage. I do not mean to suggest that such work has

no value for the novelist. Creative writers have always been attracted to discursive prose forms, and have written very distinguished nonfiction (though some—Saul Bellow, for example—seem to flounder when they work outside the novel). Even the best of these essay-writing novelists, however, have treated this work as secondary, a pause in the midst of creative labors.

If critics continue to condescend to the novel as a form, writers may begin to take the easier path. The great seductive lure of journalism lies in its directness, heat, and communicability. The journalist is not required to subordinate his own personality to that of imaginary characters, nor does he often have to plod for years on exhausting projects: journalism is the medium of immediate gratification. It is the speediest method of getting an idea into print, and—in a country which worships the literary personality but cannot be bothered to read books —it is also becoming the speediest road to fame and fortune. As a result, journalism is fast developing into a mode of performance—an actor's medium rather than a writer's. One thinks of Tom Wolfe, and, even more, of Norman Mailer, who, in ten years, has written only one novel (a potboiler composed in journalistic fashion, as a serial), but who has achieved celebrity status primarily on the basis of his reportage. There are those who admire this reportage a good deal more than I do,* but even his admirers will usually concede that it is largely a gesture of self-promotion. When Mailer writes off open letters to Castro and Kennedy, when he measures his muscles against those of other contemporary writers, or when he confides to Sonny Liston after his championship fight

* My own admiration for Mailer's journalism, as a matter of fact, has increased since these lines were written, as a result of his work in *The Armies of the Night* and his reportage of the 1968 conventions. In those works, his role playing, while still conspicuous, was at least occasionally exposed to ironic scrutiny by the author. My admiration for Mailer's fiction, however, has suffered a corresponding decrease, and it may be that he is essentially a journalist, after all.

how Liston can increase the gate of the rematch, we know we are in the presence of a star personality rather than a serious writer—a celebrity who uses prose for the purpose of acting out roles.

Yet, inevitably, Mailer's depressing development—his theatrical strutting and fretting—is described by Podhoretz as an "exemplary career." And why? Because it is "devoted to what I take to be the primary question of American life: whether the pursuit of success need cripple a man spiritually, whether a man can work his way through the corruptions inherent in that pursuit without falling into the equally disabling corruptions inherent in the stance of hypocritical highmindedness." One is grateful to learn what the "primary question of American life" is, and to be told the two possible attitudes one can hold toward it. But there are those who will persist in the delusion that American life offers other alternatives than these, and other primary questions—as, for example, how the artist can do serious work in a culture which is continually exhorting him to do everything but produce art. Actually, Mr. Podhoretz's concern with the "pursuit of success" has nothing whatever to do with the writing of fiction; it is simply a self-conscious idea about the writer's *role*.

Podhoretz describes Mailer as "one of the most powerful and subtle minds I have ever encountered." Yet, the "primary question" they both ask can be answered by any college sophomore. By now, we have had—besides Mailer's—enough "exemplary careers" to prove that gifted men in America are inevitably wasted by the "pursuit of success": F. Scott Fitzgerald is only the most obvious example. But it is essential to remember that even Fitzgerald's pursuit of success would be of little interest today had he not left behind him an important body of work to stimulate interest in his life. Without this literature, we are left with nothing but role playing, and to pretend that this role playing has intrinsic value in itself is merely a form of hypocritical *low*mindedness. But, in the end, is Podhoretz prescribing for the writer anything more than a role, a stance, a posture? What is he finally telling us but that American writers who are animated by the culture boom and their own appetites for notoriety can reach their goals more quickly through journalistic activity? Where does his advice lead us but precisely to those same degraded values of success that used to be excoriated in American politicians and businessmen?

1965

Criticism as an Arm of Show Business

Of all the superfluous nonbooks being published this winter for the Christmas luxury trade, there is none more demoralizingly significant than a monster volume called *Nothing Personal*. Manufactured in Switzerland by a special process, boxed and unpaginated, set between snow-white covers with sterling silver titles, and measuring eleven by fourteen inches in size, this tome consists of enormous photographs by Richard Avedon and alternating commentary by James Baldwin, the text set in huge type with about an inch of space between each of the lines. I stress the physical makeup of the book because it reveals the book's ambitions: no expense has been spared to induce an awe-inspiring effect. One is obviously supposed to handle such a volume with unspeakable reverence, similar to that humility of spirit with which Charlton Heston held Cecil B. DeMille's papier-mâché Commandments upon descending from his Hollywood Mount Sinai. But for all the money that went into both productions, the revelations of both are equally synthetic. *Nothing Personal* pretends to be a ruthless indictment of contemporary America, but the only readers likely to buy this extravagant volume are the female subscribers to the fashion magazines, while the moralistic authors of the work are themselves pretty fashionable, affluent, and chic.

Such show biz moralists have for some time now been a fixture of our cultural life, ever since it became apparent that Americans were eager to reward certain critics who abused them (the reception of Baldwin's *The Fire Next Time,* not to mention its publication in the *New Yorker,* did a lot to make this apparent). Vance Packard's muckraking bestsellers, television's *That Was the Week That Was,* Paddy Chayefsky's *The Americanization of Emily* (to name a few such commodities of pop criticism) are all attempts to capitalize commercially on an increasingly self-critical national atmosphere, where even Barry Goldwater can run a campaign complaining about the weakness in the American moral fiber. Now comes Richard Avedon, high-fashion photographer for *Vogue* and *Harper's Bazaar,* to join these other outraged exploiters, giving the suburban clubwoman a titillating peek into the obscene and ugly faces of the mad, the dispossessed, and the great and near-great—with James Baldwin interrupting from time to time, like a punchy and pugnacious drunk awakening from a boozy doze during a stag movie, to introduce his garrulous, irrelevant, and by now predictable comments on how to live, how to love, and how to build Jerusalem.

The book, however, is mainly Avedon's, and the really curious thing is why a photographer who spends much of his career flattering celebrities with soft lights and hazy filters should also wish to transform these same subjects into repulsive knaves, fools, and lunatics. This has been done with a rush of fury and spite that belies the book's title. Except for a few sanctified figures like Norman Thomas and John L. Lewis, who, along with most of the Negro subjects in the book, enjoy a relative normality, everyone present is seen with a hideously jaundiced eye. Perle Mesta, for example, photographed from the chin up, has acquired a wagging dewlap of a proportion equaled only by the male orangoutang at the Bronx Zoo, while Dorothy Parker—though no Aphrodite to be sure—has been provided with the decaying look of a fresh corpse, her face paralyzed, her teeth rotting, her eyes bagged like diseased pouches. Bertrand Russell and Linus Pauling both enjoy the luxury of two-page spreads, Russell looking like Cro-Magnon man—with his chin and nose jutting, and a hearing aid curling out of his ear like a worm—and Pauling like a lifetime inmate at Bellevue, his mad eyes gleefully lit up as if by an explosion of the hydrogen bomb. Even Marilyn Monroe, a perennial Avedon favorite, appears before us in an obviously unguarded moment, slack and listless, stupefied by drugs, drink, or merely life itself.

Along with these appetizing glimpses into people people are talking about, Avedon has supplied a few pictorial contrasts and comparisons, apparently to give his revenge some thematic purpose and structural unity. A group portrait of George Lincoln Rockwell being given the Nazi salute by four uniformed thugs is juxtaposed with a very naked and very hairy Allen Ginsberg offering a Hindu blessing, his other hand forming a shelf above what should be his genitals. A terribly old ex-slave, with watery eyes and elongated suffering features, is cheek by jowl with Ambassador Adlai Stevenson, pursing his lips like a prissy old queen. Cheryl Crane, her face a total vacancy, peers out at us beside Martin Luther King's

beautiful and purposeful young son, whom she unaccountably resembles. And Harold Arlen and Arthur Miller
share facing pages, both looking equally worried about
the human race, and equally incapable, for sheer fatigue,
of doing a thing to help it.

Although the best photograph in the book—a double
spread of the DAR ladies in ceremonial dress—is taken
absolutely straight, very few of Avedon's subjects are
freed from his satiric comment, which he insinuates by
means of lens distortion, foreshortening, and brutal close-
ups under hot lights that expose every black root in a
freshly shaved face. Putting aside the question of whether
it is exactly ethical to employ a portrait camera in this
manner, we are still left with the unhappy fact that
Avedon's editorializing generally falsifies rather than reveals reality. Consider his treatment of famous political
and religious leaders. By making Billy Graham, for example, into a used-car salesman in an early stage of
paresis, or by transforming George Wallace into a smug
Napoleonic egotist, or by giving Eisenhower the dazed
stare of one who has been wholly lobotomized, Avedon
actually obscures the problem of American leadership,
for he suggests that high-level stupidity or malice wears
no mask, when it is the very surface attractiveness of our
politicians, demagogues, and adventurers that most en-
dangers the body politic. Worse than this, Avedon is not
above staging a picture in order to make his comment.
He thus presents Claude Eatherly—identified as the
"pilot at Hiroshima, August 6, 1945"—holding his hand
across his anguished brow in the throes of agenbite of
inwit, even though Eatherly's claim to his well-publicized
conscience has for some time now been exposed as
phony.

Still, it is characteristic of show biz moralists to care
less for truth than for sensation, just as it is characteristic
of them to hedge their fraudulent protests with equally

fraudulent affirmations. True to this spirit, Avedon concludes his book on a note of tremulous uplift. Immediately after harrowing his readers with the nightmare faces of those condemned to mental institutions, he tranquilizes them again with scenes of Love and Brotherhood, returning to that grainy texture he employs to give the skin a Helena Rubenstein glow. Avedon apparently associates happiness with sun and surf, for it is on the beach that his string section begins to swell, mounting through pictures of a smiling young man patting his wife's pregnant belly, a Negro child and a white young woman holding each other close, and a father balancing his infant son aloft. At last (and here an angelic chorus joins the fiddles), Avedon closes the book with a large sharp photograph of the Atlanta Chapter of SNCC—clean-cut, wrinkleless, determined men, women, and children looking forward into some bright future, presumably when other Americans will no longer expose such nauseating dewlaps, shriveled lips, furrowed brows, carrion flesh, bad teeth, pockmarks, pores, double chins, pimples, or any similar evidence of a malevolent, deteriorating spirit.

The quality of mind revealed in these photographs is, I am afraid, matched by the quality of mind revealed in the text; and this constitutes one of the few unifying links between the pictures and the prose. Like Richard Avedon's, James Baldwin's rage is here inspired largely by the occasion, but while the photographer is taking advantage of the times, the writer is letting the times take advantage of him. Once direct and biting in his criticism of American life, Mr. Baldwin has repeated his revolt so often that it has now become a reflex mannerism that curls his fingers around his pen and squeezes out empty rhetoric. In *Nothing Personal*, certainly, Baldwin has either adapted his ideas to the intellectual chic of the women's magazines, or he is putting his readers on.

How else is one to explain such Norman Vincent Peal-
isms as "I have always felt a human being could only be
saved by another human being"—and "One must say
Yes to life and embrace it wherever it is found"—and,
again, "All that God can do, and all that I expect Him
to do, is lend one courage to continue one's journey
and face one's end, like a man"?

These are some of Baldwin's concluding affirmations,
designed to harmonize with Avedon's surf symphony. To
accompany Avedon's rogues' gallery, Baldwin supplies
vestpocket indictments of TV, advertising, architecture,
psychoanalysis, and the New York police force. But
Baldwin's attacks are significant less for their familiar
content than for the conditioned response they are expected to provoke in the reader—and, especially, for the
format in which they appear. By lending himself to such
an enterprise, Baldwin reveals that he is now part and
parcel of the .very things he is criticizing; and this
curious assimilation accounts in part for something in
his writing first noticed by Marcus Klein—his ambiguous
use of the word *we*. Constantly shifting between objective
nouns and first-person-plural pronouns ("talking to
Americans is usually extremely uphill work. We are
afraid to reveal ourselves because we trust ourselves
so little") or between the generic and the personal ("our
opulence is so pervasive that people who are afraid to
lose whatever they think they have persuade themselves
of the truth of a lie . . ."), Baldwin exposes a highly
uncertain critical identity, never sure whether he is talking for himself, for Negroes, for Americans, or for the
whole human race.

This uncertainty leads him not only into contorted
grammar but also into incredible self-inflation. My
favorite Baldwinism—and a typical one, though it comes
from another context—is this: "If you pretend that I
hauled all that cotton for you just because I love you,

you're mad." When the messianic fit is upon him, Baldwin frequently develops a bass-baritone voice and starts singing "Let My People Go," confusing himself with the whole of Negro history. By the same token, he is presumptuous enough to generalize wildly about the American young ("we have no respect for children"), even though he himself is childless, and to deny the existence of any happy marriages, though he has never been married. The author of *Notes of a Native Son* was a highly aware and complicated individual; the author of *Nothing Personal*, and many of his recent writings, is merely a self-constituted Symbol bucking hard for the rank of Legend. Baldwin's advancement, however, may be a long time in coming, because as a salvation peddler, he has nothing to offer but opiates. "God help that innocent here," he writes, "that man or woman who simply wants to love, and be loved." God help him indeed, if such an "innocent" really exists, and that is all he "simply" wants to do. But Baldwin pretends to be that innocent, reducing all our complexity to this one simpleminded notion, making Love the single remedy for all the spite, hatred, and ugliness he sees around him: "For, perhaps—perhaps—between now and that day, something wonderful will happen, a miracle of coherence and release . . . It is the miracle of love, love strong enough to guide or drive one into the great estate of maturity . . ." This sounds like Ibsen's Nora walking out on Torvald, but it is a Nora who has read nothing but the *Ladies' Home Journal*, seen nothing but Inge and Chayefsky plays, learned nothing but the routine wisdom supplied by Dr. Franzblau. And with the invocation of those tired words—love, miracle, release, maturity— and a few more lines of self-hypnosis, James Baldwin's slippery prose skates along this glossy paper to an end.

Nothing Personal shows us an honorable tradition of revolt gone sour, turned into a theatrical gesture by cafe-society performers. The participation of Richard

Avedon in this charade is not of very great moment, since Avedon's photography—whether he is blandishing or subverting his models—still remains an arm of show business. But the participation of James Baldwin signifies the further degeneration of a once courageous and beautiful dissent. Whether this is temporary, one cannot say. Let us fervently hope it is. But meanwhile it is serious enough to merit our deepest apprehension and regret.

1964

Boris and the
Second Avenue Muse:
A Memoir

When Boris called me in the summer of 1952, it had
been a full three years since I had last heard from him;
yet he launched into his proposition with only the most
peremptory greeting. "How would you like to play General MacArthur?" "Play who?" "General MacArthur! It's
a fat role, I promise you, and you're perfect for it."
"What have you got going now," I asked, "a war play?"
"A Jolson play," he answered. "But the general is a very
important character." "I think you should know that
MacArthur is not one of my favorite people," I replied.
"Who wants you to love him?" asked Boris with exaspera-
tion. "I only want you to play him." "Is this for money?"
"Certainly. You get paid by the performance plus four
days' rehearsal pay. We rehearse beginning of the week
and do the show on the weekend: once Friday, and three
a day Saturday and Sunday—seven times in all." "I see,
I see," I said, trying to combat my temptation to accept,
"so you're working Off Broadway now." "Hell, no. Second
Avenue," replied Boris, triumphantly. "You're talking to
the new sweetheart of the Yiddish theatre." "Yiddish
theatre," I repeated, in a panic, "since when am I supposed to speak Yiddish?" "You're going to speak English,"
said Boris impatiently. "Who ever heard of a Yiddish
General MacArthur? Don't worry, you'll be a sensation.
On Second Avenue they love well-bred Jewish boys who
speak good English. Anyway," he added, "I'm the only
one has to be bilingual. We got pros for the Yiddish parts

and for the English roles I'm lining up all my goyishe
friends—like you."

This was altogether typical of the shafts Boris used
to aim in my direction when we were students together
at the Yale Drama School. What Boris was doing at Yale
I have never been able to determine, but it was clear that
the place baffled him and that third-generation Jews like
myself baffled him even more. To me, on the other hand,
it was he that always seemed the outlander. A thickly
set tatterdemalion with Slavic features, drowsy lids,
corpulent lips, and an enormous number of teeth, he
had been born in Russia and emigrated to Detroit as a
child. He was a bit older than the rest of us, having
matured in Depression America, and the Depression still
clung to him even when we first met in 1948. Boris was
devoted to talk, speaking English, Yiddish, and Russian
with equal volubility, and I suspect he originally turned
to the theatre to indulge his compulsive oratorical strain.
Anyway, he'd had some success before coming to Yale,
having toured with Maurice Schwartz and played bits
with the Group Theatre.

My relation to Boris at that time was rather equivocal.
He had enormous charisma, but I was fresh from Am-
herst, valued detachment, and often found Boris too
truculent and engaged. We shared a certain contempt
for the mushy pabulum ground out by the student playwrights at Yale, but my own stage heroes were from the
Old Vic Company, and my style of acting was better
suited to the classics of dramatic literature than to the
realistic plays that Boris favored. Nevertheless, I soon
found myself drafted into the Odets group, a coterie that
Boris had formed in opposition to prevailing Yale
methods. Admission was simple, all you needed were
three qualifications: a respect for the reforms of the defunct Group Theatre, an infinite capacity for argument,
and a willingness to lend money to Boris. The loans were

most crucial. Debt was Boris's natural condition, his connection with the social world. By the time the year was over I had socialized with him to the limit of my bank account.

When I met him on Houston Street a few days after his call, I noticed that he had grown more prosperous looking, but he was still stone-broke. He had recruited most of the Odets group for this venture and was hauling them into a cafe one by one, ostensibly for individual instructions but actually to touch each individual for something to eat. When my turn came, he explained that he had decided to give the part of MacArthur to another actor. "Since you say you don't like him, I got you a better part. You'll be playing Jolson's announcer and arranger. It's a part with a lot of character, you'll love it." He ordered a second glass of tea (at my expense) and went into detail.

"You see, since Jolson's just died, Finegold's decided to exploit his popularity with the Yiddish audiences. Finegold's the manager of the theatre. He's so crazy about the idea that he stayed up one night and tossed off the script himself. Frankly, it stinks. But it will only run a half hour between the other acts." "What kind of theatre does this Finegold run?" I asked. "Difficult to describe now," said Boris. "But it's had a distinguished history. A long time ago it was a burlesque house. Then it did legitimate shows. Then it turned vaudeville. And now that the Yiddish audience is disappearing it's slowly going over to films. I guess you could say the house is in transition. In a typical program, Finegold gives the customers three movies and eight vaudeville acts—the Jolson bit will be an extra added attraction. It's a long program all right. In a theatre like this, you don't attend a show, you enlist in it." "You're playing Jolson?" "Naturally." "And MacArthur? How does he work into the story?" "Another stroke of Finegold's," answered Boris. "Mac-

Arthur's a great hero on Second Avenue and Finegold suddenly remembered that the general had met Jolson once when he was entertaining the troops in Korea. He'd really like to work Roosevelt into it, too, but he figures he can't be too cavalier with history." I squirmed in my chair. "Now look," said Boris uneasily, "don't give me a hard time about the script. Just play your part with conviction and you'll be surprised—the audience will eat it up. C'mon now, I'll show you around, and then I'll introduce you to Finegold." Boris scrambled out of his chair, pocketing fifteen cents of the twenty-cent tip I left on the table.

Before entering the theatre, Boris called my attention to a large blowup of his face, spread from ear to ear in a huge smile. Underneath the picture, printed in block letters on the plasterboard, were his name and the appelation *Wunderkind.* "A wonder child in the Yiddish theatre," explained Boris, who was still bitter about his perennial failure to get into the Yiddish Actors Union, "is anyone under forty-five years of age." He was very vain about his billing, but once we got inside the empty theatre he lost some of his cockiness. The house dwarfed him. From the balcony we gazed down on an estate of 2,000 seats and a stage the size of the Music Hall. You could understand how much the declamatory style of Yiddish acting owed to these enormous theatres. "Twenty years ago," said Boris impressively, his voice hollow and reverent in the empty house, "Boris Thomashefsky was the idol of this stage. And when he died, they laid him out on the apron and charged admission to see the corpse. They say there were lines, three deep, right up to Fourteenth Street."

We padded down the carpeted steps from the balcony. "I'll get the others together and we'll meet Finegold," Boris said. "I ask only one thing—restrain yourself when you see the script. Finegold has had a few successes in the legitimate theatre and he's very sensitive about his writing. If you want to help me keep my job, don't hurt his feelings."

To confirm Boris's characterization of him, Finegold—a diminutive man with a pinched face, an autocratic manner, and a bad case of the sniffles—opened up the meeting with a long discussion of his career. In an oratorical voice, he affirmed that he was a misunderstood artist whose literary powers were drying up in this vulgar vaudeville atmosphere, and that only in masterworks like *The Jolson Story* (which, not unexpectedly, turned out to be the title of the skit) were his talents fully expressed. Handing around the scripts with extreme solemnity, he warned us not to deviate from the text, but rather to enrich its meanings with our most powerful performances. With Boris nodding in mock-serious agreement, we proceeded to the first reading.

The role of MacArthur had been assumed by a stiff, slightly pompous actor named Harry Steinbeck, one of the two Gentiles in the cast. The other was Rose Gregorio, a tiny but fierce Italian girl with beautiful skin and night-black hair. Rose had been cast in a nonspeaking Jewish role: she was to carry an Israeli flag across the stage, crossing it with an American flag carried by another actor while Jolson sang "Hatikvah"—a tableau effect of the kind that Finegold often used.

Finegold had decided to improve on the Jolson movies. We too were going to use a Jolson sound track (we had his voice on records), but our Larry Parks was to be a split personality: Boris playing Jolson the dramatic character, and an impersonator named Sammy imitating Jolson singing in blackface. As Jolson's announcer, I was expected to do a Smith and Dale routine with Jolson's manager, played by a laconic designer from Yale named Al Hurwitz. Our problem, with Finegold impatiently vetoing all suggestions for substitutions, was to make something funny out of the most ancient wheezes in the business.

Boris, who was giving us secret instructions about how to play to a Yiddish audience, tried to help us here, but he encountered a lot of resistance from me. He had hired me despite my skepticism and despite my lack of training in his kind of theatre because I was a Jew— he thought he could burrow his way back to this essential fact. He had to cut through my standard stage diction, my trilled *r*'s, my classical stances, and my critical detachment to the actor he hoped was underneath. "Play it true!" he would scream at me in rehearsals. "Stop commenting on your role. You're crucifying me with your ironic readings. Don't you know I have a reputation to uphold?"

He tried to get results the way he borrowed money, by holding me personally responsible for the advancement of his career. When this didn't work, he started to lecture me on "truth in the theatre" and how this depended less on Finegold's lines than on my honest portrayal of character. This idea, which he had inherited from the Group Theatre, was blasphemy to me, an open invitation for the playwright to write badly. He countered that I was overeducated. I replied that he had an affection for clumsy plays. He spoke about visceral emotion. I talked about ideas. It was a debate that continued past the rehearsal hours, an argument that went on late into the night.

During the rehearsal period, we got to see a lot of Yiddish vaudeville, most of which was heavily influenced by TV variety shows. But one exceptional artist appeared on the program—an old-timer named Aaron Lebedoff, in whose work there was substantial evidence that Yiddish vaudeville had once had its own special style and genius. His record "Rumania, Rumania" was a great favorite in the Yiddish community; and when he sang the song in the theatre, you could tell that he had been an important influence on Danny Kaye. He was aging then, but his mighty talent was still intact. With his face absolutely impassive, except for his expressive eyebrows, he wrapped his voice around his listeners and almost literally squeezed a response out of them. He put all his dissatisfaction with life and experience into his singing, and the audience went with him all the way. He sobbed with the song and they sobbed with him—oh, how they loved to cry. And when, after innumerable encores, he finally bore his shaking figure off the stage, he snapped out of the mood immediately—like Garrick winking at a lady in a box after a supremely tragic moment—and aimed a good-hearted goose at Rose Gregorio, watching admiringly from the wings.

On the day of our first performance, we sat through the three movies as well, to which the audience paid no attention at all. Local conversations were bursting out all over the house. Almost everyone had a basket of food on his lap and, though it was barely 3 P.M., some were already eating. A woman to my left had put her feet over the seat in front of her and gone off to sleep; a man behind me was calling in loud stage whispers to someone he recognized in front. I felt my usual opening-night jitters enlarging into a full-scale panic.

For, with the exception of the Jolson records, none of our show was amplified, and, considering all the noise in the audience, I hadn't the vaguest idea of how we were going to be heard. As it was, the theatre was so large that every line had to be shouted. No modern actor likes to look into the house any more than necessary; yet we had no choice but to stare the audience down on every speech. The technique was to start off a line, directing it at the character we were addressing—"Hymie!"—then to swivel around, front the audience, and bellow the rest toward the gallery: "THIS IS WHAT I WANT TO TELL YOU!" Direct address, we were told, was a convention the audience willingly accepted, but it played havoc with our notions of the fourth wall.

Backstage, Boris explained the audience and what seemed to us its rather bizarre behavior. "These spectators are the most demanding you'll ever face. They come in for half price—it's Friday and they have to see the entire show before sundown. All that eating is going to continue right through your performance. Don't worry about it, it's traditional. This bunch has been coming here regularly for years. They're very skeptical, but at the same time they're easily moved. Nothing is really going to upset them except a phony performance. Don't worry about the script; they're not here to judge literary values. If the situation is one they can recognize, they'll buy it. What they like best though is powerful acting. So play it true, project a lot of warmth, and, if you can manage it, give them a good cry."

Not very heartened, I went up to my "dressing room," which was really the men's john, hastily converted to accommodate some of the extra cast. I sat next to Sammy, the Jolson impersonator, and watched him apply the complex facial paraphernalia of the black-faced minstrel man. Under the cork, his eyes and teeth became very white, and, making mouths in the mirror, he suddenly erupted into one of these extended sheep noises which are the stock in trade of everyone who imitates Jolson, waving his white-gloved hands beside his face. Well, he had a character, but Finegold had neglected to write a character for me, so I decided to play myself with whatever conviction I could muster, and I made up my face accordingly.

A few minutes later, we all took our places behind the curtain. The technicians were still setting the lights. We had never had a dress rehearsal and had never worked with props; but considering the improvisational nature of the whole affair, I guess we were lucky even to have written lines. During the hiatus, Finegold was making a speech out front and even getting a few laughs. When this was over, the house lights went down, the curtain rose, and we found ourselves staring into a couple of thousand expectant faces.

The opening scene was located "somewhere in Korea," the Korean atmosphere signified by a paper moon, a cut-out palm tree, General MacArthur, and a few extras in khaki shirts. Center stage was Sammy in blackface, gesticulating wildly into a dead microphone in synchronization with a record of Jolson singing "Sewanee." The song over, Sammy bowed and exited, and Finegold cut in with the applause record. This was my cue. Leaping from my seat, I grabbed the dummy microphone and waved for silence from the audience. The applause record died suddenly—Finegold was very heavy with the sound effects. At the top of my lungs I proceeded with a short harangue about how great Al feels to be out here in Korea, entertaining the troops and doing his duty as an American—and in tribute to the exuberance of the reception, he was going to sing another song. The applause was again put on the turntable, after which Sammy gestured through "Sonny Boy," a record which had an unfortunate tic from the rim to the label. As the music jumped a couple of bars with each revolution of the disc, Sammy's eyes grew desperate, and I found myself getting more and more nervous.

After the song, Sammy made an overhurried dash for the wings while I announced that Jolson was now going to honor the audience with a speech. This was the cue for Boris's entrance. He emerged from the wings where Sammy had exited, wiping his face with a towel as if he were just removing the last trace of cork. He grabbed the mike with an assurance that I envied, showed his teeth to the audience in a broad smile, and began lecturing the spectators as if they were Korean soldiers.

"General MacArthur and fellows. I just want to take a few minutes to tell you what a great and wonderful honor it is for me to be here among you wonderful fellows who are every day shedding your blood for democracy. At times like this, I feel proud—proud to be an American Jew. Like you fellows here, I am ready to give every drop of my Jewish blood to help win this war. I was just talking with your general here, and that talk brought back memories to me which have gone deep in my heart. I mean the days when I was a poor Jew living in the Bronx." (Finegold, who prided himself on being a shrewd psychologist of Yiddish audiences, was certain that the success of his script was largely dependent on the number of times it mentioned the word "Jew.") "That talk," Boris continued, "brought back memories of my Jewish Mama and Papa and how they wanted, with all their hearts, I should become a *chazan* in the synagogue. I remember those poor dead parents of mine, may their souls rest in peace, like it was yesterday. And I remember the fights we used to have over me becoming a jazz singer. Yes, I remember them well . . ."

The lights, which had begun to fade during Boris's speech, now blacked out completely, and we groped our way offstage in darkness while the set was changed. After having seen a few of his own movies, Finegold had discovered the flashback technique, and he was now introducing it into the Yiddish theatre with experimental fervor. The lights came up on what was supposed to be Jolson's home in the Bronx, forty or fifty years before the Korean action. Finegold gave us a rest here and brought in the Yiddish-speaking professionals; and, at last, the audience began to show signs of consciousness.

There were three people on stage: Mama, Papa, and a comic named Yankele who was supposed to be an uncle (I later learned there is always a character named Yankele who is supposed to be an uncle—he is a stock figure like Sganerelle and Harlequin). Papa and Yankele began ad-libbing gags which, so far as I could tell, were irrelevant to the plot, but which drew explosive laughs from the audience. When they felt the audience slacken, their conversation turned to Asa. He was giving his father great *tsores* with his *meshuggeneh* notions about being a *teaterzinger*. Mama defended Asa, but Papa indignantly told her to shut up and mind her own business. His face reddening, Papa proclaimed that if this *geschmatter yid* ever showed his face in the house again he would throw him straight into the garbage. Enter Boris, with his shirt sleeves rolled up (a touch intended to make him look forty years younger).

Mama, with a bone-crushing hug, indicated that she at least still loved him in spite of his renegade profession. But when he held out his hand to Papa, it was vigorously slapped down. A short duet followed between Boris and Papa: Boris pleading, meek and respectful; Papa autocratic and unyielding.

Throughout the latter part of this scene, I had become aware of another voice on stage, gabbling through the actors' speeches, which was growing in volume and vigor as the scene progressed. But it took me a little time to discover its source. It was coming from the prompter, a dome-headed little man in an open shirt, who was sitting serenely in his cubicle declaiming every line of the script with histrionic flourishes of his arms as if he were the only person on stage. When Boris, after a tearful exit, came into the wings, I pressed him urgently for an explanation.

"Don't worry about him," he said, wiping away his sweat and powdering his makeup. "He's your insurance policy. He reads the script aloud at the same pace you do, and if you ever blow a line, you pick it up from him as you go along." "Look, wonder boy," I growled, with some rancor, "I'm having enough trouble with these lines. I'll be sure to dry up altogether if he doesn't keep quiet." "Please, don't give me a hard time," answered Boris. "He doesn't prompt in English. Anyway," he added impatiently, "you should learn how to adjust to the conditions you work in. What kind of actor are you?"

Digesting his rebuke, I turned my attention back to the stage. Mama, Papa, and the prompter were having a debate: Mama conciliatory, Papa adamant, the prompter alternately conciliatory and adamant. Papa and the prompter absolutely refused to have any *teaterzingers* in the house and that was their last word. Mama and the prompter wanted Papa to stop being stiff-necked and give Asa one more chance. Boris made another entrance to pick up his luggage, and Mama again planted a kiss on his mouth. At Mama's secret signal, Boris held out his hand once more to Papa, who once more refused it, though with somewhat less conviction. Boris walked sadly and melodramatically to the door, opened it, and gave one last tearful look at Papa. Suddenly, Papa threw out his arms and let out a heart-rending cry: "Asa!" With two tons of water cascading from his voice, Boris yelped, "Papa!" and the two rushed center stage to embrace. While they groped each other like two wrestling bears, the audience let out an audible gasp of approval, and the prompter wiped his brow. Reconciliation between father and son. Blackout.

During the set change, Finegold's tableau of Israeli and American flags passed irrelevantly in front of the curtain, the audience applauding right through Jolson's rendering of "Hatikvah."

The next scene was a flash forward to New York, forty years later, right after the Korean expedition. It was a moment that Al Hurwitz and I had been dreading for four days, for the two of us were alone on stage with Finegold's jokes. "Hymie, I could use a drink," I said, brightly and loudly. "Yeah," answered Al, "was there ever a time when you couldn't use a drink?" "Sure," I answered, shrinking inwardly, "when I'm asleep." Silence from the house. We picked up on it again. "Let's play some rummy," said Al. "You're always playing rummy," said I. "Yeah? Well, better to play rummy than be a rummy," said Al. The audience let that one ride too. After a few more side splitters of this type, we turned back, with relief, to the plot and discussed Jolson's failing health. We both agreed that he looked exceedingly pale and ought to get a checkup.

"You know, Hymie," I offered, to emphasize my concern, "every time I look at Al, I shiver in the *kishkes.*" There was a lone hoot from somewhere in the fourth row.

Boris entered and we both told him he ought to visit a doctor. "No, boys," he answered bravely, "you wouldn't want me to let down those Jewish boys over there in Korea or those Jewish folks at home who are expecting me to give everything I got for the war effort?" He did admit, however, that he wasn't feeling too good, and a blackout prepared us for Boris's big scene.

He was seated in a chair, full front, with his collar open, Al and I supporting him on both sides.

"I'm goin', boys," said Boris, gasping for breath, "I'm goin' fast." It was a death scene, but in trying to illustrate his agony, Boris had bared his countless teeth in what looked like a fulsome, jovial smile. I felt a bubble of laughter beginning to form in my throat. "I'm remembering my life," continued Boris. "They say when you're dying, you begin to see your life parade before you." Actually, Boris's life was beginning to parade *behind* him, in single file in back of his chair. "Hey, there's Mama," said Boris, suddenly sitting up straight. "And Papa, too. Look, there's poor dead Papa. Hey, Mama, Papa, look here, don't you recognize me? I'm your son, Asa. Remember when I sang for you 'The Anniversary Song' and you waltzed together in the new house I bought for you?" The record played as Boris proceeded to die some more; then it faded under. "And look! There's General MacArthur." Harry Steinbeck, wearing a faded private's shirt with five stars painted on the shoulders, appeared behind the chair, compressing his lips around his corncob in sorrow. "Ah, General MacArthur. With President Truman he only spent an hour—but with me he spent *two!*"

Boris was going into his death rattle. The closer to death he came, the wider grew his grin. Now it looked to me as if it were going to swallow up his face. "I'm goin' boys, I can feel myself goin'." He was gripping the arms of the chair and pumping himself up and down in it. "No, Al," we cried in unison, "you can't go. We need you too much. The country needs you."

"This is it," Boris concluded. "I—got—no—pulse." His head was now over the back of the chair and he was pumping harder than ever. The bubble that had been forming in me finally burst and I let out a huge cough in a last effort to quell it.

But it was careening around in my throat, ripping out of my nose. I was trying desperately to glaze my eyes because I couldn't look anywhere without busting up entirely, neither at Al Hurwitz, who was having trouble himself, nor at Boris, who lay on the chair—dead—with a grotesque smile splitting his face from ear to ear. It suddenly occurred to me that my only chance was to bury my head on Boris's corpse and stifle my painful gasps on his shoulder. Boris shifted uncomfortably under my weight, twisted his mouth around, and began to whisper fiercely in my ear. "What in hell you doing? Stop screwing up the death scene!" I burrowed my head even further into his arms and struggled for control.

All this time, MacArthur was delivering a eulogy: "Al Jolson, you are gone. You were a great American, a true soldier, and an honor to the Jews." When I felt Al Hurwitz bring his head down on Boris's other shoulder, I knew that we both were done for. Tears of laughter had swarmed into my eyes—and then it suddenly occurred to me how I might salvage the situation. Tears, after all, were tears, no matter how they were inspired, and it was not too fantastic, considering the magnitude of Yiddish stage emotions, that my heaving on Boris's shoulder might have been interpreted as sobs of grief. When I finally got control of myself, I tested this theory by presenting my tear-stained face to the audience, and was rewarded by a little gasp from that part of the house near enough to see me. Even Boris was stirred. "That was pretty good," he told me, after we had squeezed two curtain calls out of the audience, "but don't try to run off with the scene." He punched me affectionately on the arm. "What did I tell you? Even this junk carries if you play it with the proper spirit."

I was never able, in the six shows that followed, to repeat this singular triumph, but I am sure my performance improved. For I began to play my part with a greater degree of seriousness and intensity—not much, I confess, but more than I had ever been able to lavish on such a role before. In my inner ear, I was hearing Boris shout again, "Play it true! Play it true!" and there was still enough shame in me to see the justice of his demand. Though my skepticism never completely left me, I held it for a while in partial suspension, in homage to something which had brushed by from another world —the Second Avenue Muse, then growing rapidly more shabby and déclassé, but still hovering hopefully over the stage. Around Boris, the Muse still lived, and I watched with grudging admiration, amusement, and a little envy as he wrapped himself snugly in the folds of its gown.

1960

First Year at Yale:
An Interview

I actually went into drama criticism because I thought it would help me get practical work in the theatre. I had been making the rounds as an actor with small success. I had done a couple of things at Equity Library Theatre and on TV, and I had spent seven summers as an actor at Group 20, a classical repertory company in Wellesley, Massachusetts. But as far as the commercial theatre was concerned, I was hitting a blank wall. You couldn't get a job unless you had an agent, and you couldn't get an agent unless you had a job—the typical runaround. The idea about reviewing came from my friend Elliot Silverstein, who cast me in a TV show (a ghastly U.S. Steel Hour about Aaron Burr and his daughter). When I complained about the difficulty of getting acting jobs, Elliot said, "You're a good writer, why don't you write? And if you reach a certain level of prominence, then you can direct, act, do anything you want." That's what led to my eventually becoming drama critic at *The New Republic*.

But years later, after I'd become a fairly successful critic, I didn't go out after work in the theatre. I felt the theatre had had it. I was even considering leaving theatre criticism and trying a more free-wheeling cultural criticism—movies, books, occasional drama. I certainly never thought I'd be in a position to affect the American theatre or even to give leverage to a reform.

The position at Yale came to be offered to me by a fortunate accident. As I understand it, the faculty of the School of Drama took a vote and came up with the names of Howard Taubman and Walter Kerr. My name was suggested by an English Department member, Robert

Penn Warren, a very kindly man whom I had just met
the summer before. He enclosed a copy of a note that
he had sent to the president of Yale, Kingman Brewster,
Jr. In essence, Robert Penn Warren said he wanted to
propose me because, in addition to the necessary academic background, I had had professional experience and
possessed the nerve to transform things.

Yale's president followed up and interviewed me in
New York. At that time he asked me who I thought
might be qualified to take over the school. I responded
with the name of George Devine (founder of the Royal
Court Theatre and English Stage Company. This is the
group that first produced John Osborne and founded
the whole new movement in English drama). Devine was
a very beloved man, a great man. I also mentioned
Michel St. Denis, a Frenchman who trained with Jacques
Copeau and who later became one of the formative minds
behind the Old Vic Company and School. He's particularly noted as a teacher of acting and has written a
fine book on the subject, *Theatre: The Rediscovery of
Style*. I think his ideas combine the discoveries of Stanislavsky with all the technical and vocal virtuosity that
belongs to the English. However, as far as the opening
at Yale was concerned, both of these men were soon to
be unavailable. George Devine died of a heart attack,
and St. Denis had a stroke upon hearing of the death of
his close friend.*

Kingman Brewster also asked me whether I would be
interested, but I said no, I wouldn't be interested in the
existing School of Drama, frankly no. The school had
become stultified, and had been, for as long as I could
remember, preparing its students either for Broadway or
for what was then called "civic theatre," which was just
Broadway transported to the provinces. In fact, I'd been
a student there in 1948 and had left after a year, very

* I am very glad to report that Mr. St. Denis has since recovered his
health, and is now helping to develop the new drama school at Juilliard.

disillusioned. The intellect was frowned upon: everything about the play was discussed except its meaning. There was only one acting teacher in the entire school. Activity was always *around* the play and centered almost exclusively on its physical environment. I seem to remember classes being suspended for six weeks while we put together a production of Goethe's *Faust*—an overwhelming spectacle designed by the faculty but a perfectly awful show, really a costume parade. Yet the condition of the Yale Drama School was perfectly representative of academic theatre generally in this country. The standards were those of Broadway—not today's Broadway but Broadway as it was in the twenties. Brewster replied to this that he was not interested in perpetuating the existing situation and that, if I were interested, I might think it over and perhaps present him with a list of the people I would want as additional faculty.

On vacation in the Virgin Islands, I thought about it a great deal. It was one of those luscious jobs one likes to toy with—as I had toyed the year before with the job of *Times* theatre critic knowing all the while that I would turn it down. But this time my friends were urging me to take the position at Yale. I'd reached the end of the line with drama reviewing; and I wasn't making any breakthroughs in teaching anymore. Finally, my wife and I wanted to get out of New York. Much as I cherish it as a place where eccentricity is possible and where advanced work in theatre is at least tolerated, New York as a physical environment is depressing.

While we were in the Virgin Islands, then, I dreamed up a list of faculty members. Gordon Rogoff, Herman Krawitz, and Stella Adler were among those who actually did come up. Others, like John Blatchley, Jean Vilar in directing, and in design, George Devine's associate, Jocelyn Herbert, proved impossible to hire. In general, I wanted people whose work I respected, who were not only technically proficient but who had tried to raise the theatre above its present level and had made some sacrifices in order to do so.

You might say that I had ethical as well as aesthetic criteria in mind. I knew we would have to do more with students than simply teach them their craft; some sort of spiritual regeneration would have to take place as well. We would have to make students conscious of what the theatre was at its best. Since this is a fading vision in America, I anticipated a constant attention to indoctrination, discussion, and almost fanatic expression of an ideal. Looking back, I saw that I had formed my own professional values with the help of my most idealistic teachers, and that when I had fallen short, I felt as though I had let those men down. It seemed to me, then, that the best contribution a university could make to theatre training was to set up the ideal, assuming all the while that people would always fall short of it, but assuming, too, that they would remember this ideal and try to recapture it. If we succeeded, our students would not be as likely to betray their talents as Marlon Brando and Kim Stanley and Geraldine Page and so many other people who never fully realized their promise. One never gets the feeling, for example, that Kim Stanley has had a desire to play Phèdre. I sometimes wonder whether she knows the play exists. Of course she knows; but I think she is much more comfortable with the sort of thing William Inge does or N. Richard Nash. I suppose—to get back to the main subject—what I wanted to do was to insinuate a superego in the people we train and then hope that in the next generation the best values would manifest themselves on the American stage.

The ideals we're striving for come from the great English and European companies. In England much exciting work—new playwriting, new acting techniques—has come out of lower-class ferment. This has helped create such companies as the English Stage Company at the Royal Court Theatre and the Royal Shakespeare

Company, particularly at the Aldwych Theatre in London, and, to a lesser extent, the National Theatre, whose roots are more traditional. In general, the repertory ideal moved from the provinces to London and became permanent as a result of subsidies from the government. On the continent, the Berliner Ensemble, the Barrault Company, Jean Vilar's TNP, the Piccolo Teatro Milano, and any number of other European companies have affected the techniques of the new English theatre and shaped my own ideas. In this country the Actors Workshop (erratic but fascinating when it was in San Francisco) and, most of all, the Living Theatre have exerted influence. The Living Theatre has even begun to affect the Royal Shakespeare Company through Peter Brook's work with the group. His recent production, *US*, was helped along by Joseph Chaikin, a former member of the Living Theatre and founder of the Open Theatre, which grew out of it. A workshop connected with the Royal Shakespeare Company and run by Michael Kustow, called TCG, was also sparked by the radical energy of the Living Theatre. By stirring up a kind of theatrical anarchism that is wilder than anything that has been seen here or abroad, the Living Theatre has literally given life to theatre. I think it has affected us all more than we know.

When it comes to playwriting, I think we're moving ahead of the British. Their writers are competent, but, with the possible exception of Harold Pinter, they aren't producing any breakthroughs—certainly nothing as brilliant as their staging techniques. I think we may be at the beginning of a renaissance in American playwriting, largely inspired by the boldness of the Living Theatre— its willingness to take chances, to be awful occasionally, even to bore you.

I have hopes that we can develop a special sort of repertory theatre here at Yale. The idea of connecting a professional repertory group to a university theatre isn't new in this country. I believe the APA was associated with the University of Michigan. Stanford has been bringing in actors who are also instructors (Gerry Hiken and Paul Richards, for example)—and that is proving to be a successful experiment. Brandeis has a group of resident actors who work with the students; thus, students learn not by doing things badly (the usual situation) but, first, by watching them done well and, second, by attempting to match those standards.

My own belief is that there's no sense training people in this country unless you're training them for repertory theatre, for permanent company work. One-shots don't go anywhere, are futile and wasteful. I feel that we have to do our own producing, so the students can observe professionals at work and then participate in this work. The main reason for having a repertory company is to give the best students a professional theatre to graduate into. My hope is that someday, like the English provincial reps, our resident theatre will influence the theatre in New York so that along with the fly-by-night commercial theatre the city will have three or four solid repertory companies.

My first responsibility at Yale was hiring new people, and this was a very pleasant and very affirmative task. However, I ran into trouble getting the people I wanted from England. Although they were attracted by the idea of a repertory company connected with a school, they were unwilling to pick up and leave a creative situation in order to come to a strange country. After all, we are engaged in a war of which they disapprove; we are still trying to recover from an assassination which, along with all the other violence in this country, has scared the life out of the world. Though I spent a week in England, holding five or six appointments a day, I struck out almost completely. Happily, I did get Michael Annals, a designer from the National Theatre, and that turned out to be a marvelous appointment. He's an excellent teacher and a first-rate artist.

Some funds existed for the new faculty, but the money had to be stretched. We were given a $390,000 declining, five-year grant by the Rockefeller Foundation, which allowed us $140,000 for the first year. With the university providing matching funds as the grant declined, this was designed to give us seven new positions at $20,000 apiece. I managed to increase the seven to twenty-two by obtaining the cooperation of people who were willing to work part-time or people who preferred the opportunity to the money. In contrast with the original faculty of twenty-five, we now have a faculty of forty-three, while the emphasis of the school has shifted from commercial practice and technical expertise to an emphasis on the art and literature of the theatre.

First-year actors at Yale, for example, are being prepared as rigorously in the practice of their craft as conservatory musicians and dancers; they average more than twenty-five hours per week in acting, movement, and voice classes (as compared with eight hours per week under the old program) and are taught by an acting faculty of eleven (as compared with two under the old program). Indeed, our heresy consists precisely in this assumption: that American theatre people can be trained, and do not come out of some form of spontaneous combustion. The directing department (taught by a faculty of four), the playwriting department (a faculty of four), the design department (a faculty of three), and the technical department (a faculty of five) have all increased proportionately, with a proportionate number of participating professionals taking part.

We also have a new program in administration for would-be repertory theatre producers, headed by Herman Krawitz, assistant general manager of the Metropolitan Opera, and including Harvey Sabinson and Thomas Burrows, the managing director of our theatre operation. In addition, a new Doctor of Fine Arts program has been instituted for the training of theatre critics and teachers of dramatic literature.

At first the general atmosphere at Yale was grim, with the exception of a few genuinely helpful and friendly faces, especially the late John Gassner. The faculty looked like Mount Rushmore trying to crack a smile. I was shown through the school by an obviously angry man, and it was like entering King Tutankhamen's tomb: closets stuffed with eighteenth-century costumes that were never touched or used; prop rooms that were constantly kept locked; musty, gloomy interiors; beige office with horrible lighting fixtures; a peeling theatre built along the dimensions of a Shubert house. When the president first asked me whether these facilities were adequate, I—in my innocence—had said, "Well, as long as we can work here, it's all right. I don't put that much emphasis on brick and mortar." I didn't realize how limited these facilities were, or how fiercely they were competed for by other groups at the university. The same theatre is now used by the undergraduate dramatic society, the intercollegiate drama festival, and for school dances. The first thing we did was get the place repainted. And this paint job brought the first signs of hostility from the community, particularly from wives of well-established faculty members who claimed that the red we had chosen for the theatre was in bad taste and that—worse—by painting the "Green Room" red, we had committed a serious break with tradition. This was just the first of many complaints we were to hear about every policy we initiated.

Looking back, it does seem odd that Kingman Brewster should have hired me—not only because of my age (I had just turned thirty-nine when I was chosen) but also because he must have known all the trouble I was likely to cause him with the community. He was faced with a choice: either to close down the school or to completely regenerate it. Transform it utterly. He knew he was in for a radical transformation of school policies, and I think he was willing to go down the line with it. That's why he responded immediately when I said, "not the existing school" and that's why he went immediately to Rockefeller to get the money for the additional faculty salaries.

There were other reasons the first few months were tough. Publicity created a lot of problems. We received a great deal of it, I suppose because there's general feeling that the theatre has reached a dead end, and anything new seems to promise salvation. And then attention was attracted by the fact that such an obvious transformation was going on—and that it was being conducted by a critic. Stanley Kauffmann's Sunday piece in the *Times* was the first of many articles on the new school. After it appeared, the whole publicity world fell in on us. The television networks wanted to do shows. *Time* asked to do an article; I refused permission, but they did it anyway. *Life* did a piece, which still has to come out.

In the beginning I had been reluctant about publicity, and I had considered refusing *Life* when they asked. But when I was told that they were doing an extensive report on university theatres and that we would be left out, I suddenly realized that I was no longer my own man. We have a school, and we have to advertise it; we have a theatre and we have to advertise that. I began to think that publicity might help us attract a different sort of student to the school and a different sort of audience to the plays. Nonetheless, we turned down the networks. We turned down *Time*. We turned down *Mademoiselle* and another fashion magazine: I felt I should refuse any coverage that was going toward fashion as opposed to information. But whenever I thought the information would be properly disseminated, I welcomed it. We have no other way of advertising our new policies except through the various media, and we have no other way of attracting money to the school. Frankly, I also began to feel that we were not going to be accepted in New Haven very readily, and that wider acceptance might protect us against the growing hostility. I was hoping for national support to buttress us against local criticism. On the other hand, we did not wish a developing school to be subject to the same vogues and fashions as commercial theatre properties. It is for this reason that I tried so hard to prevent Walter Kerr from reviewing *Viet Rock*.

We brought *Viet Rock* up to New Haven actually to solve some problems we had encountered with Jules Feiffer's *Little Murders*, the play I had wanted to do originally. I discovered Jules intended to transfer the play to Broadway very soon after its production at Yale, and I did not want the school to function simply as an out-of-town tryout for a commercial producer (we had no such qualms about Off Broadway presentations). I asked Jules to postpone his Broadway production until the following season, and when he, very understandably, refused, we had to put something in its place.

I had seen a production of *Viet Rock* in an Open Theatre workshop and decided to bring the group up, as a visiting company, until we could get our own production arm functioning. We had already decided to use visiting companies in order to expose our students to every possible kind of theatre, as long as it was good theatre. At the very beginning of the year we invited to Yale the brilliant Philadelphia Theatre of Living Arts' production of *Endgame* to show the students new techniques in the staging of what had already become an established avant-garde play. This work caused a lot of tremor in the community because, for a few moments, Hamm and Clov make masturbatory motions. I believe the members of the Chamber of Commerce complained that there was obscenity on the stage at Yale. Just in passing, the president told me about this; I think he was getting the feeling that I was riding a hobby horse. When he heard we were doing *Viet Rock,* he said, "It's too bad William Buckley hasn't written a play. You could put it on to show you're really eclectic." I said, "I would be delighted to do so if it were a good play." (Actually, the hobby horse belongs to America. I don't have any particular admiration for political plays, but the Vietnam war is the event that seems most to be exercising our more interesting playwrights these days.)

Next came *Viet Rock,* which, as readers of the New York papers know, kicked up more fuss. We got an enthusiastic first-night response. The second night there was an interruption of the performance by two drunken former drama students. One, a Negro, complained that there was no Negro on stage. As it happened, there was a Negro woman on stage. "I'm not exactly white," she yelled. A policeman ejected the Negro, who then complained that he was being thrown out because he was black. This incident got into the *Yale Daily News,* and to this day many people think we planted those people. But on the whole, the general feeling about the play began sympathetically and then was followed by backwashes of hostility in the form of letters charging obscenity of language and bad taste.

Similar letters have followed every one of our productions. Despite these and other problems, the *Viet Rock* experience was useful. The cast who came up was not the same cast I had seen in New York (almost half the actors had been replaced); most of these new actors were inadequately trained in the fundamentals of acting, let alone the experimental techniques. Nevertheless, the production was of instructional value; we hoped our students would profit from the advanced techniques it employed—and they did. Their own work for the next few months was highly influenced by *Viet Rock.*

To the community, though, we seemed to be bringing on an avant-garde holocaust. After *Endgame* and *Viet*

Rock came *Dynamite Tonite,* the most innocent, charming, sweet, poetic play; it, too, was found offensive, though not for reasons of obscenity. Many people didn't understand it. They couldn't categorize it; they didn't know how to respond to it. One alumna buttonholed me at intermission: "What is this?" she demanded. "It's not a comedy. It's not a musical. What is it?" "Well," I replied, "it's an opera." She retorted: "The audience doesn't like it either. Look, the house is only one-third full." To her, the size of a Tuesday-night audience indicated the quality of the play. Once more, the college paper didn't like the play; the local papers thought it was sophomoric. *Dynamite Tonite,* I am convinced, is an excellent piece of work; some of its performances I would match against anything. I was staggered to discover that so few people were aware of its originality or capable of acknowledging its quality. Even among our students there was great puzzlement over the performances, which were neither conventional nor way out but contained something extraordinary in the use of the voice and the body, and in certain improvisatory techniques. The director was Paul Sills of the Second City, who came up and demonstrated his game theatre techniques in the production. For example, during one rehearsal the actors went through the entire play speaking their lines without emphasis; but they weren't allowed to read a line without touching each other (a technique that paid off in some wonderful physical relationships on stage). In an earlier rehearsal they went through the whole play just handling the props. I thought that the chance to see these concepts in rehearsal would open up students' eyes to whole new worlds of theatre that the old rigid rehearsal techniques had never touched. I also thought we'd never get a cast like that one together again, except under repertory circumstances. They had done the play many times, in the Actors Studio, Off Broadway, and on television. They were charming, decent, intelligent, good-hearted people—and a pleasure to work with.

Our audiences have been a problem all year. The theatre in New Haven is dominated by Helen Hokinson ladies who taste plays in the same spirit they nibble mints after dinner. At a symposium we held after *Endgame*, Arnold Weinstein got up and bawled out the people who had been complaining about "obscenity" and about the "mutilation" of their favorite play. "You ought to be ashamed of yourselves," he said. "You've seen a splendid production with two of the most marvelous performances you'll ever see in your lives, and all you do is whine about a few dirty gestures. What kind of people are you anyway?" I loved him at that moment. He was really heroic. But these people attend the theatre in order to go away feeling more cultivated. The idea that theatre reflects their own lives, their bodily functions as well as their spiritual development, is a heresy that scandalizes them. Even people who are sufficiently sophisticated to know they should not react in this fashion register the same complaints camouflaged in the charge of "boredom."

To take *Volpone*, as we did, and try to make it more immediate signified to these audiences nothing more than the violation of a time-honored classic. They wanted to see *Volpone* in Elizabethan trappings, thinking that Elizabethan tights and doublets insure a correct historical style. But I am more and more coming to think that a period approach to a play is merely a way of keeping the play at a distance, of keeping it academic and genteel. The Bristol Old Vic does this sort of production and so does the APA. After you see one of these shows, you understand just what Antonin Artaud meant when he said, "No more masterpieces." If you approach Shakespeare as a museum piece, you're wasting your time and you're wasting the audience's time. And yet, I fear, that's precisely what a university audience wants. By far the most popular presentation we did all year was the John Gielgud and Irene Worth reading of *Men and Women in Shakespeare*. The audience was kept in ecstasy by two actors (excellent ones to be sure) behind lecterns vocalizing Shakespearian set pieces. I'm sure the audience left feeling more cultivated than when it arrived.

These remarks sound puritan, and I know some people call me a fanatic. Over the years there has been a definite stiffening of my ideals, but this has been accompanied by a softening in the application of these ideals. I think I know what the job needs, and I am convinced that if I begin to moderate, compromise, or back down from my position, the whole enterprise will collapse. But for the first time in my life, I'm faced constantly with the consequences of putting an ideal into action—and they're painful consequences. I have to find ways of softening these consequences without giving up the ideal. This is hardly a new dilemma, but it's the first time I've been faced with it. Frankly, I'm agonized by it.

Here's an example. There's always been a lot of slavish crew labor in this school. All classes would stop while the entire school—actors, directors, playwrights, designers, technicians—would settle down to the work of banging sets together. In 99 percent of the cases, this labor added nothing to the instruction of the students. One of my first pleasures in coming to Yale was the emancipation of students from crew labor. A humane idea which, when put into practice, caused a lot of inhumanity. It soon became clear that we didn't have a sufficient labor force and therefore the design and technical students were bearing the killing burdens of "crew." What could I do to rectify this situation? Hire carpenters? We don't have enough money. Hire part-time seamstresses? We hired the only one who responded to our ad. We asked the actors to volunteer for crew work. Lots volunteered. None showed up. What could I do? I found myself in the same authoritarian, vaguely totalitarian situation I had tried to reform. It could only be relieved by money—and we don't have enough.

Money, in fact, is our major problem. We don't have sufficient funds for anything. Our equipment is old; it's breaking down, but we can't afford to replace it. The physical plant is underequipped. We rent lights from our own students who have lighting businesses; we can't afford to buy our own. We have almost the same expense and equipment budget as the old school though we have quadrupled its activities. We introduced professional productions; that means paying performers. But we have the same production budget as for the old student majors. Lack of money affects our plans for next year as well. The university is currently tightening its financial belt, so we've had to apply to foundations for additional funds —so far unsuccessfully. We've asked for the minimum to satisfy our needs but we really need double our request. We can function effectively with $200,000 a year in addition to our present university budget. We're afraid to ask for more than $100,000. This means we will have to cut down on the number of actors in our company. If we had the funds, we would build a company large enough to handle both the acting and the teaching. The same people would not be performing in every play; those who weren't acting could teach. But our present company is too small; we will be overworking every member. While they're rehearsing, they'll also be teaching. Also, one of the great advantages of the repertory system is that it enables you to keep an interesting but unpopular play in the schedule with the help of other plays that are interesting and popular. However, under our current circumstances, true repertory is impossible. We're all using the same facility; there's only one place to work; and plays must therefore be produced one after the other.

It may sound as though this has been a gravely troubled year, but I have not really been surprised by anything that's happened. I knew in advance that the

productions were going to have tough sledding, and so I
anticipated the rough spots (I had the Living Theatre's
experience as my guide). As I have explained to the university administration, I did not accept the position in
order to entertain the city of New Haven. I never intended
to produce community theatre. (If I wanted to run a
culture center, I would have applied in a city like New
York, where at least there is an audience.) My concern
was for training—and for training in relation to a conservatory situation. There is a vacuum in the American
theatre, a vacuum that becomes more apparent each day.
Our job is to try to find out what might fill this vacuum.
I want the same privileges as a scientist working in a laboratory situation; this, in fact, is the great attraction of
the university for me. Here, I felt, the theatre could function freely as a laboratory where experiments could be
tried in a test tube, where we could determine how to
change things, how to inject a little vitality, a little
novelty, a little excitement and immediacy into a mori-
bund art. This has to be accomplished by trial and error.
You can't do it by the hit-flop system, and you can't do
it by getting yourself a majority audience immediately.
And this may explain why I think it has to begin outside
of New York. I want to feel that I have the freedom to
do this kind of experimentation without the pressure to
produce results immediately.

We are developing toward something which we don't
quite yet understand. We have to explore. If we were
simply starting another repertory company, we'd offer a
more balanced program: a comedy, a serious play, a revival, and maybe—if we could afford it—a new play. But
we are primarily committed to the production of new
plays because these change our minds about what the
theatre can be, even change our minds about the classics.
We hope to develop an identity which will help us to approach the new plays and the classics from a single point

of view, though the training in the school will remain eclectic. This identity—this concern for our own development—may result in our cutting ourselves off from the community, but I feel that the crisis in the theatre has forced us more and more into an increasingly radical position. I started out to reorganize a school. I discovered that I couldn't have a school without a company into which to feed the best students—a company to serve as a model. Next, I discovered that you can't build such a company until you have an audience that responds to the work and is interested in the kind of development the company is committed to. Of course, you can't have the audience until you have the community, because an audience is a community in miniature. You can't have a community until you have a country, and you can't have a country until you have a civilization.

The disease is at the roots. To be blunt, though I'm sure we shall succeed in part, I very much doubt whether we can realize the initial vision at present, given the fact that the culture is so much against it. Our culture thinks it's for art, but it's against art. I think that more and more we are discovering that all the current talk about the cultural explosion is very empty. In every city where advanced theatre has been tried, it has failed for one reason or another. Philadelphia's Theatre of Living Arts has just lost its driving force. Andre Gregory was fired. The Actors Workshop closed. There were two different managements in two years at the Pittsburgh Playhouse: William Ball was fired, and now John Hancock has been fired. The Front Street Theatre in Memphis was recently on the verge of collapse. Lincoln Center has just lost its second artistic director, Herbert Blau. And there will be more. It seems obvious that communities that think they want culture want it only as long as it doesn't touch them —or as long as it doesn't cost them anything. In almost all of these cities, the resident theatre has either produced a deficit (as all theatres do, if they are any good) or has produced plays that the community considered outrageous.

By now we've certainly learned that our country is primitive culturally. But the one encouraging thing is that theatre people are still willing to function in such an atmosphere, discouraging as it is: I'm speaking of people like Ball and Gregory. Personally, I think Americans ought to stop all this pretense about loving culture. Then, at least, we'll be free of hypocrisy, and we'll know precisely where we stand. And you know, once all the cocktail parties and fund-raising drives and the fancy dinners before the ritualistic visits to the culture center are all over, then we shall be faced with exactly what culture means. With how connected it is with your soul— or how cut off it is from the roots of your inmost being.

1967

A Note on the Type

The text of this book was set on the Linotype in a face called Primer, designed by Rudolph Ruzicka, who was earlier responsible for the design of Fairfield and Fairfield Medium, Linotype faces whose virtues have for some time now been accorded wide recognition.

The complete range of sizes of Primer was first made available in 1954, although the pilot size of 12-point was ready as early as 1951. The design of the face makes general reference to Linotype Century—long a serviceable type, totally lacking in manner or frills of any kind— but brilliantly corrects its characterless quality.

This book was composed, printed, and bound by The Haddon Craftsmen, Inc., Scranton, Pa. Typography and binding design by Bonnie Spiegel.